ROOS, RABBITS, AND RUGBY LEAGUE

HOW AN AMERICAN BECAME AN AUSTRALIAN BUNNY RABBIT

BY JARED SCHNABL

Glory Glory to South Sydney

www.mascotbooks.com

Roos, Rabbits, and Rugby League:
How an American Became an Australian Bunny Rabbit

©2017 Jared Schnabl. All Rights Reserved. No part of this publication may be reproduced, stored in a retrieval system or transmitted in any form by any means electronic, mechanical, or photocopying, recording or otherwise without the permission of the author.

This book is not associated with or endorsed by the National Rugby League. Although the author and publisher have made every effort to ensure that the information in this book was correct at press time, the author and publisher do not assume and hereby disclaim any liability to any party for any loss, damage, or disruption caused by errors or omissions, whether such errors or omissions result from negligence, accident, or any other cause.

For more information, please contact:
Mascot Books
560 Herndon Parkway #120
Herndon, VA 20170
info@mascotbooks.com

Library of Congress Control Number: 2016920971

CPSIA Code: PBANG0217A
ISBN-13: 978-1-68401-068-4

Printed in the United States

Dedicated to my mother and father, Bailon Johnson,
and Reggie the Flemish Giant (a.k.a. "Mr. Bubba")

"All the world will be your enemy, Prince with a Thousand Enemies. And when they catch you, they will kill you. But first, they must catch you."
—Richard Adams, *Watership Down* (1973).

"Ooh, you don't wanna race a rabbit, mate!"
—Bunnymund, *Rise of the Guardians* (2012).

"You can take me now, I have seen it all! I have seen everything! The Rabbitohs have returned the favor. And there is a new chapter in the book of feuds!"
—Warren Smith (2012).

CONTENTS

INTRODUCTION:

The rabbit: one of nature's most beloved, cherished, and often misunderstood animals. A creature beloved by many, but viewed as a menace by some. Depending on whom you ask, it is either a gentle soul that means no harm, or a four-legged nuisance that robs humans of vegetables and shrubs. To children, they are adored on an immense scale from cartoons, to pets, to symbols of a beloved holiday in spring. In Australia, however, the rabbit is considered less of a cute friend, and more of an ugly plague. Well, for over a century they certainly were.

In 1859, a native of England named Thomas Austin brought twenty-four wild rabbits more than halfway around the world, just to release and hunt them. The rabbits multiplied like... well, like rabbits! The loose lapines ate their way across the country, devouring everything left and right to the point where kangaroos nearly went extinct. For decades, it was an ugly chapter in Australia's history. It was the Down Under equivalent of what Europe went through during the Middle Ages, minus the disease and religious superstition brought about by the Black Plague. Okay, so maybe that comparison does sound melodramatic, but it was a terrible mess that greatly affected the fragile ecosystem of the Land Down Under.

Around the early 1900s, while Australia was fighting to contain its rabbit infestation, somewhere in the streets of South Sydney, history was about to be made. In a blue-collar, working-class neighborhood of Sydney known as Redfern, a group of boys in myrtle green jerseys were practicing the sport of rugby league on their training ground. But it was hard to train with rabbits leaping and bounding across the field. To clear this problem, while attempting to make some extra cash on the side, players would be hired to catch the rabbits, skin them alive on the spot, and then sell them for food and fur on the streets while chanting, "Rabbitoh! Rabbitoh! Rabbitoh!" to the people passing by. Rabbit meat was the choice food of peasants in Australia back in the day. The blood from the captured rabbits would spill onto the boys' green jerseys, thus giving them the two-tone shade that looked eerily similar to a Christmas sweater; myrtle green and cardinal red to be precise. Despite the grim picture that I paint, this rather bizarre beginning would set the stage for one of the most celebrated sports teams in Australian history: The South Sydney Rabbitohs!

For those of you who flunked history of Australian rugby league teams, or at least those who don't follow rugby league, allow me to clue you in on this renowned team. The South Sydney Rabbitohs are a rugby team from Sydney, Australia. They are one of the sixteen teams that play professionally, or "first-grade" in the National Rugby League, or NRL. The club has won more championships, or Premierships, than any other team in the NRL; twenty at last count. But their last Premiership was in 1971, and their fans have been through a roller-coaster ride of tumultuousness and controversy since the last time they were official champions. Winning the Minor Premiership in 1989 (that's finishing first atop the team leaderboard with the most wins/points), being barred from the league for three years from 1999 to 2002, finishing in last place several times, and being privately owned by Hollywood A-list celebrity Russell Crowe and Aussie billionaire Peter Holmes a Court are just a few of the highlights from their long history. But despite these highs and lows, their fans are among some of the most dedicated and jovial in the whole world; it would take more than just forty-plus-year Premiership drought to break their spirits. Not bad for a group of fans and athletes who proudly don a uniform with a bunny rabbit on it!

Actually, I am incorrect in saying that the Rabbitohs have won twenty Premierships. On October 5th 2014, the mighty Australian Bunnies, as their fans lovingly refer to them, won their twenty-first Premiership! To say that it was an historic moment for both Australia and the club would be a gross understatement. Forty-three years of waiting, heartbreak, close-calls, missed chances, and bloody tries all culminated in a magical night for the red and green Bunnies of South Sydney. Fans from Redfern to Mascot celebrated as if they all had won the lottery, but the jackpot they had hit was something more valuable than a giant check. I promise, before this book is through, we shall discuss that happy memory in detail.

How did an American from Long Island, New York manage to wander into the world of Australian rugby? There are many reasons for my utter fascination with the savage ballet that is rugby, specifically the Aussie underdogs (or rather, "under-rabbits") in red and green. Now to be fair, I am still new to rugby; I'm still learning the positions, penalties, and basic rules. I also have never lived in Australia, but that hasn't stopped me from falling in love with not just the country but the people, especially the fans that I've come to identify with as my Aussie family away from home! Actually, I refer to them as my "Australian Bunny Family." Being an American fan of rugby league, especially the Rabbitohs, is the ultimate way to make new friends in the Land Down Under. Whenever I visit Sydney, I make it a habit to wear mostly my Rabbitohs jersey and see what friendly faces come my way. I cannot begin to express my love for the Souths fans that I have come across in my many visits to Australia's largest city. I may have traveled alone, but they practically have made me a part of their extensive family. And like rabbits, their numbers are great.

Before I go any further into recounting what led me to

follow a team of Australian rabbits, I'd like to take a moment to recap some important factors that influenced my love of Australia and rugby. Oh, and rabbits.

THE RUGBY WORLD CUP:

Having missed most of it back in 2007, I'll never forget this one move where a New Zealand All Blacks player on defense ran toward a player at full speed, reached out his massive forearm, and went straight for his iron neck! For a split second, I gasped in horror, thinking that the player's head had come off! Of course, no heads rolled, but it remained an awesome memory from that game. Fast forward to 2011, when the RWC returned to New Zealand, where I watched almost every match. I was, however, disappointed with America's performance; I knew that the odds of us winning this was a huge longshot. In the end, host nation New Zealand captured the Webb Ellis Cup, in front of tens of thousands of fans in Auckland. It was a fitting end for a country where rugby is held in high regard and who can resist the intimidating power of the haka, the traditional war-chant presented among all rugby teams from South Pacific countries? No one, that's whom! The NFL has a hands-in huddle, but the All Blacks have the haka! Advantage, New Zealand.

INVICTUS:

This 2009 hit film deals primarily with the end of Apartheid in South Africa, Nelson Mandela, and the South Africa Springboks capturing the 1995 Rugby World Cup. And while there is nothing Australian in this movie, it was the first time, at least in American cinema that a film revolving around rugby became such a smash hit. The film mainly revolves around how the Springboks united the once-segregated nation of South Africa, especially at a time when many Afrikaans and non-Afrikaans were unsure of the new feelings of unity. Not to mention how the non-Afrikaans wished to do away with a team that for years was synonymous with racism; blacks were barred from the team and events. Mandela (brilliantly played by Morgan Freeman), however, stepped in to assure people that keeping the team whole under the Springbok banner would be the right thing do, as to show feelings of unity amongst their fellow citizens. *Invictus* was an inspirational film, but the rugby scenes were not to be ignored. I'm not sure if I bought Matt Damon's Afrikaner accent, but I believed his powerful grit as he channeled former Springboks captain, Francois Pienaar. Nonetheless, it made me a fan of the RWC. It also taught me that rugby can unite everyone no matter what the odds!

THE TEAM'S LOGO:

Much like a popular brand of clothing and breakfast cereal, fascination with a popular product can begin with an attractive or eye-catching logo. And the same can easily be said for a professional sports team; and can you think of a more unique symbol than a bunny? Especially if the sport tied to that logo is rugby? I mean, seriously, who would think of having a rabbit be a symbol for a brutal contact sport like rugby?

I can still remember the day when I first discovered this Australian Bunny: It was December 31st 2008, and I was perusing some merchandise inside an apparel store in Alice Springs, of all places. I came across one jersey with a bunny on it. My initial thought was, *A rugby team represented by a bunny rabbit? C'mon, really?* Of course, I said that all in my head, and without an ounce of meanness or cynicism. Still, one cannot deny that there is no better attention getter than a rabbit. It's against human nature to see a rabbit and not fawn over it. Eventually, I saw highlights of their games over the Internet, learned about their history, brushed up on the NRL, and before I knew it, I had four Rabbitohs jerseys hanging in my closet! And I wore each of them with pride, strutting my rabbit like a proud peacock. Of course, in America, where image is everything, and looking tough is worshipped like a golden calf, people would make fun of me for wearing a uniform with a cute animal on it. Some call it cute, I call it cool. The logo looks rather sleek and handsome, and reminds us not judge a book by its cover. And if you're still unconvinced that rabbits aren't tough, go read or watch *Watership Down*. I dare you! If that doesn't convince you that rabbits aren't worthy of athletic representation, then what is?

BUNNYMUND:

DreamWorks 2012's *Rise of the Guardians*, based on the Guardians of Childhood book series by William Joyce, reimagined the Easter Bunny not as a cute deliverer of eggs, but as a tall, handsome, tattooed, boomerang-wielding, ass-kicking, artistic Australian with the ability to manipulate nature. Not only that, but it was voiced by none other than Aussie superstar Hugh Jackman. That's right, Wolverine himself bringing hope to the children of the world! This was, by far, the best interpretation of the beloved holiday icon. But I digress. While watching this movie, I felt the same curiousness as when I encountered the Rabbitohs logo for the first time. I asked, "Why make the Easter Bunny an Australian, especially when the rabbit nearly wiped out Australia?!" But it didn't take me long to really appreciate just how awesome Jackman's character was. Maybe it was the floral tattoos on his fur that looked eerily similar to Aboriginal or Maori war paint. Maybe it was the gentle way he said "anklebiter" (then again, no one can resist an Aussie accent or slang!). Or it could be because he was a giant rabbit with an Australian accent that could easily kick your ass. Sounds like a Souths player to me! After watching it, I thought, *How do the Souths not know about this character, or this movie?* Suddenly, I felt even cooler donning my jersey and not giving a you-know-what if someone were to tease me about the logo. And for the record, Jackman is known as a fan of the team from Manly, the Sea Eagles. It would have been even funnier if Russell Crowe had taken that role! Still, I'll bet when Jackman isn't wearing maroon and white, I'll bet he's asking his *Les Miserables* co-star for a red and green jumper (at least I hope). In another world, Bunnymund would be a perfect mascot for the team. But that rightfully belongs to Reggie Rabbit. Do you suppose those two are related?

WARREN SMITH AND ROUND 19:

Every fan remembers where they were when they witnessed a memorable game that would forever define their fandom for a certain team. The same can be said for broadcast announcers and team members. Babe Ruth had his famed "Called Shot" during the 1932 World Series against the Chicago Cubs at Wrigley Field in Chicago. Bobby Thompson had his "Shot Heard Round the World" from the 1951 National League Championship at the Polo Grounds in New York City. Al Michaels uttered the now famous "Do You Believe in Miracles?!" at the 1980 Winter Olympics at Lake Placid, New York. For me and the South Sydney Rabbitohs, it was the nineteenth round of the 2012 NRL season at Allianz Stadium in Sydney, Australia.

By 2012, I had just starting following the team, but I'd been watching games and clips via YouTube, so it wasn't perfect, but I made do. The Rabbitohs were playing their historic arch-rivals, the Sydney Roosters. The game was a veritable seesaw match that I could not keep my eyes off of, despite me still having to learn the roster of the Rabbitohs. The best moment came down to the last two minutes when the Bunnies had the ball and ran it across the field for a try. After converting a two-point kick, the score was 22-18, in favor of the Roosters. As the clock wound down to just one minute left, announcer Warren Smith would vocally write a historic play-by-play that would make Al Michaels, Vin Scully, Red Barber, and Howard Cosell very proud. As the play began, the Roosters kicked the ball, and Smith, carefully watching the melee, said…

> *"…try and stop the Rabbitohs. He goes down to Sutton, who gives it Taylor, who brings it back! And gives it to McQueen! They're away! Merritt's there again! Here he is! Merritt, Merritt's linked up with Luke! Luke for the line! Keeps it alive. Reynolds! Reynolds! You can take me now, I have seen it all! I have seen everything! The Rabbitohs have returned the favor, and there is a new chapter in the book of feuds!"*

Hearing those words coming out of Warren Smith with that great Aussie tone of voice only added to the ambiance of the moment. The sheer, unadulterated joy from the players' faces was unlike anything I had seen in American sports in quite some time—not since the New York Rangers won the Stanley Cup back in 1994 or when the New York Giants won Super Bowl XLII in 2008 by destroying the New England Patriots' perfect season. What was even more special about that win was how the team did something that I never see in sports nowadays: the players jumped into the stands to embrace their loyal fans! Nowhere else is that sense of camaraderie present than at an Australian rugby match. If there is any proof that the Aussies love sports, that game and that reaction from the team is more than enough proof. After that game, and prior to going into the next season, I was determined as ever to see this team and their fans for myself, in person!

Put it all together and you have the makings of an American who would eventually find his way into a strange, yet exciting world where sports fans are jubilant, friendly, and can proudly say "GO BUNNIES!" with the utmost pride! A place where the beer is always flowing, the crowd wears red and green, and a giant rabbit mascot is as beloved as the players themselves. I write this as a tribute to one of my favorite places on Earth. I already loved Australia—from the lyrics of "Midnight Oil", to the fanciful bush of Blinky Bill, to the spirituality of Aboriginal culture. But my discovery of this breed of bunny only made me more fascinated with a subculture of Australia that, in my opinion, should be the envy of the world! It is indeed a most wonderful place that I saw with my own two eyes, and I want to share it with you: a land of kangaroos, rabbits, and rugby.

PART I:

The 2013 Minor Premiership

CHAPTER 1:
Olympic Park Station

SEPTEMBER 6, 2013:

It was a sunny afternoon in Lidcombe, a large suburb just 11 miles west of downtown Sydney. I grasped the yellow handrail inside the train good and hard with my right hand; my left hand gently patted my pocket. I firmly caressed the red-and-white envelope that I had been guarding for weeks like a priceless jewel. I was dizzy with anticipation as I was surrounded by a bevy of red and green fans. I didn't even mind that they were a little drunk and a few smelled of tobacco. There was Brian, with his sharp stubble; Brigitte, who welcomed me with a beer and a hug; Carmelo, an older gentleman with a rather firm handshake and a thick accent. These were just a small fraction of a larger contingency of fans that bled red and green and welcomed me as a member of their family.

As the train dove into a tunnel, I was keeping close tabs on my poster that I had worked on with such care—a tribute to my new favorite team, made possible by the last person you'd expect: an American who follows footy! But I was not here to steal anyone's thunder. This was the day of the Minor Premiership; the game that would decide what team would finish high atop the NRL's leaderboard. I did not plan on being the star attraction of this highly hyped event. Instead, as Andy Warhol would put it, I was a celebrity for about fifteen minutes. Or in the Rabbitohs' case, sixteen minutes.

I could see the glorious fortification of Sydney's massive ANZ Stadium in the distance. You know that feeling you get when you see something in real life that you've only seen in pictures or on TV? That's just how I felt staring at the grandeur of one of Australia's most amazing structures. And I hadn't even walked inside it yet! I felt as if I was levitating from the train toward the stadium. It felt like a dream, only it wasn't. But before the game could begin, I had business to attend to: I had promised to meet with several other Bunny supporters outside the stadium at The Brewery. And boy was I thirsty.

CHAPTER 2
A Miracle in Tribeca

JUNE 24, 2013:

To really get this story into motion, I need to go back to how this adventure all started. Not to when I first discovered the Rabbitohs, but to how I made it to my first rugby match. Sorry—I mean, rugby league. How I ended up 10,000 miles from home happened, you might say, because of a miracle. Or an amazing stroke of luck coupled with a few dollars.

I had just finished an afternoon of swimming in Amagansett, a small town in the east end of Long Island. While drying off, I was checking my Facebook status and something caught my eye. It was an ad on a page for my favorite bar in New York called The Australian NYC, which was hosting a food and wine tasting party where the theme was all Australian food. The Australian NYC was my favorite watering hole in Manhattan due to the fact that it was the only place that showed rugby matches. Not to mention it had kangaroo on the menu and an ice cream sundae made with Tim Tams. The party was known as "A Taste of Down Under." The instant I saw that ad, I knew I had to attend this Australian soiree. My emotions went from excitement to panic when I realized it was that night, and in only a few hours. Throw in the fact that I was over one hundred miles from Manhattan, and I knew it was a race against the clock.

Without missing a beat, I dried off, threw on some clothes, grabbed my wallet and phone, and hit the highway. Without getting pulled over (relax readers, I didn't drive recklessly!), I made it home, showered, threw on my suit jacket, and headed to the train station. Realizing my train would arrive in only a few minutes, it was time to hit the gas once again. Making it onto the train with a minute to spare, I had forty minutes to catch my breath between Rockville Centre and Penn Station.

The party was atop a loft on Desbrosses Street in the neighborhood of Tribeca. After ponying up a hefty cover charge at the door, I entered the shindig with a straight face and a wet brow from the exhausted sweat of a humid day. In between noshing on roast lamb, spiced kangaroo, and sausage rolls, I noticed there was a silent auction of items up for sale. Australian mementos like NRL jerseys (no Rabbitohs gear, unfortunately), artwork, Australian candy, and other expensive knick-knacks from the Land Down Under. There was one thing in that showcase that piqued my interest: a raffle for a pair of Qantas tickets to anywhere in Australia (Sydney, Melbourne, or Brisbane to be precise). Realizing that I could hedge my bet by buying up to twenty-five tickets, I threw in my money. Unfortunately, I had only ten dollars left, since I dropped most of it on the cover charge at the door. My ten bucks bought me only three tickets in the jar. I figured my chances were incredibly slim and I thought to put it out of my head by concentrating on watching the sunset over the Hoboken skyline across the Hudson River.

When it came time to announce the winner of the Qantas raffle, I was mildly paying attention. That's when I heard a woman's voice over the microphone say those four words: "*Where is Jared Schnabl?*" Noticing that she slightly mispronounced my last name, I practically levitated toward the stage inside the loft, completely beside myself. As she told me with a straight face, "*You won!*" I couldn't believe it. It was one those surreal moments where time seems to stand still around you for just a split second. You want to smile, but your brain is swimming in a sea of emotions. "I won?" I asked, trying to smile. "*You won!*" she again exclaimed. All I could do was hug every last person on stage; I put more energy into those excited hugs than I did racing to catch my train. I had never been on a game show and I had never won the lottery. But this trip that I had just won was, dare I say it, a miracle.

All I could do was stare at the big manila envelope with the words "RAFFLE PRIZE" scribbled on it, and think to myself, *I'm the luckiest guy in the world right now! Or perhaps the luckiest guy in Long Island!* I immediately ran all the way from the party in Tribeca to The Australian NYC to break the happy news. More importantly, I now had a reason to return to Australia. I knew what I was going to do the instant I got there: I, Jared Schnabl of Rockville Centre, New York, was going to see the South Sydney Rabbitohs. I could just hear the roar of the crowd while staring at that free Qantas voucher.

While on my way home, I clutched that prize envelope to my chest, nursing it like it was an infant. I knew that until my flight and hotel was booked, it was my job to keep this thing secure until my departure. Of course, now came the other task of acquiring a ticket to see the mighty Rabbitohs! There was so much planning to do.

CHAPTER 3
The Posters

In Tennessee Williams' *A Streetcar Named Desire*, Blanche Dubois says, "*I have always depended on the kindness of strangers.*" Those words were never better used when it came to getting to know some of my new friends via the world of the Rabbitohs. Knowing my trip to Sydney was imminent, I wasted no time getting to know some of the most dedicated fans of the red and green via the Internet, specifically Twitter and Facebook. While I had no problems with Facebook whatsoever, Twitter and I had started off on a cold note. I was hesitant to join because I was repulsed by who was always on it: MTV reality show stars, gossip columnists, and more teenagers talking about buying shoes and salad. Not to mention it sounded so dumb; you can only communicate in 140 characters or less? Anyone ever hear of texting? Or calling?

Despite this, one of my cousins talked me into joining so I could get the word out on my travel blog and talk to other fellow travel bloggers. And while it did work now and then with others in the travel/photography cache, it worked even better for talking with fans of the Rabbitohs. I had found a new use for the social media site. By the time the 2013 season began, I began tweeting with fans from Australia, and even parts of the US who followed the Bunnies. Having missed being in Australia for almost five years, it was nice chatting with others who seemed to take interest in an American who had an uncanny knowledge of the Lucky Country. The more I watched the game and the more I tweeted with the fans, the more I got into the game. In fact, throughout 2013, I always looked forward to talking with my fellow Bunny followers. My favorite part of the day was when I had a chance to check Twitter to see if any of my friends in Australia had left me a shout-out.

One fan I found a real connection with was a man named Bill Gotsis from Schofields, a town in the western suburbs of Sydney. He and I seemed to hit it off because he was a Souths fan, but he was also a New York Giants fan as well. When I told him that my family was season ticket holders, he was excited to say the least. And when I told him I was a fan of the Rabbitohs, he and I began tweeting to each other almost every day. We went from talking about just sports, to talking about where we were from, to family life, cooking, my love for Australia, his wish to see a Giants game, and how impressed he was with my knowledge of Aussie slang. Bill soon became my favorite Bill from Australia, second only to Blinky Bill. He and I seemed to have so much in common. But that was just the beginning.

Over the next few weeks came more new Twitter followers who sported red and green, or at least a picture of them posing with Reggie, their beloved mascot. Since I could not stay up late enough to watch the Rabbitohs matches live, I would send shout-outs to all of my Rabbitohs followers, asking them the musical question, "*Are You Ready For Some Footy?!*" It wasn't long before I was getting shout-outs from the teams' Twitter feed, game announcer Warren Smith, and even former Rabbitohs captain and NRL great, Mario Fenech, who said fans like me made the club great! I was something of a celebrity to the fans, but alas, I was just a fan who loved the team and the game.

With my hotel and flight taken care of, I still needed my Rabbitohs ticket. Since I wanted to go while the season was still going on, not to mention when the weather would be most welcoming, I chose the beginning of September; summer to Americans, but an early spring for Aussies. The weather, however, wasn't my prime concern. The match I chose to attend was a doozy! It was the last regular season match, a bout between the Rabbitohs and their long-time rivals, the Sydney Roosters. This was the NRL equivalent of seeing the Yankees and the Mets. Or the Cubs and the White Sox. Or the Yankees and the Red Sox. To pick this match as my inaugural NRL event was indeed a fine selection. From the second they went on sale, I bought my ticket and knew just where I wanted to park myself: The Burrow. This was the prime seating where the most hardcore fans sat and sung during every second of the match—the ultimate cheering section where one could be lost in a sea of red and green, and be full of joy and pride!

My purchase was successful, but now came the long waiting period for my ticket to come. And with three weeks until my trip, I hoped to God it would come before I left. To kill time, I decided to make a little something to bring with me to the game, so everyone would know who the American Bunny would be. Armed with a poster canvas, a color printer, markers, scissors, glue, and a few stencils, I went to work. I shuttled back and forth between red and green markers so much, one might think that I was constructing the world's biggest Christmas card.

I worked late into the night, carefully measuring the distance between letters and numbers with the stencils I bought. It read: **"I TRAVELED OVER 10,000 MI FOR MY VERY FIRST GAME!"** Each letter and number alternated between red and green. The coup de gras were all the images of Rabbitohs players and Reggie, all in a glorious montage of red and green. But it wasn't finished yet. On the blank reverse side, I did a second design to illustrate that this is one American who is an Australian Bunny on the inside! The reverse side read: **"I'm Red, White, and Blue. BUT... I Bleed RED & GREEN for SOUTH SYDNEY RABBITOHS!"** At the top, I glued a miniature American flag, but at the bottom, I glued a miniature

Australian flag right where the word Rabbitohs was written. Like the other side, I had to include images of the two coolest rabbits in Australia: Reggie and Bunnymund; I even pasted an Aboriginal Dreamtime sketch of Bunnymund, including a pair of boomerangs.

The most noticeable pictures were a pair of images of Reggie, in a sort of enraged state. Think of a rabbit, combined with The Incredible Hulk and Cujo, minus the green skin, rabies, and dripping fangs. This popular image of the Rabbitohs features a demented-looking rabbit complete with a huge torso, pulling apart a chicken's head, showered in blood, with the phrase, "THERE CAN BE ONLY ONE!" Creepy to some, but to Rabbitohs fans, we couldn't love this image any more if it was emblazoned on a flag. It shows the coolest mascot of the NRL ripping the head off our most hated rival. That'll show any outsiders that rabbits are not to be taken lightly!

With my posters complete, I uploaded both images to my Twitter feed and my Facebook page. Within hours, every Rabbitohs fan from Botany Bay to the Central Business District began forwarding and trading the poster images. I had created something of a groundswell; it attracted fans like a beacon. I was getting major praise for my artwork, and I knew it wouldn't be long before I would be showing this off to the good people in The Burrow. More importantly, if this didn't attract any cameras or any of the commentators at the match, then I'd be most upset. "*An American coming all this way for his first footy match? Camera 3, shoot into The Burrow, and get a look at that beauty!*"

CHAPTER 4
The Royal Oak

SEPTEMBER 5, 2013:

The morning that I arrived in Sydney after winning the raffle at the party, I had just cleared customs and was pushing my luggage through the arrivals hall. On the other side of those wide doors was a crowd of both tourists and cabbies, all of whom were holding up signs for incoming passengers. There was one person I was keeping an eye open for: Tony. My dear friend had previously agreed to pick me up from Sydney Airport on the morning of my arrival. Sure enough, there he was with his mate, Warren, or as he called him, Wazza! It was so good to see my old tour guide again. We chatted away over a flat white and a plate of muffins at this small café just across the street from the line of taxis and buses outside the airport. Instead of driving me to my hotel, Tony and Wazza took me to their apartment in Brighton Le Sands, a waterfront neighborhood in South Sydney, just a short distance from the airport.

Tony and Wazza, being the kind innkeepers, offered me a hot shower, a plate of Devonshire cakes, a cuppa coffee, and a long nap to catch up on some much-needed rest after that endless flight. I couldn't imagine a nicer surprise than Tony's hospitality, but he and Wazza had an ulterior motive. Wazza presented me with two amazing gifts. First, he had a Qantas gift pack which included a backpack filled with all sorts of Qantas gear that is usually given to the passengers in first class going on long flights. But inside that backpack with the kangaroo logo was my second present, and boy was it a doozy! It was a Rabbitohs footy ball. But not just any ball.

This ball came complete with the signatures of every member of the 2013 Rabbitohs squad including Michael Maguire's! Tony said that since Wazza worked for Qantas, he got a lot of free swag from the airline. It just so happened that he was piloting a plane that was carrying the entire Rabbitohs team on board. Tony asked him if he could persuade the team to do a favor for a die-hard Bunnies fan from New York. According to Wazza, he just handed the boys a blank ball and they all happily put their John Hancock to pigskin, or rubber, if you please. It was just like that.

All Wazza had to do, according to Tony, was mention that the fan was from America and they said they were only too happy to autograph the ball. I just stood there, speechless, trying to find the words to express how stunned and happy I was. If this wasn't a moment of pure joy, then I didn't know what. I just went in for a big hug and happily thanked Wazza for this gift courtesy of the red and green boys. Oh, and Qantas. After that gift, I was too excited to catch up on some sleep in their apartment. All I could do was fantasize about showing off the ball to my friends and family. The only other autographed ball I ever got was from legendary Brooklyn Dodger Carl Erskine at an autograph signing at a mall. As much I loved that, and he was very nice when he signed it, I gave it to my uncle since he was a bigger baseball fan than I. Now, I had a piece of history I could display for all to see!

SEPTEMBER 6, 2013:

I had been in Sydney for just under thirty-six hours by the time the day of the game arrived. I spent the first day catching up on some much-needed rest; a fifteen-hour flight from Los Angeles will drain all the life out of you. I spent the afternoon picking out exactly what to wear: my Rabbitohs jersey, my poster, and a comfortable pair of khaki shorts.

Around 2:15 pm, I received a call. It was Tanya, another one of my Rabbitohs Twitter followers, a Souths fan from Brisbane who came all the way to Sydney to see her beloved Bunnies play for the Minor Premiership. As I listened to her voice for the first time ever, I'll never forget the other end.

"*Jared, its Tanya. Where are you, we're all waiting for you here at the pub! Listen everyone, it's Jared! *crowds cheering in background* Come on over! We're at The Royal Oak at Lidcombe station. Just hop on the train and walk across the overpass, across the street to the pub. We're waiting for you!*"

I cannot remember the last time someone called me up and I overheard the raucous sound of a crowd of people waiting for me to come! Not even on my birthday have I been treated with such recognition. And in another country, mind you! Without wasting a second, I grabbed my camera, my camcorder, my poster, my phone, my wallet, and of course, my ticket, still in its Australia post envelope, headed out of the hotel, and nervously ran to Town Hall station to catch the next train to Lidcombe, which Rabbitohs fans use as a juncture point for getting to Olympic Park.

While on the train, I began to breathe like a pregnant woman in labor; I just couldn't believe all this was happening! It is such a marvelous feeling to watch something that you've only dreamed about unfold before your eyes. As the train slowly approached Lidcombe, I stumbled off the train and spotted the bar. I took a deep breath, knowing I was diving into my first sea of red and green. One step inside, two steps inside, three steps inside. "Are you Jared?" someone asked from behind me, to which I replied, "Yes, that's me."

It was Brigitte and Brian who greeted me. They were standing right next to a pool table when it happened. "Good on ya!" Brigitte exclaimed when she saw my poster unraveled. I was escorted to a small patio just to the side of the pub, where I met my new friends. It was the scene I had envisioned, only with more cigarettes and booze. Granted, I am not a smoker whatsoever, but I was willing to overlook the sour odor of tobacco in exchange for staring at a friendly group of faces who were only too excited to meet me! So many smiling faces met my four-eyed grin; I think some of their smiles reminded me less of rugby players and more of ice hockey players! I think I saw one smile that reminded me of Leon Spinks on a good day!

Dental hijinks aside, I took a seat at the front of the table, and was introduced to the bevy of Bunnies. A bloke named Shawnee introduced himself to me; a cigarette limped off his lips while he flashed me a wink and smile. "G'day, cobber!" exclaimed Brian, a fan with a sizeable amount of stubble. "Eh, we're givin' ya a bit of the Aussie lingo, mate!" said Mick, another fan who was nursing a pint of beer. Frankly, the sound of "*good on ya*" and "*mate*" coming from every end of the table was like music to my ears; a symphony of slang, served with a side of beer.

I watched the bubbles in my beer float to the top in a rich, amber liquid. In between sips, I told everyone the unusual story of how I discovered the Rabbitohs. When I mentioned the unforgettable win over the Roosters from 2012, I saw their faces light up. It was like I had turned on a switch; a Pavlovian response that resulted in raucous laughter and merriment, at least for Brigitte. When I told them that I also got into the game from watching the Rugby World Cup, which is rugby union, they were immediately quick to point that out. I had mentioned it on purpose so that I could see the look on their faces. To mix up rugby league with rugby union in Australia can be one hell of a faux-pas! I had only known these people for a few weeks over the Internet, and I had just met them only a few minutes ago, and yet I felt like a member of their close-knit family. But since this was a fan base of the Bunnies, I prefer the term warren; a series of underground tunnels where rabbits live.

Since I wanted to pace myself with my beer, knowing I didn't want to fall asleep at the match, I spent long sips on my second glass. Of course, in Australia, where taking your sweet time on a beer is considered improper etiquette, I knew better than to be disrespectful in front of my new friends; first impressions do matter. The longer I talked, the more excited I got; I could hear myself stuttering at certain points. Frankly, I could have gone on chatting away with my Australian rabbit family for hours and hours more, but alas, footy waits for no mate.

Once our glasses were empty, we headed out the door back to Lidcombe station. For the Rabbitohs fans, Lidcombe is the jumping point toward Olympic Park Station. I have to say, the trains sure were fast and reliable around that city. I also loved the fact that the computerized voice that announced the stops had a thick Australian accent. It sure made commuting feel less mundane, at least from an American commuter's perspective.

CHAPTER 5
The Brewery

SEPTEMBER 6, 2013:

When we began this story, I was sitting nervously on the train, heading toward the stadium with my newfound friends. There was one funny event I left out at the start: one of my Rabbitohs friends brought a rooster-shaped piñata to the Royal Oak that he also brought with him onto the train. Tying a noose around its neck with a small rope, he hung the paper plucker from a safety railing inside the train car. Suddenly, everyone began taking turns whacking the bug-eyed bird with everything we had. Using my poster as a stick, I gleefully began whacking away at the avian effigy, while passengers all around cheered me on.

My friends began breaking out their iPhones, and took numerous shots of me; I looked angry, but deep down, I was so happy! I felt like I was an outsider taking part in a rare ritual. The native Bunnies invited me to take part in the ceremonial *whack-the rooster-piñata-with- an-angry-grin-on-your-face.* Suffice it to say, I made it through a Rabbitohs rite of passage.

Every team has rituals or traditional places they meet before heading inside their home turf. New York Yankees fans congregate along River Street, noshing on burgers and beer at Stan's Bar. Boston Red Sox fans gather along Yawkey Way or Lansdowne Street. New York Giants and New York Jets fans tailgate out of their car trunks at the Meadowlands in East Rutherford, New Jersey. Some of them don't even bother leaving their car and going inside; it is all about barbequing and never leaving the parking lot. It's as American as apple pie served on an American flag! The Rabbitohs fans congregate at The Brewery, a popular sports bar located just outside ANZ Stadium.

Outside, a horde of red-and-green Bunnies swarmed the place like a mob of drunken rabbits. Inside, several TVs broadcasted horse races, while viewers placed their bets on the winning pony. It is no secret, by the way, that Australians love to gamble and dance with Lady Luck. All the while, cans of Pure Blonde, VB, Tooheys, and XXXX glistened in everyone's hands. I was holding up my camcorder to my red and green entourage, trying to get them to give a big shout-out to my friends and relatives back home. It was at this moment that I was introduced to even more fans and followers whom I had met previously on Twitter and Facebook. I felt like I was at a Hollywood party sans the arrogance, well-dressed A-listers, and make-up. Instead, I was rubbing elbows with the most famous fans in Australia. One recognizable individual was the Rabbitohs Warrior, who was very hard to miss. A man who had his face painted in red and green two-tone (not a square inch of facial skin was unpainted). Accompanied by a giant afro, glasses, and a giant sword (which was fake), he was practically the unofficial mascot of the team, let alone The Brewery. His enthusiasm was the envy of all the fans, but I decided to confront him and see if his outfit was any match for a fan from halfway around the world.

The Warrior came over to where I was drinking; Brian introduced me to him. He was as boisterous as you could imagine, but a fun-loving fan, as you might guess. He had a gleam in his eye when I told him who I was and how far I had come for my first game. He pulled me in for a big hug and posed for several pictures. Suddenly, I felt like I was at Disneyland; every fan felt like being in a parade of fanciful characters, but with more drinking and cursing! He held aloft his mighty sword, and as he did, I saw Mick hanging the rooster piñata over a tree branch. The Warrior ran to it with his sword and pierced the dreaded bird! I have to say, if this was the kind of entertainment that was going on outside the stadium, I could only imagine the mayhem that existed inside the stadium.

I also met Ursulla and Darren, a married couple in their matching jerseys. Darren shook my hand and exclaimed, "*You know my wife Ursulla? You two chat together on Facebook. I've seen your poster, mate. That's a real nice job there!*" Everyone was so eager to shake my hand and introduce themselves to me. I hadn't had this much attention since my Bar Mitzvah.

It was at that moment that I finally met Bill Gotsis, my first Rabbitohs Twitter follower. Like me, he wore a pair of thick black glasses, was sporting red and green, and was excited to finally meet me. Soon enough, Bill started showing me off to other fans. A rare creature was I, an American fan of footy, as was he, a New York Giants fan from Australia. The other fans were so curious to know why a Yank would come all this way for a game, an important game of the year, nonetheless. They just couldn't believe their eyes and ears. Still, whenever I shook their hands, they made me feel more than just welcome. They made me feel like I was family; a genuine Australian Bunny!

What was even weirder was how many people I saw at The Brewery recognized my poster, even though they did not recognize me. One unforgettable fan was Dingo MacNaughton. Yes, you heard me. An Australian rugby fan named Dingo! The instant he got a look at my poster, he did something no fan in America has ever done that I know of: he literally gave me the shirt off his back! It was a t-shirt, or rather, an undershirt with an adorable picture of a bunny in a red and green jumper angrily fornicating a rooster, with the inscription "F**k the Roosters!" And yes, it came with a pair of genitals! Still more tasteful than what Red Sox fans have to say about the Yankees! I wasn't even inside the stadium, and already, I was being showered with gifts. But that shirt was just the beginning.

Then, I met Wendy Celarc, another fan I was introduced to

on Twitter. When she heard of an American who was coming to Sydney to see the mighty Rabbitohs play, she was impressed to say the least. I had requested to her that I would like one of the trademark South Sydney "Till I Die" scarves worn by almost every Rabbitohs fan. She told me that it was sort of a members only thing and you had to know certain people to acquire one. Either that, or bid on one on eBay. Realizing that I had no PayPal account, but knowing someone associated with the Rabbitohs, I asked Wendy if she could hook me up. In return, I promised her one of my New York Giants scarves. Not worth the same value, but as a sign of international friendship among sports fans. Sure enough, within weeks of my departure, Wendy posted me a picture of the scarf in her possession, and I kept my end of the deal with my Giants scarf.

By the time we met face to face at The Brewery, it was an historic moment between two friends. As she handed me the beautiful and soft scarf bearing the two-tone red and green colors, I handed over my scarf bearing the NY insignia of my beloved Giants.

This, my friends, is one way of practicing the lost art of diplomacy. Why bother dealing with negotiators, politicians, military experts, and angry mobs when you can just connect to other human beings via professional sports? That's one reason we have the Olympics and the World Cup, so that people from other nations can meet each other on and off the field. But on a personal level, it can work wonders. When two fans meet and form a friendship based on their love of a favorite team, it can snowball into something great, like a domino effect. If we could just put politics aside and just talk about the similarities of rugby and football between nations, it would be so much easier than dealing with things that go boom. I don't mean to go off on a tangent, but sports can work wonders when it comes to learning about one's culture. It worked with Ping-Pong when Richard Nixon visited China in the 1970s, and it led to open relations with the Asian nation. Granted, Australia is not Red China from 1972, but I've learned that friendships Down Under form when sports are the topic. Nothing is a better ice-breaker in the land of kangaroos and koalas like talking about the NRL, the AFL, or anything involving guys in uniforms with unusual mascots clobbering the crap out of each other. Whether it's talking about the differences between cricket and baseball on the Chunnel or how Aussies practice the devoted art of rugby worship, sports can really bring the world together.

CHAPTER 6
The Clubhouse

SEPTEMBER 6, 2013:

The entrance to ANZ Stadium, or "The Warren" as I referred to it, approached closer and closer. There wasn't a bevy of security guards that gave me repeated pat-downs; I noticed how many fans were allowed to bring in flags of all sizes. One little step through the turnstiles, and "*Bonza!*" I had entered the hallowed hallways of Sydney's most famous stadium! I took a deep breath and inhaled the wonderful aroma from inside. It was so big and spacious. Bill took my hand and whisked me into a world where Rabbits speak Australian and curse the name of a Rooster!

I noticed that there were not a lot of concession stands. Except for a couple of beer stalls and perhaps one or two sausage stands, food items were not to be seen everywhere. While watching the NRL on TV, it occurred to me that binging on stadium chow was not the norm at these venues. Everyone was so busy cheering, singing, taking pictures, and waving flags, that no one had the time to stuff their faces! Chugging away at a few beers, definitely, but eating during the game was something I did not see a lot of. At a Giants game, I'm used to seeing everyone shove a sausage or hot dog in their face; it's hard to cheer loudly when your mouth is full. At the Rabbitohs games, everyone's singing comes in clear as a bell. The food they were serving however, did look good, but I didn't want to miss a micro-second of the action. But I would definitely find enough time to have some of Australia's amber nectar!

Before heading to our seats, Bill took me up to a special

reserved area of the stadium called "The Clubhouse." Bill flashed a badge to a sentry and we rushed up the escalator. Without warning, I was escorted into yet another dwelling of the Bunnies. This was a "fans-only" area, featuring a panoramic view of the stadium. The Clubhouse felt like being in a giant skybox, minus the fancy food, TVs, and slight arrogance. Then again, I have a skybox at Madison Square Garden, so who am I to complain? It seems that the favorite activity among footy fans, when they're not cheering or playing, is drinking and talking. They are a social bunch who can carry on a conversation even after a few beers. One thing I always look out for whenever I go places is not to believe in stereotypes. Thanks to the inaccuracies of Outback Steakhouse and Fosters, Americans have been force-fed on the image of Australians being obsessed with beer; rowdy drunks that are the byproduct of campy beer commercials with a redneck flavor.

I always look to reality to debunk the silliness, but if my round of drinks at The Royal Oak taught me anything, it turns out that image is somewhat true, but not in some déclassé fashion; one that does not reduce the Aussies to cartoonish images. The footy fans with a cold beer in their hands are but a jovial bunch who love to recount sports memories with good company, peppered with a casual swear or two. In short, no different than Americans at a tailgating party. The one difference: Aussie beer tastes slightly better and footy fans are just the coolest! If only Americans knew more about rugby culture, and how it goes so well with cold beer and friends.

Bill Gotsis was a most cheerful individual. He was as forthcoming and friendly as I had envisioned; I had only known him through our tweets and emails. To say that he is a most enthusiastic bloke would be quite an understatement. During the time I was at the game, along with my two weeks in Sydney, Bill took me under his wing as the newest member of The Burrow! He showed me around the stadium, introduced me to his friends and family, brushed me up on the basic rules and positions, and gave me some insight into the team's history. He was sort of my Rabbitohs sensei; my Australian Bunny brother from another mother! Frankly, I was most lucky to have someone as knowledgeable as Bill. When it came to knowing the sport, I was out of my wheel house; I was a little afraid of getting quizzed on the spot about the game. But no one made me feel pressured, especially Bill. He seemed so relaxed, even for a night where so much was at stake. Either he had purged all the nervousness out of his body, or he was secretly sweating and shaking on the inside. Talk about calm under pressure!

Another Bunny who was looking out for me was Tanya, a big Rabbitohs fan from Brisbane. She was another fan I had met courtesy of Twitter. I recognized her from a Rabbitohs tattoo on her arm; the Rabbitohs Bunny logo in black ink. From the minute she saw me at The Brewery, she had practically squealed with delight. Like Bill, she too was an enthusiastic fan, and very friendly. While I was not too crazy about the smoking, the two of us hit it off. We had chatted about the Bunnies on Twitter, but not in person.

While rubbing elbows in The Clubhouse, I was introduced to a cute girl from Sydney named Morgan. Surprised to see an American among the Souths faithful, she asked, "Did you really come all this way for the game?" Blushing, I admitted yes, but not before bragging about my raffle prize from New York. I couldn't help it; it was just so worth bringing it up. Trying hard to not reek of any such arrogance, I calmly stated that I was a fan of the team, and that it was my first match ever. Morgan then said, "I've not ever met anyone who came overseas for a game!" To which I responded, "Do the Roosters have a fan like this? No!"

She then lovingly pointed to a poster of Sam Burgess, her favorite player. She asked if there was anyone in America like Sam Burgess. All I could come up with was the Manning brothers, Eli and Peyton from the NFL.

The Burgess Brothers, for those who are not familiar, are four brothers who all play for the Rabbitohs: Sam, Thom, George, and Luke; four natives of England who have become big footy stars Down Under. I told her about how two of the best quarterbacks in the NFL were brothers. She seemed rather interested, until I segued into how Eli Manning helped the New York Giants usurp the New England Patriots' perfect season back in 2008, the year they won Super Bowl XLII. Her eyebrows shot straight up when I told her how a rag-tag group of underdogs beat an undefeated team to win the biggest game of the year.

America has the Manning brothers, and Australia has the Burgess Brothers, or as I like to refer to them, the "Bunny Brothers!" Regaling Morgan with this true story of underdogs made sense of why she seemed so interested; Rabbitohs are often looked at as the underdogs of the NRL, despite their illustrious history and numerous Premierships. Or perhaps she was enthralled with my retelling of an otherwise memorable championship! Frankly, I could have spent the entire night talking to her about the similarities and differences between the Giants and the Rabbitohs. But, we had bigger things to attend to...

CHAPTER 7
The Bunny in the Burrow
(First Half of the Minor Premiership)

SEPTEMBER 6, 2013

> *"In The Burrow, we sing. Many fans have questioned why, when it is such a foreign concept in this country. Yet in many stadiums around the world, singing embraces all aspects of football fandom. It celebrates the triumphs, rallies support behind the team, enhances the ground's atmosphere, and intimidates the opposition through the creation of home-ground advantage. Our vision is to have these songs not only sung loud and proud in The Burrow, but all around ANZ Stadium, uniting Souths fans in voice for the greatest football team in the country."*

In the spring of 1994, I went to my first baseball game at Yankee Stadium. In April of 1995, I went to my first hockey game at Nassau Coliseum. In September of 1997, I went to my first football game at Giants Stadium. In December of 2000, I went to my first basketball game at Madison Square Garden. And now, in September of 2013, I, Jared Schnabl of Rockville Centre, New York, attended my first rugby (I'm sorry, rugby *league*) game, ten thousand miles from my home! The closer I headed to Section 110, the faster my heart beat. Actually, sections inside the stadium are referred to as "bays." My toes curled up into my sneakers. I could feel my tongue getting drier by the second. My heart began thumping, like... well, a rabbit's foot! A few steps through the tunnel, and there it was: the green field that was ANZ Stadium. The rugby goal posts looked even taller in real life. I couldn't believe I was actually there!

I made a 360-degree turn, taking in all the sights, sounds, and smells. This was truly a memorable moment, beyond comparison. Not missing an opportunity to show off my artwork, I held my poster high in the air for all the fans to see. I saw a few fingers pointing at it, while a few others applauded for my long journey. "Mate, is this your first time?"

"Mate, is this really your first match?"

"Did you really come all this way for the Bunnies?!" asked every fan who seemed bewildered at my signage. I tried not to let my head swell, but when would I ever feel this kind of admiration again? "Yep! This is my first footy match ever! You're looking at the only Bunnies fan from Long Island, New York!" I said in a most boastful manner. I tiptoed into my row and plopped down into my seat. I had finally made it!

As the clock ticked down to kickoff, I could see the rows around the stadium filling up. Normally, a regular season NRL match doesn't always have a sold-out stadium, but that does not mean that the team, let alone the sport, is unpopular. With nine NRL teams playing within and around Sydney, and with a population of around 4.6 million, everyone has their favorite club; it would be very hard to fill those games to maximum capacity. Every time I would watch a Rabbitohs game, I would notice that the entire stadium was not filled like a World Cup soccer match. Rest assured it is not an issue regarding ticket prices, popularity, TV coverage, or a lackluster record. It is just hard to find over 65,000 Rabbitohs fans among hundreds of thousands of other fans in a city where other clubs compete for top dollar.

And for the record, the NRL, despite its popularity, is not the same cash cow like the NFL. Team jerseys don the names and logos of sponsors that financially support the club, like a NASCAR racecar. The Rabbitohs, at the time, had DeLonghi and The Star Casino front and center on their jerseys. Despite the corporate influence, it didn't bother me that the team jerseys look a little like a miniature billboard. All that mattered was that I was watching some gigantic Aussies stampede up and down the field, crushing all those in the way!

One of my newest friends I met in The Burrow was Lachlan, a tall fellow with a wild crop of hair and a beard that seemed to match. There was also Joe Mancusi, whom I had first befriended on Twitter. Like Bill, he too was an enthusiastic fan who was quite delighted to meet me. He and I had quite a rapport on the Twitter-feed; he seemed rather impressed by my knowledge of Australia and my love for the Rabbitohs. A real cheerful bloke if I ever met one.

The time finally came when the Roosters came out of the tunnels. The entire stadium erupted in an angry howl of boos, save for a small section of the stadium reserved for those in navy blue, white, and red jumpers. It reminded me of the moment when the visiting team lineup was read aloud at Yankee Stadium while "The Empire March" from Star Wars played over the loudspeakers. But then, the moment that everyone else had been waiting for. I heard a drum beat. And then another. It was the opening theme of the South Sydney Rabbitohs' fight song, "South Sydney Marches On." Sung to the tune of the Battle Hymn of the Republic, this could be my favorite team song. It starts off like the beginning of a parade with the drum rolls, then it segues into a melodic humming, and then it jumps into the lyrics in which the team boasts its many accomplishments in a voice that would be on par with the Marine Corps choir.

SOUTH SYDNEY MARCHES ON....

CHORUS
Glory, Glory to South Sydney
Glory, Glory to South Sydney
Glory, Glory to South Sydney
South Sydney Marches On

When speaking of the champions
One stands above the rest
Of glories old and records proud
When often put to test
Of fine traditions, history
That others cannot best
They wear the RED & GREEN

REPEAT CHORUS

They mauled the Balmain Tigers
Slew the Dragons from St. George
The Seagulls and the Mounties next
Were crushed with mighty force
They humbled Parramatta
And the Berries in due course
They wear the RED & GREEN

REPEAT CHORUS

They plucked the Western Magpies
Slashed the Newtown bag of blue
The Eastern Suburbs rooster crowed
And then was conquered too
The greatest name in any game
Within South Sydney grew
They wear the RED & GREEN

REPEAT CHORUS (twice)

I look forward to the day when I can find this song on iTunes! With the opening of the song, I finally laid eyes on the Rabbitohs' beloved mascot, Reggie. For most teams, the mascot is usually written off as superfluous. It is in that nature that Reggie Rabbit stands alone. To the Rabbitohs and their fans, he is practically part of the team, let alone their red-and-green family. When he storms out of the team tunnel, the crowd erupts in an ear-splitting cheer. I mean, you have to love the humor of it; a giant smiling bunny that leads an athletic army into eighty minutes of brutal physical contact.

Standing at nearly seven feet tall if you include the ears, Reggie the Rabbit is the South Sydney Rabbitohs' beloved mascot, not to mention one of the most recognizable faces in the National Rugby League, and maybe all of Australia. After all, when your team is comprised of seventeen gigantic rugby players that can charge up the field in a flash, and their mascot is a giant white bunny in a red-and-green jumper, people are going to take notice. And he doesn't just hang on the side of the field like some wallflower. Reggie, much like the team, gets in on the action, at least with the fans. He spends most of the game shaking hands, or rather paws, with his adoring public on the front rows from the stadium's edge. It seems that everyone practically clamors for a photo or a hug with him. And you thought the Easter Bunny was popular! But you didn't hear that from me!

They say that behind every great man is a great woman. Well, behind every great rabbit, is a great man. For years, Reggie has been portrayed by Charlie Gallico; faceless to the fans, but not to those at South Sydney, who hold the pint-sized seventy-year-old Australian dear to their hearts. Gallico has been involved with the club for the past thirty-three years, and you would be hard-pressed to find someone who would gain greater pleasure in a South Sydney premiership than him, let alone the fans. Like any superhero, he leads a double life;

a native of Matraville, a suburb of South Sydney, who works as a mechanic by day, but transforms into a giant rabbit come game time. Take that, Clark Kent, mild-mannered reporter for the *Daily Bugle*!

Earlier this year, however, while Mr. Gallico was having dinner with the Rabbitohs players, he received a phone call that turned his world upside down. His lovely wife Sofia, who had been in the stands for every South Sydney home game in his twelve years as Reggie, had taken a sudden turn for the worst and tragically passed away. The fans, along with friends and family of Mr. Gallico mourned from Redfern to Maroubra, and even thousands of miles away in Long Island where yours truly sent his condolences halfway around the world.

It was during Round 12 of the 2013 season that Reggie took center stage at ANZ Stadium. The Rabbitohs took the field against the Newcastle Knights in front of thousands of Rabbitohs fans at ANZ Stadium and Reggie still found the strength to lead his beloved South Sydney into battle. In a turn of events, instead of leading the team out onto the field, the players came out first and then led Reggie out onto the field. This became a key moment in which I became enamored with the team. I mean, since when in American pro-sports do the fans pay that much of a tribute to their mascot? I even listened as the commentators and coaches saluted Reggie like a proud solider. The game looked like it would be Newcastle's during the first half, but the Rabbitohs went on to win 25–18 after a drop-kick field goal sealed the game. The climactic moment came when the players hoisted Reggie onto their shoulders, and carried him off the field as the fans stood up and cheered like crazy!

Since I was at home watching the game over the Internet, I stood up and clapped, then attempted to hold back a tear or two. That kind of love for someone on your team, even if they're not someone who takes the field to score or the strongest individual, is something so seldom seen in pro-sports nowadays. It's no wonder that Reggie is the "Rabbitohs' 18th man." Beneath Reggie beats the heart of a man. But beneath that man, beats the heart of a proud, Australian Bunny!

Bryson Goodwin kicked the ball with a mighty blow, and the game was on! Just three seconds later, James Maloney of the Roosters caught it, but was swiftly tackled at the 10-meter mark. On the fourth tackle, the Roosters punted the ball and none other than Greg Inglis himself scooped it up. After getting tackled ten meters from their try line, Dylan Farrell got the ball but went down on the second tackle at the 20-meter line. Adam Reynolds, our star kicker, recovered the ball at dummy half and was tackled at the 25-meter line. Then, Ben Te'o was tackled at the 35-meter line for fourth tackle. On the fifth tackle, Roy Asotasi went down at the 40-meter line. At 1:20, Adam Reynolds punted the ball from the 45-meter line, just shy of midfield, and that drive became my first witness to the Rabbitohs in action on offense! I'd have to wait a couple more minutes, however, before the Bunnies would score.

If you think glee club members or Broadway chorus dancers love to sing, then you haven't met these blokes. For the entire match, I was drowning in a sea of music, beer, and red and green. The Burrow is the fans-only section of the stadium. That may sound redundant, but this place is special. It is a marked off area; there are separate tickets just for this section. Then, in an effort to kick subtlety to the curb, the section is clearly marked with a giant red-and-green banner with "THE BURROW" written across. And lucky me, I was sitting right behind the banner. But not to worry; it didn't obstruct anyone's view. The Rabbitohs even take The Burrow with them to away games; they sit in a specific section of the visiting stadium, and proceed to make camp. For me, an American making his first visit to a Rabbitohs game, let alone his first footy match, sitting in this part of the stadium was a real honor!

You'd think I'd stick out like a sore thumb, but instead, I was welcomed with open arms.

The fans sounded loud on TV, but being there in real life, my ear drums and vocal chords became sore like you couldn't imagine! It seemed that every few seconds, The Burrow would segue from one cheer to another. They even had a whole catalog of cheers and songs that were sung to the tune of some already familiar favorites. It wasn't just "Glory Glory to South Sydney"; The Burrow's Facebook page had a downloadable songbook that featured twenty-three fun-filled chants. In between holding up my poster, hoping it would attract a cameraman or two, my ears took notice of all the songs. Luckily, I have a great memory, and I managed to pick up on the words and melodies of each cheer. The fast-paced game of tackling, combined with the musical enthusiasm of the fans made for such an ambiance that I had not previously experienced in any major sporting event.

As if a noisy choir of footy fans wasn't enough, Reggie came toward The Burrow, leading the chants like a long-eared conductor. With each note and lyric that I belted out, I suddenly felt like I belonged there! Everyone was so psyched to be there, and not just because it was one the biggest games of the year. One of my favorite moments during the first half came when The Burrow began chanting "Rabbits!" over and over, along with a rhythmic clapping. And then, right on cue, Reggie faced The Burrow, waved his fists in the air, and led the chant. Moments later, he returned with a cowbell; so that's what was missing from the game—more cowbell!

I have to say, the members of The Burrow are but an obedient mob; they know when to shout joyously, and when to keep quiet during key moments of the game. Reggie, however, wasn't the only long-eared pied piper in the warren. A member of The Burrow had brought a drum with him; he was pounding away, giving the section a much-needed rhythm section. Come to think of it, The Burrow was a footy version of the old Brooklyn Dodgers Sym-phony band! In fact, from my perspective, the Rabbitohs *were* the Australian Brooklyn Dodgers. Sure, they may have had way more championship wins than the sorely missed ghosts of Flatbush, but they had the same loveable, underdog appeal. And like the Dodgers, the Rabbitohs came out of a working- class neighborhood. Back in the day, Redfern was practically the Brooklyn of Sydney. I think I just realized why I enjoyed rooting for this team. The fact that the club hadn't won a Premiership in over forty years made them both underdogs and perennial "let-downs" among NRL fans. The fans, despite the tumultuousness, stuck with them through and through, while other clubs wrote them off as either irrelevant or has-beens.

At around 10:38 into the first half, Tom Burgess with the ball was delivered a first tackle inside the Roosters' 45-meter line, then Roy Asotasi got a second tackle inside the 35-meter line, then Sam Burgess got tackled inside the 25-meter line for a third tackle, and then Adam Reynolds got the fourth tackle just 15-meters from the try line. Then, at the 11:00 mark, Reynolds gave the ball to John Sutton, who passed it to Greg Inglis. Then, at 11:08 in the first half, I saw my first try and it was made by none other than Rabbitohs' fullback and superstar, Greg Inglis. ANZ Stadium erupted in a cacophony of happy screams; the noise made inside Madison Square Garden during a Rangers game is the only thing that can come close to the volume I was immersed in that evening. And it wasn't just the cheers. Flames shot up into the sky from pyrotechnic cannons in the end zone, and the scoreboard showed a rather awesome animation of a giant, fanged rabbit going all "Incredible Hulk" on a rugby ball. It certainly confirmed my belief that a rabbit was not only a cool choice for a rugby team, but intimidating as well! As Greg Inglis took a moment to acknowledge the fans, Adam Reynolds took the field to convert the four-point try into a six-point try with goal kick. I first became aware of Adam Reynolds after the historic come-from-behind win against the Roosters from last year. He was the one who carried the ball across the try line to secure that amazing win. When I look at Adam Reynolds, I can still hear Warren Smith crying, *"Reynolds! Reynolds! You can take me now, I have seen it all!"* Throughout the season, I have seen him step up to the line, and practically kick the ball high through the goal posts, and into the stratosphere! And I'll tell you what—his first big conversion didn't disappoint!

With the first try came a slew of sayings echoing from every corner of The Burrow. "*Get'em outside, ya pink poofta!*" "*You bloody bastard!*" "*Give it to those f**king scum!*" and the always classic "*Crikey!*" It was whole lot more melodious than the cacophonous "DE-FENSE! DE-FENSE!" heard in the NFL. Sports just seem more fun when you throw in a little culture, or at least something that you don't always see on a daily basis. A giant rabbit? Australian slang? Oceans of beer? A barrage of tackling sans helmets? Yes, please! The NFL ain't got nothing on this!

CHAPTER 8
Still Hate The Roosters!
(Second Half of the Minor Premiership)

The South Sydney Rabbitohs and the Sydney Roosters are arguably the most famed rivalry in Australian rugby league, if not the most heated rivalry in Australian sports. While America has the New York Yankees and the Boston Red Sox in baseball, Australia has its own famed sports rivalry. For as long as the NRL and rugby league have been around, these two teams have been duking it out for footy supremacy in Australia's biggest city. There are many reasons why these two teams are always at odds with one another. For starters, they are two of the original rugby league clubs in Australia, dating back to over 100 years ago when the NRL was founded as the New South Wales Rugby League (NSWRL).

The Rabbitohs and their fans have built up rivalries with other clubs, particularly the Sydney Roosters, the only other remaining foundation club. The Rabbitohs and the Roosters share inner-Sydney territory, resulting in a strong rivalry since 1908 when the Rabbitohs beat the Roosters in the first Grand Final, 14–12. From that point on, the Rabbitohs have racked up twenty more titles; more than any other club. In addition, many NRL trophies are all named after former Souths stars like JJ Giltinan (JJ Giltinan Shield; awarded to the winner of the Minor Premiership), Clive Churchill (Clive Churchill Award; awarded to the most valuable player of the Grand Final) and Ron Coote (Ron Coote Cup; awarded to the victor of the first Rabbitohs versus Roosters match of the season). These athletes are not just some of the best players to ever don red and green, but they are considered by almost all Australians as some of the greatest rugby players in history.

In Round 1 of 2010, the Rabbitohs and the Roosters became the first clubs to play 200 matches against each other. To celebrate their rivalry, the Rabbitohs and Roosters contest the Ron Coote Cup annually. When it came to home turf, the Rabbitohs came from the working-class suburb of Redfern, while the Roosters came from the middle- to upper-class neighborhood of Bondi, which is why the club also goes by the name Eastern Suburb Roosters. However, recent history had not been kind to the Bunnies, much like Australia's human population was to its actual bunny population a century ago.

Okay, maybe not that cruel, but the team's last premiership win was, until recently, in 1971, two years before the Sydney Opera House opened to the public in 1973. The team had a few years of glory in the late 1980s under the leadership of Mario Fenech, another Rabbitohs legend who gave South Sydney its last Minor Premiership in 1989. But only a year later in 1990, the team was awarded the dreaded Wooden Spoon, which is given to the team who finishes in last place for the season. Think of it as the footy equivalent of the Razzie award in Hollywood. But I digress. The Roosters were stealing the Rabbitohs' mojo; they had racked up an additional three Premierships (1974, 1975, and 2002), bringing their total to twelve. And to really add insult to injury, the Rabbitohs were barred from the NRL for three whole years thanks to the Super-League War that forced the Rabbitohs to either merge with the Sydney Roosters, thereby reducing the number of clubs in the league, or simply cease operations and fold.

Wait just a minute. For my American friends and readers, allow me to backtrack and clarify that fact. The Super League War was a corporate dispute that was fought in and out of court during the mid-1990s between the Rupert Murdoch and News Corporation-backed Super League (Australia) and the Kerry Packer and Optus Vision-backed Australian Rugby League organizations over broadcasting rights for, and ultimately control of, the top-level professional rugby league football competition of Australasia. Prior to News Corporation's Super League proposal, the New South Wales Rugby League (NSWRL) and Australian Rugby League (ARL) had planned to rationalize the number of footy teams based in Sydney. In a nutshell, the plan was to expand and create new team franchises from various parts of Australia as well as parts of New South Wales. During the 1980s, when this grand idea came about, some teams were eliminated from first-grade competition for not being profitable or not attracting mass crowds anymore. Some, however, were forced to merge with other more profitable clubs; the Illawarra Steelers merged with the St. George Dragons and the Western Suburbs Magpies merged with the Balmain Tigers.

After much court action from the already-existing ARL (Australian Rugby League) to prevent it from happening, Super League ran one premiership season parallel to the ARL's in 1997 after signing enough clubs disenchanted with the traditional administration to do so. At the conclusion of that season, a peace deal was reached and both Leagues united to form the National Rugby League of today. But one infamous casualty from the Super League War was the forced merger of the South Sydney Rabbitohs with the Sydney Roosters.

Not wanting to abandon their fans, logo, or history, the team did the unthinkable and chose to not merge, but saw themselves in a sports-like limbo. For the NRL to not have the Rabbitohs in the club would be like major league baseball not having the Yankees or the Cubs. It took the rallying support of their fans, former players, as well as some much-needed cash for the National Rugby League to see what kind of a Pandora's Box they had unleashed by locking the Bunnies out of the proverbial garden that was their own league. The cry of red and green fans could not be ignored; in 2001, the NRL relented, and the Rabbitohs were reintroduced to the league come the 2002 season.

The power of the fans had won. In fact, some of the most vocal in their support for South Sydney were none other than the Roosters and their fans. Why? As much as the Roosters hated the Rabbitohs, they had much respect for their red and green rivals, and felt that they needed to exist as it was a matter of simply needing them. After all, light cannot exist without darkness and vice versa. With the Rabbitohs reinstated, a part of the Roosters was reborn, as was also the historic rivalry. But I digress. Now back to the Minor Premiership.

With the score tied up, I was awaiting the moment where the Rabbitohs would do what they did best: make an amazing come-from-behind win in the second half, which I saw a lot of during the 2013 season. I didn't even see a tinge of fatigue in any of the players. Then again, I was so caught up in a sea of jovial, drunken footy fans screaming "*Bunnies!*" that I began to lose track of the game itself. Unfortunately, so did the Rabbitohs.

The second half became a 180, so to speak, from the first half wherein the Roosters just couldn't be stopped. Somehow, they had zeroed in on our Achilles heel that I had seen all throughout the season: defense. We could run, tackle, and weave in and out of the opposition at dummy half to score a try, but defense was where we seemed to come up short. It was like watching football players in the NFL get totally blindsided by the offense, and jumping just a second too late in. Now, I am not saying they were playing terribly, far from it. Maybe it was the overconfidence or the pressure, but two unanswered tries by the Roosters in the second half practically sealed our fate. There was one moment during the second half when we all thought we Bunnies had a try late in the half. It was such an exciting moment, Lachlan, the tall, bearded fan sitting next to me hoisted me high into the air. He lifted me with such force; I think I almost got a nosebleed! Giants fans at the Meadowlands aren't this athletic and excited!

Alas, our pandemonium was not to last when our try was called off from the video refs. The feelings in The Burrow ran the gamut from sheer disappointment to more swearing than I had ever heard in my life, and I've seen the Yankees play the Red Sox at Fenway Park! Now there's a great source for utter profanity! It appeared that Lachlan was going through the five stages of grief, judging from how upset he was at the unrewarded try. But the Rabbitohs fans were not about to let the Roosters have the last laugh. It was then that the red and green fans, at least a select bunch in The Burrow, began unveiling a giant banner.

In the thick of it all, I was a bit confused by the ruckus going on, so I just went with the crowd. I had no idea what we were unraveling; being behind the massive banner doesn't help much when you're trying to read the freakin' thing. I slyly ducked under my seat, under the banner, and scooched my way toward the aisle in the bay. It read in black and white letters: ROOSTERS SCUM: FOREVER IN OUR SHADOW. I didn't know it at the time, but I was in the thrall of what would become a small controversy amongst footy fans over proper behavior at a game combined with the inner workings of just how those loyal Rabbitohs fans really felt about their Eastern Suburbs rivals. I heard several security guards and ushers scolding the people holding the banner to take it down immediately. This did not sit well with the rather sore lot of fans who were going to sit by silently and let the Roosters walk off with just a win. While I'm all for sportsmanship, I couldn't help but join in with the sign bearers who defied the ushers in their black-and-white protest. And in their defense, there was no profanity on the banner and it wasn't like they weren't saying something foul that wasn't on every Rabbitohs fan's mind.

Still, I decided to slink away so as not to get in trouble. By the last few minutes, it was a foregone conclusion that none of us Bunnies wanted to face. But, being a team that is "always a bridesmaid, never a bride," the fans were just getting what was coming to us. It was a painful reminder that Rabbitohs fans knew all too well: they came so close, but they just couldn't make it all the way.

The game ended with a 24–12 Eastern Suburbs win, and the Rabbitohs fans booed as they shuffled out of Olympic Park. This certainly was not the way I wanted to remember my first professional rugby match, much less my first match in Australia, much less my first Rabbitohs game. Then again, my first New York Giants game didn't end in a victory, and I'm still standing to this day. I certainly don't mean to sound bitter, but I did not enjoy my long walk back to Olympic Park station. As I exited the magnificent venue, it didn't take me long to see a horde of bitter Bunnies chanting, *"Ya know we still hate the Roosters, still hate the Roo-sters! Ya know we still hate the Roosters, still hate the Roo-sters!"*

As much as I wanted to join in their merriment, I was too busy nursing a broken heart. Well, not a broken heart as much as a bruised ego and dashed hopes. I was also trying to steer clear of any Roosters fans, what with their smug sense of self-satisfaction rubbing it in all of our faces, forgetting that the Bunnies hadn't finished the season atop the ladder for the Minor Premiership since 1989. It was just like when every last Red Sox fan in Boston would not stop talking about how they came back to beat the Yankees to win the pennant in 2004 from three games down.

As the train pulled into the station, I noticed that the platform was packed with Roosters fans from left to right; the Chookies outnumbered the Bunnies heavily, and I could rule out crying on someone's shoulder. I slumped into the only open seat I could find, whipped out my iPod, and attempted to escape into sonic solitude to soothe my disappointment. But not even the upbeat catchiness of Men at Work and Weird Al could cure my blues. The train ride seemed longer than usual as I kept looking out the window for Central Station. I just couldn't help but notice all those Roosters supporters on the train and found myself wishing they were cheering Bunnies fans instead. Is this what the red and green army has to put up with every year? Is this what it's like to be emotionally invested in a sports team that is always a bridesmaid, but never a bride. I have a desire to root for an underdog team out of sympathy for the fact that the fans have been infinitely impatient with wanting to see their home team win the big one.

Of course, it wasn't the first time I had experienced heartbreak in sports. I had my fair share of being let down from Major League Baseball to high school basketball (that last one I still carry with me to this day). This one, however, felt different. I guess maybe because I was a newcomer to this sport as well as the culture it came with. Also, I hadn't been around as long as the other Rabbitohs fans who had been through several Wooden Spoons, and the years in which the team was barred from the NRL. But this loss introduced me to what every red and green Aussie has had to put up with. And yet, they always find a way to come out of their funk, and still keep showing up ready to fight again. It is the undying love and admiration that comes with being a fan. And when you're a Rabbitohs fan, it is a love and admiration that few can fathom.

As the train finally pulled into Central, I headed downstairs to catch my connecting train to Town Hall. It was from that day forward that I said to myself, *I am a Rabbitoh! I am an Australian Bunny Rabbit! I wear the red and green!* Well, at least I had the playoffs to look forward to! The Roosters may have won that battle, but they had not yet won the war. Touché, Chooks.

PART II:

My Bunny Brethren

CHAPTER 9
The Rabbit from Rockville Centre

I spent most of my life in Rockville Centre, a large suburb on Long Island, just twenty-five miles (40 km) east of New York City. I can't say when my love affair with the Land Down Under began, but I like to think it began when I was seven years old and in the first grade. It was at that age that I was introduced to an author named Mem Fox and the story of Koala Lou, an ambitious little koala that wants to climb higher and faster than any other animal in the bush. It was memorable because it was the first time I was introduced to koalas. I just couldn't believe that there was such an animal that resembled a real-life teddy bear. And quickly afterwards, I was introduced to more titles by Fox, like *Possum Magic*, which was memorable for introducing me to Australian delicacies like vegemite, pavlova, and lamington.

A country with adorable animals, amazing eats, and beautiful beaches? This would be more than enough to pique any child's interest in wanting to visit, except for one tiny detail. It's thousands of miles away from America, and no child has the will or patience to sit still for a fifteen-hour plane ride. Alas, my fascination with Australia cooled down and it would be a few years before I discovered rugby. In the year 2005, I rekindled my love of Australia thanks in part to two factors: *Oyster Farmer* and Midnight Oil.

The former was a foreign film from Australia, which might sound silly since English is spoken in Australia. *Oyster Farmer* was a romantic comedy that took place along the scenic Hawkesbury River. Prior to this movie, I never knew this place existed. Within the first few seconds of the movie's opening credits, I was mesmerized by the beautiful the winding scenery, accompanied by the most beautiful-sounding music I had ever heard. It was an ethereal mix of violins, fiddles, banjos, acoustic guitars, mouth harps, and a didgeridoo. In my humble opinion, it sounded what I imagined Australia to sound like. If the bush could talk, it would sound just like the first four minutes of *Oyster Farmer*. I also enjoyed the film because it featured the longest sex scene that has ever committed to celluloid; a wonderfully tasteful fornication done on an old fishing dock tucked away in the mangroves. What's more, the movie had such a limited release; I saw it at a tiny indie movie house in Manhattan in a theatre that was nearly empty. Still, I walked out of that little cinema with a feeling of awe. I thought to myself, *if I ever visit Australia, I* must *visit this place!*

The latter, as most Aussies would know, are the oldest music band to hail from the Land Down Under. Americans know them from their 1987 top-ten single *Beds are Burning,* in which the band sang about the plight of the Aborigines, as in most of their songs. I was watching VH-1's *I Love the 80s* and their music video for the titular hit was brought up as a topic. I thought the song was really catchy, and I went out and bought their album *Diesels and Dust*. While perusing their music, I discovered another album called *Head Injuries*. One of the tracks was called *Koala Sprint*. I thought to myself, *a rock song about koalas?! Now, this I gotta hear!* After uploading the CD to my iTunes library, I immersed myself in the 1979 single. It was not about the iconic Australian marsupial, but rather about escaping the city to the country. The best part was at the end when the song would segue into a trippy guitar solo that seemed to mimic Pink Floyd; you could easily see someone lighting up a joint while this solo plays, whilst looking at the stars and weeping. It was a trippy, psychedelic, catchy, and amazing song that sounded like something a surfer would compose.

No surprise, as I learned that the band began its career in earnest playing to the surfies at Bondi and Narrabeen; all their early music from the 1970s sounded like what would happen if the Beach Boys and the Ramones got together and combined their music. To me, this band is one my favorite discoveries and a reminder of just how awesome Australia truly is. With their music, Midnight Oil managed to somehow romanticize Australia in such a way that made it more than just a colorful land of kangaroos and koalas.

The Oils, as they were also known, were a socially and politically conscious band that always had something important to say while cranking out some of the catchiest music I had ever heard. It wasn't long before I bought every one of their albums and memorized almost every song by them. The group disbanded in 2002 when lead singer Peter Garrett left to pursue a career in politics, which irked a lot of fans who saw it as act of selling out to the very people Garrett fought against in his music. While I am upset that the band is no more, at least for now, it shouldn't surprise fans that Garrett would pursue this. He has a law degree, originally ran for Prime Minister in 1984 under a third-party ticket (the Nuclear Disarmament Party), and one could make a case that he got more involved in politics to actually make a difference; why just talk the talk when you can also walk the walk? If I had the chance, I would love to shake Garrett's hand as being a big influence in nurturing my love for Australia, as well as taking up a lot of space in my iPod!

But Australian movies and music weren't enough to satisfy my appetite for this exotic land. In 2007, during my last year at Nassau Community College, I attended a seminar about a study-abroad trip in Sydney and Auckland. While my ears were tuned into the lecture, I was getting buzzed on my cell phone; I had a gym appointment that I couldn't miss. I ducked out of the lecture early and in hindsight, it was not a wise move, as I missed out on when to sign up and how much to pay. Eventually, I missed the deadline and they wouldn't even accept a check at that point. I had missed the boat and I was depressed for days and days. Little did I know that this unfortunate miss would be one of the best mistakes that ever happened to me!

Fast-forward to December 26, 2008: I boarded a plane from New York City to Melbourne. As a Christmas present, my family had arranged a two-week tour of Australia for me. I would rendezvous with a group of tourists at my hotel in Melbourne. I was so excited that I couldn't even sleep on the flight, let alone sit still. It seemed like the quickest fifteen hours of my life had just flown by in a heartbeat. I will never forget waking up (Okay, okay, so I slept for a while on the flight) to a glorious sunrise over the South Pacific. My flight was 30,000 feet above the island nation of Vanuatu and I sat witness to the sky morphing from night to day. The sky opened up with a tinge of navy blue, then cerulean, and then a cornucopia of orange, yellow, and pink stretched across the horizon. It is so rare to see a sunrise, but even rarer to see one from nearly six verticals above one of the most remote island countries in the world.

Once I touched down in Melbourne Airport, I headed into downtown Melbourne to my hotel, just around the corner from Chinatown and the QV Centre. It was here that I was introduced to my first friend in Australia: Tony De Quintal. On the surface, he was my tour guide for two weeks. Little did I know that this lovable bloke from Corrimal would play a big role in my affinity for Australia. On every bus ride, whenever he would ask the tour group a question, my hand would always be the first to rise up. It felt like being back in school; I was so eager to show off how much I knew about the Land Down Under. I cuddled up with some grey kangaroos on Philip Island in

Victoria, got drunk on Victoria Bitter beer in Alice Springs on New Year's Eve, stood in the awe-inspiring majesty of Uluru, gazed at stars underneath the expansive Outback, braved the briny deep of the Great Barrier Reef in Cairns, cuddled a koala in Kuranda, toured the Sydney Opera House, felt the sand between my toes on Bondi Beach, and took a seat upon Mrs. Macquarie's Chair. I also managed to fulfill a promise to myself: I visited the town of Brooklyn and dipped my feet in the Hawkesbury River. In the foreword, I talked about how I discovered the Rabbitohs in Alice Springs, and how that would set forward a series of events that would lead me to discover the awesomeness of Souths. I would have to wait another four and a half years, however, before my transformation into an Australian Bunny Rabbit would be fulfilled.

CHAPTER 10
My First Australian Friend

DECEMBER 28, 2008:

Tony De Quintal was more than a tour guide who showed me around the Lucky Country. This humorous Aussie became the first friend I made in the Land Down Under. While Tony may not have been the biggest fan of footy, let alone the Rabbitohs, it would be extremely rude of me not to mention him in my fond look back at Australia. Tony was a native of Corrimal, by way of Madeira, Portugal. That's right, a half-Australian, half-Portuguese living along the Illawarra Escarpment in New South Wales! He had excellent taste in fine dining, drinks, and always seemed to be in a great mood. When they say that Aussies are a friendly lot, Tony is proof of that axiom.

Over the course of the two weeks I was on the road, I seemed to become his favorite tourist in that I was always raising my hand to answer a question about Australia. Much like the biggest nerd in class, I was always vocal in answering any questions he asked the other tourists on the bus. I seemed to be the only one who knew not to pronounce the letter "R" sound in Melbourne (it's correctly pronounced "Mel-bun" for the Yanks out there!).

One of my favorite moments was when Tony taught everyone in our group the words to the old Australian bush ballad "Home among the Gum Trees," which is sort of like Australia's version of "Home on the Range." Instead of singing about deer and antelope playing, seldom being heard, and skies not cloudy all day, it's about living happily in a place filled with plum trees, sheep and kangaroos, clotheslines out the back, rabbits running 'round, and cooking up vegemite on toast. Forgive me, American heartland, but I think I'll take the Aussie bush ballad; it's just so damn catchy and fun! In addition to the lyrics, Tony also taught us the pantomime movements as well. Some might have seen this a little like a grade-school sing-along, but it sure beats the Itsy-Bitsy-Spider! I loved it so much I even downloaded the song into my iPod! Don't you judge me!

Tony sure knew how to keep everyone on our bus motivated, especially when we were on a six-hour bus ride from Alice Springs to Uluru. When you can keep everyone on the bus from succumbing to boredom and road rage in searing heat with almost no changing scenery for that long, you are born tour guide! Actually, to call that trip boring would be most unfair, as it was my first time in the Outback and the scenery was so surreal and gorgeous. What struck me was how lush and green the desert was; flowing shrubs and small trees seemed to dot much of the region our bus was driving through. When I say lush and green, I do not mean that the desert bore a resemblance to Ireland or a dense valley, but I was surprised to see that the Outback didn't look anything like the surface of Mars like so many movies depict. To call it beautiful would be a big understatement; words fail me to describe how immense and amazing the red center of Australia truly is.

Tony and I continued our trek from the Outback to the Great Barrier Reef in Cairns. I thought that after my trip to Alice Springs and Uluru, I had been to the hottest places in the world. But I took one step outside the airport in Cairns, and it was like shoving my head in an oven! The intense heatwave of tropical North Queensland was overwhelming as I took one step outside the air-conditioned splendor of Cairns Airport. Even nighttime was just as humid, as it peaked in the high 80s.

By the time Tony and our tour group made it to Sydney, he went all-out on the fun scale! He took a group photo of us at Mrs. Macquarie's Chair at the Sydney Botanic Gardens where he would not let us leave until we gave him every ridiculous pose he could think of! One of the best moments came when we were riding around downtown Sydney and Tony led our group in a rousing rendition of Australia's favorite tune, "Waltzing Matilda." And like a teacher's pet who couldn't keep himself from showing off, I belted out every word, perfectly. You'd think I was a born Aussie celebrating ANZAC Day or drunk off his ass after winning the World Cup.

Actually, like the works of Mem Fox, this was another early memory of Australia I first had around the age of four or five. The first time I heard it, it was just so catchy, upbeat, and bouncy, much like a kangaroo! Truthfully, I didn't know it was about a sheep thief that takes his own life until I was in high school, but it was a perfect tune for a nation of underdogs and rebels. For me, I just like it because it is catchy and really fun to sing. And to honor it, A.B. Banjo Patterson, the man who wrote the song, is pictured on the Australian ten-dollar banknote. Meanwhile, we have Alexander Hamilton, the founder of the US Treasury. Advantage, Australia.

By the end of the tour, I had officially fallen in love with Australia. Seeing everything up close and in real life was a real eye-opening experience for me. The way the Sydney Opera House glistened in the sun and the way Ayers Rock shone at dusk was something that I just could not put into words. I had given the tour and Tony a perfect score rating for his company; I honestly could not find one negative thing to say about either the tour or the tour guide. Before heading to Sydney airport for a long flight back to New York, I gave Tony a farewell hug and told him that I hoped to see him in New York soon. After all, he was nice enough to show me around his native land, so I thought it only appropriate to show him around my neck of the woods. However, I'd have to wait about a year and a half for that to happen.

AUGUST 16, 2010:

It was a dreary morning in Manhattan. The sky was slightly gray, it was drizzling, and almost everyone was lugging their dripping umbrellas everywhere. While most people were on their way to work, I was on my way to the Century 21 department store in lower Manhattan to rendezvous with Tony. I was so psyched that he had made it all the way to the Big Apple! I was, however, a little bummed my parents were not there to meet him; they were attending a wedding in Atlanta that day. Alas, it was me, myself, and I that would reunite with my Aussie friend.

I scoured the ground floor of Century 21 like a spy. I scurried from rack to rack; mannequin to mannequin in search of my friend. After nearly an hour, I caught him near the shoe section. I snuck up from behind and exclaimed, "*G'day*!" And the next thing I knew, I was reunited with my good friend from Corrimal. Apparently, I learned my friend was a real shopaholic; he was lugging several shopping bags from some of New York's biggest retailers: Macy's, Bergdorf Goodman, Century 21, and the M&M store. Yes, the M&M store! Apparently, that is how I learned from Tony that shopping is much cheaper in America than it is in Australia; having been back to Sydney a few more times, I can see why!

Tony and I made our way to Penn Station where we headed to my hometown of Rockville Centre for lunch. I decided it only fitting to treat him to something distinguishingly Long Island. I decided on Nick's, an Italian restaurant on Sunrise Highway that made some of the best coal-oven pizza in Long Island. Tony was surprised to learn that pizza was, in fact, a pie; he always thought pie was something big that had a filling like dessert or the quintessential meat pie. Details aside, he seemed to dig into it without any hesitation. He just picked up a slice and ate it as if he was a native New Yorker or Long Islander. So proud! For dessert, I took him to the International

Delight Café, a famous diner known for its numerous gelato flavors. Tony, deciding to go native, ordered up a scoop of Baci (containing pieces of the titular Italian chocolate) and Stracciatella (a vanilla-based gelato with dark chocolate pieces and nuts). *Mangia!*

Before heading back to New York City, I drove Tony to my house in my neighborhood for a little tour of suburbia. Suburban Long Island is so different from the Aussie suburbs in many ways. For one thing, there are a lot of big houses in Long Island; so many styles and front yards that make some wonder how yard work and house work ever get done. My house was a Georgian-style brick house on a dead-end street in a neighborhood covered with such tall trees. In fact, many of the houses in my neighborhood, compared to the suburban dwellings in and around Sydney, made my neighborhood homes look massive by comparison.

Tony explained to me that most Aussie homes are modest, to say the least. Aussies opt for practicality over spaciousness, as it suits them cost-wise, and it is easier to maintain and clean. A lot of the homes I saw on my first trip all seemed to be stuck in a 1950s-era time warp. It was as if most of them copied the cutesy look of the suburbs from post-war era Long Island when Levittown first came about in 1947. I'm surprised most of the homes didn't have white picket fences with push mowers and pipe-smoking dads.

Once we both went inside, Tony began snapping pictures of almost every nook and cranny inside my home. You would think he was a realtor or someone on the market planning to buy my home. Surprisingly, Tony said that he was most taken back by the abundance of wallpaper throughout my home. Tony explained to me that it is not a common form of décor in Aussie homes, as per the theme of practicality. Most Aussies just paint the naked walls or added a little wood paneling. Tony also noted that the wallpaper gave my home the look of a turn-of-the-century era Victorian home; one such type of paper had the fake invites and RSVPs of attending a soiree at an English estate. For the record, however, these were picked out by my mom.

Tony went upstairs to my room where I showed him all the mementos I kept from my trip to Australia. He laughed a hearty laugh when I showed him that I hung on to a few of the receipts and luggage tags from the various destinations. As someone who loves to visit places, I have a tendency to be somewhat nostalgic and hold on to as many memories as I can. After all, memories will live on in our heads and hearts, but it is nice to carry around a little something we can hold in the palm of our hands.

After shuffling through more items, it was time for my friend to return to New York City, and back to Australia. As we waited for the train at the Rockville Centre station, I didn't want to say goodbye yet. I decided to accompany Tony back to the city on the train. To pass the time, I told him the story of the Brooklyn Dodgers and how they went to Los Angeles. I don't know why I picked that topic, but probably because I wanted to give him a really riveting story about something legendary from Long Island lore. During my trip to Australia, I learned about Aboriginal legends from the Dreamtime and bush ballads, so I thought it fitting to spin a yarn about something really famous that many Long Islanders and New Yorkers remember so fondly. Tony seemed to hang on my every word all the way to Penn Station; before we knew it, was time to say farewell once again. Actually, we just said, "See you soon!" When? Well, that would be in another three years from that day. And it sure as heck wouldn't be the last time.

Tony De Quintal is the first friend I made in Australia and is also one reason why I became enamored with the travel and tourism industry. While this may be about paying respect to the South Sydney Rabbitohs, it is also about Australia, and I would not have discovered the Rabbitohs in Alice Springs if I had not gone Down Under on vacation and walked into that apparel store with our tour guide. Tony may not be a footy fan, let alone a member of the red and green faithful. But to me, he is rightfully a part of my Bunny brethren!

CHAPTER 11
The Redfern Oval

SEPTEMBER 7, 2013:

On that crisp, clear morning in September; the sky was blue and the weather was promising. It was a beautiful day, but I was still licking my wounds from last night's bout. I did not want to let this one match affect my first time in Australia since 2009. I mean, you couldn't blame me for being upset that my first Rabbitohs match ended in a loss for the home team, especially for such a crucial match like the Minor Premiership. Still, as I had stated before, this must be what so many fans feel every season. To come this close, and have it snatched away from you from by none other than your biggest rivals. The fans root together and the fans suffer together. But enough about the Chicago Cubs! Relax, I kid! And speaking of fans, I was on my way to see my beloved Bunny Brethren at the Redfern Oval.

Situated in the historic suburb of Redfern, the namesake oval is the former home stadium of the Rabbitohs as well as the training grounds. To call it a stadium would be a bit of stretch; it appeared to look like a big, high-school football field with a somewhat impressive covered grandstand and bleachers. All that was missing was the scoreboard and the cheerleaders. Maybe it's the fact that I'm an American trying to contemplate the fact that this small "stadium" was once the legitimate turf for the oldest rugby league club in Australia. I hailed a cab from my hotel in Darling Harbour; seven minutes later, my eyes came across the Redfern Oval. Actually, what I saw first was a magnificent fountain sitting under the shade of palm trees and lorikeets. In the corner of my right eye, I saw a small group of people sitting down to eat. Unmistakably, it was Brigitte, the same woman whom I was introduced at the Royal Oak in Lidcombe the day before. Tanya, the Rabbitohs fan from Brisbane was also there, along with a man in dark sunglasses and stubble. It was Brian "Ed" Rabbitoh; I had recognized him from Facebook.

"G'day, Jared! Pleasure to meet ya, mate! Tough break after last night's fight, right? We'll get'em in the Grand Final, mate. Don't worry!"

Well, Brian may have seemed calm with his introduction, but I think deep down, he was angrily cursing the Eastern Suburbs. Alas, both of us hid our disappointment from each other with a smile. The whole red and green crew was sitting down to brunch. On one side of their plate, half-eaten eggs and fruit. On the other side of their plate, an ashtray that was littered with the remnants of their cigarettes.

My friends seemed like they were in no hurry to finish. As they maneuvered their way through eggs and smokes, I explored our dining establishment. The Café on Chalmers, named after the street on which the Oval was located, was a cute place to say the least. I was expecting a noisy café filled with drunken Rabbitohs fans, just like the ones I met at ANZ. It was, however, a small place that had seating for about twenty people. Really, fifteen at most. A small array of simple items designed to tantalize your taste buds like sandwiches, pastries, and lattes were just a few of the eats on the menu. Arguably, my favorite part of the café was the fact that they had free Wi-Fi! A marvelous thing, especially in Sydney where I learned from the locals that free Internet in Australia is hard to come by. Makes sense why I was paying a hefty sum for Internet service at the hotel.

The star attraction at this eatery, next to the miniature heads of the South Sydney starting lineup, was the array of coffee choices. There's something you should know about

Aussies: they are serious coffee drinkers! For those of you who imagine the Aussies to be passionate about only beer and beer alone, turn off the Fosters' ad and pay attention! The Aussies could easily give the French and Italians a run for their Euros with their Down Under coffee.

With the end of World War II, many immigrants from Southern Europe, the Italians and Greeks mostly, found purchase halfway around the world. Unable to return to their war-torn homelands, they needed a place to make a fresh start. Meanwhile, Australia was in need of new immigrants and a massive population influx. Kismet, as one would call it, and soon, European ex-pats made their homes in the Land Down Under. As it turns out, the climate and landscape seemed to be reminiscent of their native homeland, and they flourished nicely. With their arrival, however, they brought with them their culture, their cuisine, and their coffee from their native Europe. And throw in the fact that Australia is right near Indonesia, one of the biggest coffee-producing countries in the world and you have the makings of a country that loves its brew. And not just the amber nectar made famous by those annoying Fosters commercials that have rendered Australia a fictitious land of drunks.

And for the record, Fosters beer is about as Australian as the Olive Garden is Italian. Asking for one Down Under would indeed be disrespectful; would you go to Paris and forego their haute cuisine in favor of a McDonalds? Still, coffee is a big deal for the Aussies. In fact, they are so snobbish about it, it is almost impossible to find an iced coffee. You'd think that in a country that is sunny and hot year round, that would be incredibly easy to sell. With a few coins in a pocket, I purchased a flat white, which is a simple latte, and rejoined my friends. I savored the milky wonderfulness that met my lips with the slight burning sensation. Midway through my cuppa, I saw my friends getting up.

“Where are all of you headed off to?” I asked.

“Right now, we’re going up to the merch store on Chalmers Street.”

From the minute the elevator doors slid open, it was as if I could hear the angels humming. Or that could have been the air conditioner. Beautiful bounties of red and green bunnies were stacked from end to end. Something that I never could find in America was all there for the taking! Jerseys in all sizes, training shirts, tank-tops, an assortment of caps and scarves, and a whole basket of miniature Reggie dolls that beckoned me. Like a kid in a candy store, my Rabbitohs spending spree began; this time, however, I would not need to click *Confirm* on a website to make a purchase! Within a few minutes, my arms were a mess of red and green stripes! Also on sale was a fully functioning chopper motorcycle that was painted in red and green, a Rabbitohs rabbit decal, and came with a matching helmet. Well, don’t ask how I’d get that sweet bunny-hog through baggage claim.

By the time I made it to the register, I had so much Rabbitohs gear in my arms, you could barely see my face. As the cashier began to ring up my purchases, Brian mentioned to the cashier that I was an American. And just like the fans in The Burrow, the cashier just couldn’t believe that a Yank would be splurging on all this! The cashier then reached below the counter and pulled out two sleeves of golf balls with the NRL logo on one side and the Rabbitohs logo on the other side. She offered these up as free gifts with my purchases, and even threw in a stack of Rabbitohs stickers and a stationary set for free too! First the fans bought me beer, and now I was getting a few free Rabbitohs souvenirs?! It pays to be an American Bunny!

Once my Rabbitohs spree concluded, it was game time! We headed back to the Oval for the Souths Juniors match. This was the reason my new friends were gathered at the Oval and it wasn't just for brunch. The South Sydney District Junior Rugby Football League, or Souths Juniors for short, is an affiliation of junior clubs in the Southern Sydney area. Instead of first- grade teams from major parts of Australia like the Newcastle Knights, the Brisbane Broncos, or the Melbourne Storm, the juniors are comprised of lower-grade teams exclusively from suburbs in and around parts of South Sydney. Such teams include the Botany Rams, the Clovelly Crocodiles, La Perouse United, the Maroubra Lions, the Coogee Dolphins, and the Coogee Randwick Wombats which have produced future Rabbitohs stars like John Sutton, Alex Johnston, and Jason Clark. To American readers, think of these teams as the minor league of the NRL, but located just within the confines of South Sydney neighborhoods. While they may not be major league, in American terms, they have cult followings amongst their most loyal fans, not to mention they are the clubs where possible NRL stars will begin their careers. You know when a baseball player in the minors gets called up to the majors? This is the rugby league equivalent.

Imagine if you will, a neighborhood: picture tall, massive apartment complexes, combine them with the large sporting fields that schools had that you could see from the Long Island Railroad en route to Jamaica, factor in the blue-color working class, a diverse populace, then add the English-style pubs and Australian-inspired terrace homes with verandas, an Aboriginal demographic, and palm trees. That's Redfern. From the bleachers of the Redfern Oval, I saw all the way to the other side; it was all apartment buildings, rows of trees, and terrace houses. For years, it had been a poor, working-class neighborhood that was a far cry from the lavish Central Business District and beaches of Bondi. Over the years, it was plagued by both poverty and crime. Nowadays, it appeared to be going through sort of a "Williamsburg" phase of rebuilding itself as an up-and-coming neighborhood for

Sydney's newest residents. Much like how Brooklyn went from blue collar to hipster, Redfern appeared to be mimicking Williamsburg's gentrification. Unlike Brooklyn, it was nice to see some original buildings and homes standing side by side with modern apartments and bars that looked so new, you could smell the fresh paint.

In fact, that is one more reason I idolize the Rabbitohs: their history and Redfern share much in common with the Brooklyn Dodgers of yesteryear. The Dodgers lived in blue-collar Brooklyn, always in the shadow of their glitzy Manhattan neighbors from across the East River. The Dodgers may have been professional baseball players, but they lived in the neighborhood alongside their fans; they didn't live in fancy mansions away from the public. Also, some even took jobs in the neighborhood to make ends meet. Except the Dodgers didn't have to chase rabbits for fur and food. Rather, they chased baseballs and dodged trolleys, which is how they earned their unusual name. Both teams gave their respectable sport some of the most famous players in history. Jackie Robinson became famous not just for breaking baseball's race barrier in 1947, but for being one of the fastest players to steal home countless times. There was legendary shortstop Pee Wee Reese and pitching great Duke Snider.

The Rabbitohs had Clive Churchill, who became both one of rugby league's greatest players and coaches, the Burgess Brothers, the enormous Greg Inglis, and the indestructible John Sattler, who survived a broken jaw during the 1970 Grand Final and still came back on the field to win the game and be carried off a hero. Can you imagine what would have happened if the Brooklyn faithful at Ebbets Field got together with the red and green faithful from Redfern? If you ask me, they would have been the best of friends! The Bunnies would be slinging back Tooheys while Dodgers fans would be chugging Schaefer beer.

The fans, much like the Rabbitohs fans, were also from humble backgrounds that didn't always come with money attached. The Dodgers became heroes to their "average joe" fans who only wanted to bring baseball prominence and respectability to the neighborhood of Flatbush. Halfway around the world in the neighborhood of Redfern, the Rabbitohs were doing that almost every season. It is here that the similarities between the Dodgers and Rabbitohs end. The Dodgers only won one World Series title in 1955 before being exiled to Los Angeles, breaking the hearts of countless Brooklyn natives. The Rabbitohs won numerous premierships with a roster of legendary players. In spite of its history, I would call it a beautiful neighborhood with much to offer and a place that I wouldn't mind having an apartment in. That way, I'd be close to the team and all the action.

CHAPTER 12
What Happens in Kings Cross...

SEPTEMBER 7, 2013:

I have said that the Rabbitohs are my Australian family members; my Australian Bunny family, if you please. One such Bunny family from Down Under that has been incredibly kind to me since my discovery of the Souths has been the Gotsis Family. Earlier I mentioned Bill Gotsis, the rabid Rabbit I first befriended on Twitter over the Rabbitohs and the Giants. To say that he is a fan would be a big understatement. I have never known another person outside America, much less New York or New Jersey, who knows so much about the New York Giants. He reminded me of my uncle Ed who has been a lifelong fan and season ticket holder. As I got to know him, he told me that he worked as a ground announcer for a professional soccer team in Sydney called the Western Sydney Wanderers; a soccer team that plays in the neighboring town of Parramatta and is part of the A-League of professional soccer in Australia. Actually, Bill does announcing or calling the game on the radio; a station called 2GLF in Sydney.

From the minute I told him that I'd be headed to Australia to see a Bunnies game in person, he was only too eager to meet me. He just couldn't believe a Yank would come all this way for a footy match, much less to be around drunken footy fans. As we shook hands at The Brewery outside ANZ Stadium, I noticed the look on his face was somewhere between disbelief and amazement, like a kid who woke up on Christmas morning or a star-struck fan that just shook hands with his favorite athlete. But meeting one Gotsis was just the beginning. Two days after the loss to the Roosters at ANZ, I was invited to a birthday party for Bill's cousin, Mario. I put on my best slacks, collared shirt, and suit jacket, and headed out to Kings Cross.

Kings Cross, by the way, is Sydney's red-light district, and is reputed to be home to organized crime groups. Once known for its music halls and grand theatres, it was rapidly transformed after World War II by the influx of troops returning and visiting from the nearby Garden Island naval base. Today, it is dominated by bars, restaurants (particularly cafés), nightclubs, and strip clubs. It being my first time in this neighborhood, I braced myself for what I thought would be a bacchanalian rampage. I was given the address of a restaurant and club via Twitter, and I arrived via taxi in front of a tiny marquee and a stairwell leading upstairs. But instead of heading up into what I thought was the party, I stepped into a pub next door where I saw a small crowd watching the All Blacks play on TV. Bill had told me to first come here where I'd be introduced to his wife, Rachel.

I had learned from Bill, however, that she was a fan of the Parramatta Eels club. At least she wasn't a Roosters fan! I presented her with a gift of chocolate; a box of See's candies that I had picked up at LAX Airport in Los Angeles en route to Sydney. It seemed that I picked up the perfect gift as I saw Rachel's eyes just light up! It turns out that this Sheila had quite the sweet tooth! Bill and Rachel then introduced me to Mario, Bill's cousin. I presented him with a gift as well; a sweater from Stony Brook University, my Alma mater. And speaking of gifts, I handed Bill his gift and it was a doozy: an authentic New York Giants football jersey. To say that Bill was happy would have been a gross understatement. The look on his face was akin to a kid opening his presents on Christmas Day or on his birthday. I only wish my Uncle Ed could have been there to see him; he's the biggest New York Giants fan in the family. In the middle of small talk and sips of beer, I had to take a step back and just compose myself for a second. I mean, I had only known Bill in person for less than a week, or a few months if you count the endless hours that we chatted on Twitter, Facebook, and email. And yet, here I was, a stranger in a foreign land, and he along with a couple of family members that I hadn't even met yet had invited me to a birthday party for someone I had only known for just a few minutes. I felt the same sense of camaraderie that I had felt at The Brewery and in The Burrow. I can't remember the last time a group of strangers made me feel that welcome; the many first days of school that I had as a kid and a teenager were never this cool and welcoming. Seriously, my first day of classes in elementary school and community college felt so tense. And yet, in the few minutes that I was surrounded by these jovial Aussie drinkers, they practically made me feel like family. Perhaps America should mandate that all bars and nightclubs require a handful of Aussies to break the ice and lighten the atmosphere? And while they're at it, put more rugby on TV and serve up Tooheys and VB! C'mon, people!

After shaking hands and meeting Rachel and Mario, we adjourned upstairs to the venue inside Kit & Kaboodle and Sweethearts, a small party venue that was blasting the loudest club music around. Not to sound like a stick in the mud, but I'm not too keen on the nightclub scene, mostly because the music coming out of nightclubs sounds terrible. Unless it is music from the 1980s or new wave music, or if there is perhaps a piano player, or you can at least hear what the other person next to you at the bar has to say during a conversation, then I have no interest in your cacophonous excuse for a get-together. But I digress. The place seemed to be a mockup of an old-fashioned karaoke bar and dim-sum restaurant; the place had sort of a Chinese restaurant décor. It was as tacky as you could imagine. How tacky, you ask? Well, for starters, there was a piano painted in zebra stripes! Well, sloppy looking stripes. There were bamboo screens that had Chinese characters painted on them, a leopard-print sofa, hand-carved ceiling, paper lanterns, and a giant gold hand that doubled as chair; the tired derriere would sit down in the palm of the golden hand. My favorite fixture was a chandelier made out of empty Ketel One bottles that hung in the stairwell leading up to the club. Zebra piano and a golden hand chair? Well, at least the club wasn't uninteresting!

After a few minutes, hors d'oeuvres and cocktails were being tossed around. There was so much drinking, laughing, talking, and shouting, that I just couldn't keep track of anything that was going on. I parked a seat on one of the many cushy ottomans that adorned the walls of the camp-tastic establishment. One minute it was a Jack and Coke, and the next minute it was a cold beer. Bill, meanwhile, was bringing me around the bar and introducing me to his friends and Rachel's friends. He was showing me off to everyone; he couldn't stop introducing this rare breed of human being; an American who passionately followed the Rabbitohs and possessed a pretty diverse knowledge of Australia. Every chance he had, Bill couldn't help but show me off to all the partygoers, so I playfully went along, strutting my Rabbitohs swagger like a proud peacock.

After I finished chewing the rag with Bill and his friends, I saw food being passed around. A wide variety of dim sum, or as it is known in Australia, "yum-cha" was passed around like cocktails. I was hoping that this wouldn't be my dinner for the night. About a dozen dumplings, two beers, and three Jack and Cokes later, and I was feeling a buzz. I managed to stay awake, and thankfully, sober for the moment when Mario blew out his candles. But as if the night couldn't have gotten more interesting, it turns out that no one brought plates and flatware. In other words, there were *no* plates and forks for cake! At least someone had the foresight to bring a plastic knife. So basically, every partygoer was served a slice on a napkin and ate with their hands. As if being slightly drunk wasn't enough, now everyone had cake smeared on their face like a bride at a wedding or a toddler at their own birthday! Everyone had a smile and chocolate cake on their faces.

By the time cake was served, I somehow noticed, even with my head slightly spinning, that the same song was being played in a continual loop over the loudspeakers. Modjo's *Lady (Hear Me Tonight)* was pounding in my head. Either it was on a loop, or the tune was stuck in my head. Wow, I must have had a lot to drink, eh! Thankfully, the song was catchy enough for me to keep tapping my feet while I sat on the wraparound couch trying to compose myself. Unfortunately, it was here that the evening would go from awesome to awful. Well, at least for me. Feeling the need to stretch my legs and regain myself from the booze and loud music, I slowly shuffled my feet to the bathroom. Just a split second after throwing the door open, I saw that someone had, well, "tossed their cookies!" But you might say that his aim was off and the area around the commode was a mess!

About a half-hour before midnight, Bill, Rachel, and I had decided to throw in the towel and split. We ambled out to a McDonalds just down the street where we sobered up with a Big Mac and fries. It was here that Bill decided to throw on his New York Giants jersey and brag to all the customers. One guy walking by our table thought he was an American tourist. Suddenly, I thought of a fun game: "Which one of us is the Aussie and which one is the Yank?" A few minutes later, with fast food absorbing the booze, cake, and yum-cha in our bellies, we made our way back to Bill's car. And just in case you were wondering, yes, we had a designated driver with us! Just before we got to our car, we passed by the police station near the famed fountain in Kings Cross. I was afraid our slightly raucous behavior might give off the wrong impression. That was when Bill rode to the rescue by bragging to the cop that I was an American fan of the Rabbitohs. Maybe it was the booze talking, but I like to think that Bill was riding high on the feeling of wearing his brand-spanking new Giants jersey! The cop sent us off with a wink and a smile, we found Bill's car, and I managed to make it back to my hotel in one piece. My head was spinning and my stomach was churning, and I had only been in Sydney for three days.

CHAPTER 13
A Rabbit in Search of the Oyster Farmer

When Americans think of the topography of Australia, they think of the beach, the bush, and the ochre-colored Outback. For a long time, that's what I thought Australia's landscape boiled down to. That is until the summer of 2005 when I wandered into the Quad Cinema on 13th Street and Fifth Avenue in Manhattan. I had read about a movie called *Oyster Farmer* in the *New York Times* movie section. From the minute the opening credits rolled, aerial images of a serpentine-like river winding around every turn were accompanied by a melodious mix of mouth harps, guitars, didgeridoos, violins, and banjos. If I could describe that opening music, you might say it's what the Australian bush sounds like.

The film revolved around a young, troublesome fisherman named Jack Flange (Alex O'Loughlin in a pre-*Hawaii Five-o* look) trying to make ends meet for him and his hospitalized sister. Desperate for more cash, he robs a fish market in Sydney, and mails the stolen money to himself while putting up with his tough-as-nails boss. The main star of this film, however, was the idyllic Hawkesbury River, a bush region of New South Wales just less than forty miles north of Sydney. The oddball cast of characters really made everything funny; a lot of the fishermen extras in the movie were all just local citizens taking part in this love letter to Australia captured on celluloid. My favorite moment, and I may be embarrassed in admitting this, was the sex scene between Jack and his girlfriend, Pearl. It starts off on an old fishing dock under the mangroves, slowly goes into a make-out session, and then they just leave nothing to the imagination! And to think this film was rated NR (not rated). How did this movie not get any publicity in America?! The best foreign film Oscar definitely should have gone to this Australian gem.

JANUARY 8, 2009:

During my first visit to Australia with Tony, I had been looking forward to seeing the Hawkesbury. Even when I made my way through the exotic sands of the outback, my mind was occupied with thoughts of me hitching a ride on a tinny in Mooney Mooney. It was our last day in Sydney; each member of my tour group had the opportunity to do a guided tour or choose their own adventure. Seizing this opportunity, I woke bright and early, packed a backpack, headed to Central Station, and chugged along the Northern Line toward Hawkesbury River Station in the quiet town of Brooklyn. Granted, the weather that morning was not exactly the sunny tableau I saw in *Oyster Farmer*. It was cloudy, a little windy, and rather dreary for a summer day in Sydney.

I began my trek around town to various sites like Parsley Bay and the Hawkesbury River Marina. One of my favorite moments that summed up the "laidback" vibe of Australia was when I saw this house with a giant couch on the front lawn complete with a goat on a leash that was nibbling away at the grass. Somehow, I felt like I just landed in the middle of a Jeff Foxworthy joke! It sort of made sense since some people, mostly the British, refer to Australia as "redneck England," which I find unfair since real rednecks have worse teeth! But I digress. This hilarious tableau made this train ride from Sydney all worth it!

It was such a peculiar sight to see, but I didn't come to see an Aussie version of the bayou. Well, in a way, the Hawkesbury might be regarded as sort of a Down Under bayou. A short walk brought me to Hornsby Bay, a small beach hidden by the main roads. There were a small number of wooden picnic tables, a grassy area, and a rocky shoreline. In spite of the overcast weather, I took off my sandals and let the river run through my toes. I breathed such a happy sigh of relief.

Before I knew it, an hour had passed and my feet were more wrinkled than a box of raisins. Not wanting to waste precious daylight, I explored the Hawkesbury Marina hoping to find at least one of the extras from *Oyster Farmer*. I did, however, find a small convenience store selling cases of Victoria Bitter beer just like in a scene from the movie. Inside, I found copies of the movie right next to the cash register, sort of like an impulse buy next to the Cadbury bars. I gushingly told the clerk that it was the movie that brought me halfway around the world to this river region. She seemed so stunned to learn that an American had not only seen the movie, but was inspired by it to visit the Hawkesbury. She was so touched she gave me a small Cadbury bar as a souvenir. One thing was for sure: this place was just as friendly as it was in the movie.

Before leaving the Hawkesbury, I took one look around to see if I could find at least one oyster farmer. The closest thing I could find to this elusive Aussie was an honest-to-goodness tinny. Yes, I saw a real-life tin fishing boat anchored near the train station! Sadly, no one was in it, but it was a sign that I had come to the right place. A heavy feeling came over me as I waited for my return train back to Sydney. Would I ever set foot in this wonderful place again? Would I ever come back here? Little did I know that I'd have to wait four and a half years.

SEPTEMBER 12TH, 2013:

During my second visit to Sydney, I was completely preoccupied with the Rabbitohs and getting to see the sights that I had neglected to visit on my first trip. After all, last time, I had only one free day in Sydney for myself. And time was a precious commodity for me. Still, in spite of all my new red and green friends, I had some business to tend to up north. I had remembered to keep a promise I made to myself. And that day, the weather could not have been better! No clouds in the sky, no rain whatsoever, and just the right temperature for a swim! I had packed a backpack with a change of clothes; I wasn't going to pass up an opportunity like this! I was so excited; I couldn't sit still, let alone keep a thought running straight in my head. I could just hear the opening theme from *Oyster Farmer* playing in my head.

The instant I stepped outside the train and onto the platform, I took a deep breath and inhaled the sweet aroma of Bush Country. Seconds after the train disappeared from the tracks and into the distance, I could hear the symphony of kookaburras, galahs, and magpies, accompanied by the rustling of palm leaves in the gentle breeze. It felt so good to be back. I ambled my way from the station, past the marina, past the café, and toward the beach. Actually, to be more precise, the beach where I was going swimming was a closed-off part of the river surrounded by a massive square dock as an enclosure for safety. The shoreline was rather laughable; a small set of concrete steps leading onto a small patch of sand no longer than about ten yards or so. Nonetheless, this was not something I was about to pass up.

I just had one, little problem: I had forgotten my bathing suit and a towel. But would that deter me? *No*! I went old-school bushie and just jumped into the river with my khaki shorts on! Oh, there was one more minor inconvenience: since I had come by myself and there weren't any lockers to stash my valuables, I had to keep a close eye on my backpack at all times. I tied my pack to a pole on the enclosure dock; half the time I swam and half the time, I was bobbing my head to see if it was still there. And don't you make fun of me for forgetting my swimsuit. There's a difference between not having a bathing suit and towel and not having a wallet to get back home.

From the banks of the river, I walked the short distance to the Marina Café for lunch. Being near some fertile fishing grounds (at least those portrayed in *Oyster Farmer*), I had a hankering for some seafood. The café's interpretation was as simple and delicious as you could get. There was no greasy newspaper as you might see at a chip shop along the Thames in London, but it came on a plate with fries, a wedge of lemon, and dipping cups of tartar sauce. Combine that with a cold iced tea and a view that was practically unbeatable, and it made for one of the most memorable meals that I can possible remember. I only wish my family and friends had been with me on that sunny afternoon.

With my stomach full from lunch, and the day still sunny and warm, I headed down toward the edge of the Hawkesbury River Marina to do something I neglected to do the first time I was in Australia in 2009: take a ferry ride up the river. I remember there being a small pier and shelter box next to the railroad tracks, where I remember also seeing a small barge; it looked vaguely like the boat from the Jungle Cruise in Disneyland.

As I waited for the boat to arrive, I sat next to a sweet, old lady. I introduced myself to her, after which I stated that I had come all the way from New York to see this region, along with the Rabbitohs. I knew I had her undivided attention, and she said that the Hawkesbury doesn't get a lot of tourists, let alone ones from America. I could only concur, as this region still remains a hidden gem of Australia, I was quite unlike most tourists who came to snap pictures of the Opera House, and then went home. She said the closest thing to tourists they had were locals from the city who came for a day on the river, or anyone who owned a boat moored along the banks. It seemed quite shocking that the region, in its vast beauty, had not been discovered by outside tourists. Then again, I wouldn't want to see a glut of tourists spoiling the natural scenery with too much development and crowding. It is this conundrum that makes the Hawkesbury so special to me. On the one hand, it is a place so beautiful, that I feel it is a crime that tourists neglect to see it. Still, on the other hand, it is important to remember that once something gets discovered, it doesn't stay a secret for long. And before you know it, the outsiders start to come in droves, possibly ruining the natural environment from the scourge of the inevitable. It is a dilemma that those in travel and tourism are always fighting when it comes to seeing the world and wanting others to experience it as well; it is also the reason for sustainability in tourism. I wish more knew about this place so that they would realize how beautiful it is and how it would be a crime to neglect to take care of this part of the world. But, once word gets out, you open a Pandora's Box that you may not be able to close. For now, I think I'll keep this place just between me, myself, and I.

The ferry pulled up to the dock, and I eagerly climbed on board. I was introduced to Captain Matty Doyle, as he stood behind the helm. He seemed rather interested in the fact that I was in Australia for both the Bunnies and the Hawkesbury. Jokingly, he said that he was a Manly-Warringah fan (Sea Eagles). Luckily, I had no beef with him, and not just because I was still a newcomer to the NRL culture. At least he wasn't a Roosters fan! Without missing a beat, he began ruffling my feathers by saying to the passengers, "He's a Roosters fan, mates!" It would be like saying a Yankees fan loves the Red Sox! Ugh! In an act that could be viewed as a cheap-shot at a rival NRL fan, he blew the ship's horn right as I was standing beneath it. *HONK*! As it erupted in a shrill cacophony, he said, "Sorry, mate. I didn't see ya there. I'll have to let ya know before I blow it next time." The paranoid side of me thought he was doing it because I wasn't a Sea Eagles fan. But I'm pretty sure he just forgot I was standing up at the bow of the ship. But boy, did my ears hurt!

Before pulling out, we waited for a group of passengers to

board the boat. Captain Matty said that we were picking up a group of schoolkids who were heading home. In other words, this ferry was also a floating school bus! My ferry ride was about to get a lot of more interesting; I was getting a first-hand look at how kids in this rural part of Australia get home from school. This is just another reason of why I love travel and tourism. To me, it is not enough for one to just go on a leisurely holiday and capture everything on photographs. It is important to learn about how life goes on for people living in that part of the world, so that you, the visitor, take away something important from your visit. To see the world, from not a tourist's perspective, but from one who mingles with the locals far from the comfort of civilization yields more of a meaningfulness between peoples. I wouldn't technically call the Hawkesbury River "far from civilization," but I wasn't just here to swim and hike. I wanted to see first-hand the daily life around this bushy landscape of New South Wales.

With all our passengers accounted for, the boat finally pulled away from the dock, and we were bound for Dangar Island. As the boat gently cruised up the Hawkesbury, I was quite impressed by all the cute homes I saw. I only saw them from behind, but it looked like the front, in that their driveway was where they parked their boat! It was like cruising the Venetian canals, but with a more exotic touch. Where opulent palaces and gondolas stood, my eyes laid upon bushy bungalows and colorful dinghies bobbing in the water. Dangar Island's wharf was clearly marked, as I watched all the anklebiters disembark. I don't know why I adore that Aussie-ism for small children? Anyhoo, I took notice of the kid's outfits and backpacks. All Australian schoolchildren and students are required to wear matching uniforms, but I had no idea they also had matching backpacks too. I'm not that crazy about uniforms, but they looked rather adorable, in my opinion.

After waving goodbye to our smallest passengers, our boat

continued its journey. One piece of scenery that was hard to miss was the Hawkesbury River Railway Bridge which carries the Main Northern railway line across the Hawkesbury River just north of Brooklyn. The railway bridge was built back in 1889, and it was a major engineering feat at the time. This icon of the river was one of the many bits of scenery shown repeatedly throughout *Oyster Farmer*. After trains cross the bridge, they disappear into the Woy Woy Tunnel, en route to Woy Woy, the next stop up the Hawkesbury. I watched a pair of trains traverse the bridge as one disappeared into the tunnel and one reappeared on the other side.

I was surprised to see the many number of houses on the river's edge. Not so much the number of them, but how really nice they were. There weren't a lot of the typical one-story bungalow terraced houses that were a dime-a-dozen throughout Sydney, with the cute thatched roof and Victorian-era verandah. Also, many weren't as rugged or trailer-shaped as they were in *Oyster Farmer*. It was when our boat docked at a place called Little Wobby Beach where I got close enough to see a few more residences on the river. One house looked like a big, rectangular box that was propped up by stilts. The house next to it had a cream-colored paint job with a big awning and crew rowboats leaned up against the back of the house. And just a stone's throw from the dock, a two-story house in the flesh. It was light tan and brown, with a green roof, and two big windows sticking out from the slant of the roof; from behind, the windows gave the appearance of the house having a pair of eyes, but not the scary kind like in *The Amityville Horror*. Everything around me made me feel like I was in Venice; most especially, houses built on the water where you could hop from the deck of a boat to your front door.

Just when I thought Captain Matty was busting my balls for joking that I was a Roosters supporter, he hollered to a few locals standing on a nearby dock, "This guy's a Souths supporta! From the States, he is! I got here a Souths fan from the States!" he hollered as he pointed to me at the bow of the boat. At without missing a beat, I waved to the people as if I was someone riding on a parade float. I felt like the most famous American in the Hawkesbury. In fact, I think I may have been the only famous American in the Hawkesbury.

Before I knew it, the boat had made its return back to Brooklyn. With the sun beginning to dip into the horizon, I hurried back to the train station. But not before I gave everyone on board a big goodbye! I bid Captain Matty farewell and shouted "*Go* Rabbitohs!" Call me a Roosters supporter will ya?! I kid, Captain Matty, relax! I felt a bit of melancholy wash over me as I waited for my train. I mean, would I ever come back to this little slice of paradise? Then again, it was four and a half years ago that I first visited this place and back then, even I was doubtful that I'd make it back here. And alas, I did. As I continued to wait, the Hawkesbury continued to entertain me with its vibrant flora and fauna. I spotted a magpie; that familiar black- and-white bird of Australia, perched on a rail track. I had never seen one in real life, apart from the old Western Suburbs footy team and the Collingwood AFL team. It was quite stunning with its perfect pattern and how balanced it was on the rail. I also saw another one flying overhead through the swaying palm fronds.

I may not have found any oyster farmers on this trip, let alone any of those miniature mollusks. But what I did find was a beautiful piece of paradise tucked away in a little corner of Australia. I discovered a place that looked like an Australian version of Venice. For just one day, I got to feel the river flow through my toes and beyond as I breathed in the scent of palm trees, frangipani, and low tide. This place was yet another reminder of why Australia is so beautiful and so unique. If I could say to the director of *Oyster Farmer*, Anna Reeves, from one American fan, "You should have won an Academy

Award for best foreign film! You made me want to explore this part of the Lucky Country. Good on ya, Anna!" To wander aimlessly around this part of Australia brings out such a part of me. As the tagline for *Oyster Farmer* said, "Risk is an Aphrodisiac." That's a pretty apt description for life in this rugged, yet beautiful landscape.

CHAPTER 14
La Familia Australia

SEPTEMBER 14, 2013:

One week after my dizzying night in Kings Cross, I was still eager to see the Gotsis family again. At the party, Bill mentioned that Mario and his family ran one of the best Italian restaurants in Sydney. Now this was something I had to see for myself: authentic Italian food in Australia? A taste of Italy on the other side of the planet? Back in 2008 during my first trip to Australia, finding good Italian food was a big challenge for me. It seemed that I just couldn't find any place that had a menu that reminded me of my family's cooking, much less live up to it. Or perhaps, I was just looking in the wrong places. It turns out that Sydney had a pretty good minority of Italian immigrants who brought a piece of the Old Country to the Lucky Country. One restaurant in Sydney that did both coffee and Italian cuisine right was Dolcissimo's, the one run by Mario's family in the neighborhood of Haberfield, which was home to an Italian minority of Sydney residents.

I left my hotel room dressed to the nines in a suit and tie, shined shoes, and slacks. It was going to be a traditional Sunday dinner with the family. At least this time, it would be in a much nicer place than Kings Cross. Bill gave me the address via Twitter and my cab driver took me through Haberfields in search of it. One thing that surprised me was the uncanny resemblance between neighborhoods in and around Sydney and different pockets of Long Island. Suddenly, I felt like I was back home, save for the fact that the cars were driving on the opposite side of the road. Almost all the houses were one-story bungalows accompanied by cute fences, verandas, and terrace-style awnings, which is a distinctly Australian look on most suburban houses.

I arrived in front of Dolcissimo's in the Italian neighborhood of Haberfield, just northwest of downtown Sydney, around the time twilight was present. On the corner, I took a moment to take in the surroundings. Unsurprisingly, it did feel like being back in Long Island; a cross between Riverhead, Franklin Square, and a bit of Forest Hills. Boy, so much for Australia being a rustic desert in the middle of nowhere. I was excited to see my Aussie friends again as they welcomed me with a big hug. The restaurant reminded me of Dancing Zorba's, the fictional diner from *My Big Fat Greek Wedding* except for the absence of a countertop and a neon sign. There were kids making a mess at the table, food being slung left and right, and boisterous conversations filling the place. If only it had the screeching chorus between Aunt Voula and Maria, I would have broken out in laughter and hives.

It was here that I was introduced to Bill's two children, Isaac and Charlotte. Isaac was two years old at the time; an adorable little anklebiter he was. Also, he bore a striking resemblance to my little cousin, Charlie. He won me over not just because he was adorable, but also because he was able to pronounce my name! Charlotte, on the other hand, was only ten months old, so her speech was quite limited. Nonetheless, she was adorable and had such eyes!

Just before dinner, Bill, Mario, and I stepped outside and went for a walk. It was here that my two new mates introduced me to another staple of Australian culture: placing a bet at the TAB. I learned that Aussies love to gamble, especially on professional sports. So much so, that before the start of every televised footy match, a company called Tom Waterhouse gives viewers gaming odds on who would be the favorite payout from the upcoming match. But it doesn't stop at rugby league. Aussies not only love to watch rugby league, but every sport there is! Why else would Bill be so fanatical about my Giants? Apparently, I also learned he is a Tampa Bay Rays fan and a big Golden State Warriors fan as well.

During dinner, I began to feel like I was home. A serving of hot bread and salad caprese came out, and everyone reached for their forks. Granted, I'm not too crazy about salad caprese, but the hot plate of bread was nothing short of delicious; it was more akin to pizza bread covered in melted Parmesan and olive oil. For my entree, I was brought a big bowl of Caesar salad. By the way, an entree in an Australian restaurant is what comes out before your main course. My salad had Caesar-like vinaigrette; not creamy like a traditional dressing, but it was a lighter fare. It included large shavings of Parmesan, bacon rashes (yes, bacon!), and croutons. The weirdest part of the salad was a strange dough pocket that was filled with a mixture of tomatoes, peppers, and oil. My main course was a big bowl of meat-filled tortellini, smothered in a thick Bolognese ragout. One taste and I was more than convinced that Australia definitely had food worthy of a kitchen in Little Italy! Of course, to convince my mother would be a risky endeavor; being a native of Calabria in Southern Italy, her standards for good Italian food are of the highest caliber. Nonetheless, it was one of my favorite meals Down Under.

All I could think about was how much I wished my family could be with me to share the meal. Growing up in an Italian family, good food is an integral part of the house. I'd have a pretty difficult time convincing my family that there is good Italian food in places not called Italy or Long Island. Being inside Dolcissimo's with Mario, Bill, and his family gave me a slice of homegrown goodness that ailed whatever homesickness I was feeling. The food, the atmosphere, the conversations, and the gelato were a little slice of Italy, halfway around the world! *Mangia!*

CHAPTER 15
Daniel and Turbo

MAY 27, 2013:

Back in 2013, I was introduced to the State of Origins. At first, I saw it as the NRL equivalent of an all-star game. Instead of pitting two teams from East versus West or American League versus National League, the State of Origins is an all-out brawl of the NRL's best from New South Wales (turquoise) and Queensland (maroon). To be precise, the players are assigned to each team depending on where they began their NRL careers. Greg Inglis, for example, plays for the South Sydney Rabbitohs, so you'd think he'd throw on a NSW jersey. But his career began in Queensland, so he wears a maroon jumper. All-star games in the USA can be a big deal, but if you're an NRL fan, this series is a huge deal! All over social media and the Internet, I saw countless photos of fans throwing on blue and maroon with such zeal, it would make a fight between the Yankees and the Red Sox look like a picnic.

Seeing the sheer amount of fandom that this brawl generated, I couldn't help but explore this concept further. The Australian, my favorite Aussie hangout and my own Rabbitohs HQ in New York City, was hosting the first game of the State of Origins. But because of the time difference, the game was airing at six in the morning. Nonetheless, I woke up at 5 a.m., drove to the train station in Rockville Centre, and made my way into New York. Since I did not own either an NSW or Queensland jersey, I just threw on my Rabbitohs jersey. Little did I know that I was in for one hell of a morning. I ran all the way from Penn Station to The Australian just in time for the opening kick. The place was packed! I mean, it was just an hour after sunrise, and there must have been over a hundred or so Aussies screaming at the top of their lungs! Most of them were either ex-pats living in New York, but some were on vacation and most fortunate to find an Australian bar that was showing this match. In the midst of this game, it was here that I was introduced to Daniel Phelps. A fan dressed in a blue NSW jersey, Daniel just couldn't believe that an American was proudly sporting a Rabbitohs jersey, much less showing up so early for a game that almost no American knew about. To him, I was most unique in my fandom of the Bunnies, not to mention I had come on my own accord to experience the State of Origins. We stood side by side the entire second half. There were so many fans, we practically had to stand on our toes just to see the TVs above the bar. By the end of the match, we exchanged contact information and I told him that the next time I was in Sydney, I'd look him up.

SEPTEMBER 18, 2013:

I was on my way from Town Hall station to Blacktown, a large suburb in the Western Suburbs outside Sydney. I had agreed to meet Daniel that day. I was looking forward to meeting up with him. He pulled up to the station in a black Mitsubishi and gave me a big welcome! We began our day in the Wests with a visit to Featherdale Wildlife Park, one of Australia's oldest wildlife parks. First opened in 1972 in the nearby town of Doonside, the zoo has not only been home to Australia's most well-known and beloved fauna, but it has also been visited by several celebrities like Leonardo DiCaprio, Dave Grohl, Robert De Niro, and Matt Damon.

If there's one thing I do love about Australia, it's the fauna. I mean, where else on this planet can you see creatures so unique and special in their own way? I have said before that I was introduced to Aussie wildlife through the illustrated works of Mem Fox. Seeing these colorful denizens of the bush in real life was always a rare treat. I held my breath as I cozied up to a grey kangaroo; it even playfully rubbed up against my leg! I also could not stop staring at the koalas. I mean, how could anyone not stop and fawn over these real-life teddy bears? And yes, I am fully aware that they are not actual bears! Daniel even took a photo of me up close with one the koalas.

Not all Aussies, however, are so in love with this fuzzy icon. Some call them "drop bears" due to the fact that some fall out of trees and if an unfortunate person is underneath that particular tree, the koala will panic and claw the person to death. Of course, it sounds truly ridiculous, but considering how sharp those claws are, I wouldn't be surprised if they gave someone an on-the-spot lobotomy! But watching these sleepy tree dwellers, you'd almost forget.

After exploring the friendly fauna inside Featherdale, Daniel and I headed for some tucker which is Aussie slang for some grub. Exploring koalas and kangaroos can really work up an appetite. Fortunately, Daniel knew a fun place off the road near Blacktown in nearby Kellyville Ridge along Merriville Road called The Ettamogah Pub. How unusual was the place? How about a giant red tin roof, an antique truck on top of the roof, a cartoonish font, and a fanciful poem painted on the side of the restaurant proclaiming the wonders of beer. Take that, Outback Steakhouse. My friend and I decided on a schnitzel (breaded chicken cutlet) and beer. While schnitzel is a German food, but it has been uniquely adopted by the Aussies as a favorite piece of pub grub. Served with a liberal dosage of chips (French fries), salad, and tomato sauce (ketchup in Australia), the schnitzel has somehow become a part of Australian cuisine.

With our stomachs full of fried goodness and beer, Daniel and I headed back to his apartment in Blacktown. It was here that I was introduced to another new Aussie friend—Turbo,

Daniel's pet rabbit. Being a Rabbitohs fan, I might have guessed that perhaps, in the back of my mind, Daniel bought this little fella just before I arrived, because he knew I was a big supporter of Souths. Or perhaps he too loved the Rabbitohs, even though he told me that he goes for the Manly Sea Eagles. Or maybe, it was just a crazy coincidence that he had a rabbit. He kept Turbo inside a hutch on his balcony. He gently scooped him up from his hay and laid him in my lap. I had just realized that this was the first time, perhaps in almost, well, forever, that I had held a rabbit in my arms. From the minute Turbo stared up at me, I had no words to describe how sweet he was. He was small, white, and had little patches of silver around his paws, muzzle, and ears. He seemed rather content to just relax in my arms as I nuzzled him. As I watched him scurry around my legs, I just couldn't believe something this small and cute nearly wiped out Australia all those years ago.

I had learned from Daniel, however, that rabbits were not allowed to be kept as pets in Queensland. Up North, they dealt with the long-eared pest with the use of myxomatosis. Myxomatosis is a disease that affects rabbits and is caused by the myxoma virus; it was introduced into Australia in the 1950s in an attempt to control the rabbit population that began with Thomas Austin's twenty-four rabbits. The affected rabbits develop skin tumors, and in some cases blindness, followed by fatigue and fever; they usually die within fourteen days of contracting the disease. The disease is spread by direct contact with an affected animal or by being bitten by fleas or mosquitoes that have fed on an infected rabbit.

For the next two hours, Daniel and I just relaxed on the balcony. We just took turns talking in between sips of beer, taking turns holding Turbo, and just staring at the view of Blacktown on a sunny afternoon. We chatted about—what else—sports. We talked about our favorite football teams, footy, our home lives, and when we couldn't think of anything else to commiserate over, we just watched Turbo hop around the balcony. If there's one thing I can say, it's that rabbits are never uninteresting.

With the sun beginning to dip below the horizon, I bid a farewell to my four-legged friend. As Daniel drove me to the Blacktown station, I reflected on the day. I could have been another tourist wasting precious footage and seconds snapping photos of Sydney Harbour, but instead, I spent the day with a fellow fan of footy, accompanied by beer, marsupials, and rabbits. I think it was safe to say that this was, indeed, a most wonderful day. Frankly, I think that if everyone was a bit more drunk and surrounded by Australian wildlife, everyone would be in a happier mood! Daniel's car pulled up to the station's overpass platform and it was here we said goodbye. In spite of his fan loyalty for Manly, I consider him a member of The Burrow!

CHAPTER 16
Red and Green in the Blueys

SEPTEMBER 19, 2013:

I am very fortunate to have met Rachel Gotsis. While she may be a Parramatta Eels fan, as far as I am concerned, she is an honorable member of the red and green family. She is one of the coolest and smartest people I have ever met and a great example of just how warm and welcoming the Aussies truly are, especially when you're a devotee of footy. This was the day she introduced me to the majestic Blue Mountains of New South Wales, or as the locals call them, "The Blueys."

My original plan was to travel by train to the mountain town of Katoomba from Central Station, and then take a bus to Scenic World, the iconic tourist attraction that allows visitors to explore the confines of one of Australia's largest and most beautiful valleys. Instead, Rachel offered to pick me up from the Blacktown train station and drive the rest of the way to Scenic World. In my opinion, this could not have been a better way of getting around. And this way, I wouldn't be alone for the journey. Frankly, I had been getting quite bored of exploring new places on my own.

That morning, Rachel picked me up at the Blacktown train station. We drove into the highlands of New South Wales, just northwest of the Western Suburbs. As we ventured down the highway, I looked out the window to see if any of the passing scenery resembled any part of New York; I like to find little similarities between foreign countries and my home. The ride up reminded me of driving into upstate New York from Manhattan along either Route 9A along the Hudson

River or Route 22 into the Appalachians. The roads climbed high; I could see rock wall formations in the distance, the passing scenery became more and more bucolic, and towns were suddenly few and far between. I also relished in the fun-to-pronounce names of the towns like Bullabura, Wagga Wagga, and Katoomba. Just give them a roll off your tongue and try not to smile!

When one conjures up images of the Australian bush, they think of idyllic images of koalas napping high in gum trees, kookaburras laughing joyfully, and rocky cliffs towering over the greenest trees billowing in the breeze. It is a peaceful tableau if you ever saw it. And it is quite real, if I dare say so myself. One particular place within the confides of the Blue Mountains is Scenic World, where locals and tourists alike come from miles away to get the best view of one of Australia's most beloved areas.

Scenic World is located in the town of Katoomba in the Blue Mountains of New South Wales, about seventy-five miles west of Sydney. Scenic World is home to four attractions, of which the most famous is the Katoomba Scenic Railway, which is the steepest railway in the world. The site also includes the Katoomba Scenic Skyway, the Cableway, and Katoomba Scenic Walkway, which is a one-and-a-half mile elevated boardwalk through the ancient rainforest in the Jamison Valley.

When Rachel and I arrived, I experienced something that I had never known before: cold weather in Australia. And boy was it cold! I was wearing a short-sleeve shirt and khakis; I was getting goosebumps on my goosebumps. It was barely the start of spring in Australia, and it was freezing that morning. The temperature reminded me of March in Long Island. Rachel, on the other hand, was wearing a long-sleeve shirt and a heavy coat. How I envied her warmth! We got our park tickets and proceeded to the Scenic World Skyway. Suspended 270 meters above ancient ravines, this aerial cable-car provided a breathtaking view beneath the feet of curious adventurers via an electro-glass cabin floor.

Rachel and I boarded the Skyway. I took a deep breath as we were treated to an amazing view, to which we both reacted with awe! Nothing could have prepared me for such a marvelous sight. It was kind of like the first time I laid eyes on Uluru back in 2009. Jamison Valley was covered in many shades of green, accompanied by a towering waterfall. The chilly weather was still a bother; I was rubbing my hands and trying to take pictures at the same time. I wished I had at least brought a scarf or a pair of long pants! Brrrr! I was doing everything I could to snap a picture, afraid that I may never see such a sight again. But all I could do was stare in awe of how lucky I was to be in such a place that reminded me of why Australia is often referred to as the "Lucky Country!"

As Rachel and I disembarked from the Skyway, we then headed off into the depths of the Australian bush. After checking out a map of the surrounding areas, we started uphill on what we thought was the correct path down to The Three Sisters rock formation. Instead, we began a slightly exhausting climb up a public street, and almost into a nearby residential area. Once we realized that we were nowhere near the mountain path, we turned around, but not before having a good laugh. Of course, deep down, I was a little bit tired from that uphill trot. Little did I know that I would eventually learn the meaning of the word "tired!" I followed Rachel down the walkway, never taking my eye off of her red backpack. It shone like a beacon so I would never lose sight of it. The wind rustled loudly through the branches as I whipped out my camcorder to document every last sight and sound in this verdant valley.

The path was a combination of stone rectangles, carved steps, and a dirt path. It felt pretty easy at first, because since we were going downhill, it wasn't an arduous endeavor. The sound my feet made as they shuffled along the path made sort of a crunching sound. In fact, one might say it was sort of a symphony of the bush, if you will. The crunching of the dirt under my feet, the warbling of the birds and the wind rustling through the branches all made for an ethereal experience. I had heard these sounds before in New York or in the park on a quiet day, but the fact I was in such a faraway place made it all the more special.

To me, there is nothing more romantic than a walk through the Australian bush. The idea of a bushwalk conjures up images of an adventurous, yet curious wanderer, surrounded by a chorus of Australian avian wildlife, the many friendly marsupials, the valley of trees left and right, and natural formations that hold a sacred spot in Aboriginal lore. There's also the image of the walkabout, a ritual made famous by the Aborigines when someone ventures off into the Australian wilderness in an attempt to "find oneself" or to better understand nature. Of course, we didn't ride in the pouch of a red kangaroo as I remembered from the musical sequence from the film adaptation of *Dot and the Kangaroo*:

"Hippity-hoppity, thumpity-thump, when you come with us you'll know!" "Hippity-hoppity, thumpity-thump, that's the way it goes!"

Rachel continued to lead the way. Like Alice following the White Rabbit through Wonderland, I followed my brave bush guide with the red backpack into the valley. I listened carefully for any sounds in the tree tops; a laugh from a kookaburra or a warble from a magpie. Even the smells intrigued me, triggering various memories in my head. Instead, I just heard the cool breeze waft through the branches. Rachel even got a shot of me just inches from the edge of a small cliff. Don't worry, I didn't fall! After a short climb uphill, Rachel and I finally came to a close-up of the Three Sisters. This is probably the most iconic and most famous rock formation in the Blue Mountains. They are, as the name would suggest, three vertical rock towers, all in a neat little row, towering above the Jamison Valley.

In Aboriginal lore, the commonly told legend of the Three Sisters is that three sisters (Meehni, Wimlah, and Gunnedoo) lived in the Jamison Valley as members of the Katoomba tribe. They fell in love with three men from a neighboring tribe (the Nepean tribe), but marriage was forbidden by tribal law. The brothers were not happy to accept this law and so decided to use force to capture the three sisters. A major tribal battle ensued, and the sisters were turned to stone by an elder to protect them, but he was killed in the fighting and no one else could turn them back. This legend is claimed to be an Indigenous Australian Dreamtime legend. To this day, people from all over Australia and the world come to this part of the Blue Mountains to pay a visit to the three stone ladies of the Blue Mountains.

From nearby Echo Point, a bushwalking trail leads to the Three Sisters and down to the valley floor via more than 800 well-maintained steel and stone steps called "The Giant Stairway." This was the most difficult part of the bushwalk. How difficult was this part of the trek? Let's just say I would rather climb the Sydney Harbour Bridge, twice! The steps at certain points were so steep; it was as if they were teetering around a sixty-degree angle. I was holding on to the steel railing for dear life!

I was doing everything I could to catch up to Rachel, hoping that I wasn't going to be stranded in the middle of the bush. Eventually, I caught up with her at the middle of the Meehni rock formation. I got to walk under it, and even touch the rather smooth formation; it was a pretty awesome experience! Then began the arduous climb back up! Since each step was pretty high above the next, and was angled pretty steeply, each step felt like I was getting the wind knocked out of me. I kept looking up, hoping I was getting closer and closer to the summit. Finally, I was able to catch up to Rachel and we made it back up to the beginning of the path. Despite me having to catch up to my breath, I had seen the bush up close and personal, not to mention having met the three most beautiful ladies in Katoomba. But now, I had to get back to my brave tour guide from Schofields.

A much tamer walk from the top of the staircase toward the Katoomba Scenic Railway gave me a chance to catch my breath. This is one of Australia's most famous attractions, as it is the world's steepest cable-driven funicular railway in the world with an incline of fifty-two degrees contained within a total incline distance of 415 meters (1,361.5 feet). It was originally constructed for a coal and oil shale mining operation in the Jamison Valley in the 1880s, in order to haul the coal and shale from the valley floor up to the escarpment above. From 1928 to 1945, it carried coal during the week and passengers on weekends. The coal mine was closed in 1945, after which it remained as a tourist attraction.

The path toward the railway felt like being back in Disney World; it took away from the ambiance of the place for a bit. At any moment, I thought I'd see a ride operator with mouse ears and a name tag. Even the train carriage looked more like a roller coaster, which only added to the excitement. Rachel and I stepped into a row near the rear; so much for waiting in line for the front car. Once we took our seats, we noticed that there was a lever at the end of the row that could alter the angle of your seats. In other words, as you head downhill, you can literally make your seat lean in more and more toward the abyss-like hill! Or for those who lack a spine, you can lean back against the funicular, and not suffer a case of vertigo. Sadly, our row didn't come with this cool feature.

As the train began its slow descent, I was practically leaning into the train for dear life! It was so steep that I couldn't believe I didn't scream as the train headed downhill. Then again, we were heading down at a comfortable pace; I'm not sure about the speed, but it felt like it was less than twenty miles-per-hour. The train car pulled into the station at the bottom of the hill. When Rachel and I disembarked, we stared uphill at the tracks and couldn't believe just how steep it was! The word "railway" was probably a misnomer, as "roller coaster" would have been a more apt description of what we had just ridden.

Actually, speaking of roller coasters, you'll find remnants of a roller coaster track set up around parts of Scenic World. In 1984, Scenic World began building a roller coaster known as the Orphan Rocker, named after the nearby Orphan Rock. This was the first roller coaster to be completely designed and manufactured in Australia. The highlight of this ride was meant to be a swooping banked turn that would take riders within meters of the edge of a 656 foot cliff. The roller coaster has never publicly opened due to demands for redevelopment elsewhere onsite, but the roller coaster track has been left in place for possible redevelopment in the future. In fact, if you look out over the Skyway and the Scenic Railway, you can see roller coaster track set up all over the place. The design of the track sort of bears a resemblance to the famed Revolution roller coaster from Six Flags Magic Mountain in California, the one made famous in the 1983 movie *Vacation*.

For the final part of our journey in the Blue Mountains, Rachel and I headed from the Scenic Railway and onto the Scenic World Scenic Walkway. The secret word, in case you didn't know, is scenic! In the thick of the rainforest, near the bottom of Jamison Valley, is a 2.4 kilometer (1.5 miles) elevated boardwalk that traverses through the bush, underneath some of the tallest trees in all of Australia. Along the way, Rachel and I explored the site's coal mining history, including the mine entrance, a replica miners' hut and scale bronze sculpture of a miner and his pit pony. As I previously mentioned, back in the late nineteenth century, the Scenic Railway was originally used as a means of transporting coal and shale oil from underneath the valley. Here, we saw original pieces of what miners used during their digging, along with where the miners would begin their descent.

The best part of this walkway was just slowly meandering around the bush, listening to the wind rustle through the branches, and hearing the musical warbling of kookaburras, lyre birds, and magpies. While I couldn't hear any kookaburras laughing, I did hear the distinct whistle of the magpie. I loved that swift whistle so much that I even tried mimicking it. Once, I swear, as I walked past a bench, I could hear a bird sing the exact same call I had just given! I'm no birdwatcher, but it was a pretty awesome moment! I even snapped a picture of a magpie perched in a tree.

The part of the Blue Mountains we explored has been featured in many Australian films. One of the most notable was the 1977 film adaptation of *Dot and the Kangaroo*, one of Australia's most beloved children's books, written back in 1899 by Ethel Charlotte Pedley. The story was arguably one of the first books to romanticize the creatures of the Australian bush at a time when most Australian settlers saw them as either food or things to hunt. The titular character, lost in the bush, is befriended by a gentle kangaroo that feeds her special berries that allow her to communicate freely with the denizens of the bush. The kangaroo becomes something of a surrogate mother to Dot even though the massive marsupial does not fully trust humans, let alone every other animal in the bush.

Dot and the Kangaroo was a whimsical piece of literature that brought to life all the animals of Australia long before Mem Fox introduced her books to American schoolchildren. The film was made by Aussie animating legend Yoram Gross, using two-dimensional animated characters set in a real-life background. In other words, viewers are treated to a non-animated bush throughout most of the movie. It was a trademark way Gross made most of his movies, including the 1993 animated adaptation of Australia's most famous koala, *Blinky Bill*, which was also shot in the Blue Mountains. The whole time I was walking along the Scenic Walkway, I kept an eye out for Dot and her hopping friend, as well as Blinky. Alas, not this time around, sadly. I guess I'll have to look even harder next time I come back.

Rachel and I began our long hike back up to her car. We rode the Scenic World Skyride gondola back up from Jamison Valley. Once again, the view did not disappoint. As we came close to the top, I began humming the Midnight Oil song *In the Valley*. It just seemed like the perfect tune choice for such a location. Maybe it was the catchy opening riff or the fact that Rachel and I were in a valley. Whatever it was, as the song echoed through my head, it sent a shiver down my spine, but not a scared one. It was one of those "right-place, right-time" moments.

CHAPTER 17
The Bunny and the Eel

SEPTEMBER 19, 2013

Our ride back into Sydney was a quiet one at first. Rachel and I just enjoyed the long, winding road through the Blueys. I was keeping myself occupied by trying to pronounce the town names like Bullaburra, Katoomba, and Warrimoo. What can I say? I love the names of Australian suburbs. Of course, what trip to Australia wouldn't be complete without a little shopping? Much like Rachel's plan to drive up to the Blue Mountains, she also had another special idea in mind: shopping for ugg boots.! But these wouldn't come from some high-end retailer. These boots came from none other than a leather maker found off the side of the road, just a few miles from Bullaburra. His stand was littered with hand-made leather trinkets in all shapes and sizes. One might say that it looked like something out of Medieval England; an artisan with his finest goods all set up under a massive tent accompanied by the musty scent of leather.

I spotted a pair of ugg boots that had the softest interior that my fingers gently caressed. It's kind of funny how these type of boots (not to be confused with the trademark UGG Boots) are sold as a fashion statement in America, but the origins in Australia and New Zealand began as a piece of footwear one might wear if, say, your mom wanted you to take out the garbage or pull the car into the garage. They were essentially, if you will, ratty slippers that were primarily associated with "bogan" culture, which is anyone from Australia or New Zealand that is of lower-class status. The American fashion industry took uggs, and basically made diamonds from coal. Very smooth, wooly, soft lumps of coal!

With my new uggs on my feet, Rachel and I resumed our trip back to the city. Little did I know that she had more surprises in store for me. Before heading back to Sydney, Rachel and I took a little detour through Parramatta. I had never been through this part of Sydney before, but I had heard that it was sort of Sydney's shopping capital in that it had a big mall and a big transit hub. Rachel told me that we planning on surprising Bill at his office building. We walked through the front door, slowly crept up toward his office room, and, let's just say, we both left him speechless! It was just a candid moment that still lives inside my head. In fact, it was so unexpected, Bill then starting bragging on the phone about how his wife and I surprised him at work. Even Bill and Rachel had to go and introduce me to his office receptionist on the first floor. It's almost like the Gotsis family wanted me to know almost every person and acquaintance in their family.

As if surprising Bill at work wasn't enough, Rachel told me that she was in need of a new set of shelves. And it just so happened that she was in need of a strong pair of arms to help her get them into her car. You know, when tourists come to Australia, they expect to hug a koala, hop with the kangaroos, or get drunk on the beach. Me? I helped a friend of mine do some heavy lifting and errands. Ah, adventure! But I digress.

We made a short drive to a parking garage at the Westfield Parramatta Mall and it was here I was introduced to another awesome thing in Australia: the parking garages. Dangling over each space was a skinny, black rod that had a colored light at the end over the space. Like a signal beacon, each light-stick could be seen from a good distance away. Whenever the light glowed red, it meant that a car was occupying the space; a green light meant that the space was vacant. And a blue light was reserved for handicapped vehicles. This was such a brilliant system to keep everything in order. As if that wasn't efficient enough, each corner of the garage had a counter that kept track of how many spaces were vacant. I just have one question: Why don't we have this in America? In the United States, parking lots and parking garages are practically blood sport, but these devices take all the stress out of looking for a space. Is it any wonder why Aussies are happier than Americans?! I know I sound a bit odd gushing over something as esoteric as a parking garage system, but I had never seen something so simple and yet so clever. It's always the little things that fascinate me.

Rachel and I headed for The Reject Store, a rather hilariously named discount store inside the mall. As much fun as it was carrying those heavy shelves into Rachel's car, she had one more surprise in store for me. From the parking garage, we walked underneath the Parramatta train station toward Church Street. Once again, I felt like I was transported back to Queens. The big, bustling train station, the rows of buses, the old architecture, the massive shopping choices, the slew of ethnic restaurants on every corner, and the tall office buildings. It was like an Australian version of Forest Hills meets Jamaica; the shopping and restaurant choices of the former and the transportation hub of the latter. Instead of seeing the words *Queens Center* emblazoned on the front of the mall, the words *Westfield Parramatta* were there instead.

Rachel and I strolled past the Parramatta City Hall and fountain and brought me to the coup de gras: Peter Wynn's Score. For Aussies in the know, this is the premier sporting goods store. This is more than just a place to buy a jersey; it is a hodge-podge of everything Australian sports related. I had heard of this place on social media from every Rabbitohs fan. I had asked them what place I should go to for all my Rabbitohs needs. While many of them said The Clubhouse Store on Chalmers Street, a vast majority all agreed on Peter Wynn's.

The outside of this store was lined with flags of every NRL club, pennants in all shapes and sizes, and a sign that read "*If You Don't Score Here, You'll Never Score!*" Damn, straight! Peter Wynn's Score was established in 1988 by Australian Rugby League player Peter Wynn and his brother-in-law Mark Assef. This footy great played for Parramatta for eleven years from 1979–1990. During his tenure with the Eels, he helped to lead the yellow and blue to several Premierships in the 1980s, most notably three consecutive in 1981, 1982, and 1983, and a fourth title in 1986; he was out during the 1981 Premiership due to injuries. His last three seasons were severely affected by injury, with a broken ankle sidelining him after six games in 1988 and major injuries keeping him off the field in 1990 until late in the season, when he was used on the reserves bench.

After his retirement from rugby league, Wynn went on to found the namesake store. The place specializes mostly in rugby league, but they run the gamut from footy, to soccer, to cricket. But they don't stop at Aussie sporting goods: the place also serves up a laundry list of America's pastimes: baseballs, catchers' mitts, and even basketballs can be found among the rugby goodness. In fact, baseball has gotten quite popular Down Under recently. On March 22nd, 2014, the Arizona Diamondbacks held a two-game home opener at the Sydney Cricket Grounds against the Los Angeles Dodgers. During those two matches, it was the first time in the history of Major League Baseball that a game, let alone two games, was played in Australia. To see major league sluggers in 2014 step up to the plate with white picket fences and manual clocks looming behind them was such a throwback to the days when baseball stadiums looked so antiquated; I'm surprised I didn't see ticket ushers dressed to the nines with handlebar mustaches like they were in the 1920s.

One of the most memorable moments happened not on the diamond but up in the press box. The cricket commentators were trying to get the baseball commentators to try vegemite. Unsurprisingly, the baseball commentators were resistant to the Australian spread. That is, until the Aussies tried to convince them that it was like eating spreadable beer, as the food is a yeast extract, yeast being a main ingredient in beer. Within seconds, the Americans happily ate the savory spread on bread, and another momentous moment was made in the thawing of our Americo-Aussie relationship. Now if only they could convince the Americans to assist them on the commentary for a cricket test match.

The store was a wonderland of Aussie sports paraphernalia. Without hesitation, I grabbed as much Rabbitohs gear as I could get my American Bunny paws on. I wasn't content on just settling on jerseys and shirts though. I loaded my arms up with every last sticker, keychain, lanyard, flag, pennant, water bottle, and wrapping paper with red and green on it. By the time I got to the register, Rachel was laughing from all the Bunnies swag I was holding and the girl behind the register looked quite speechless. The shock continued when I spoke with no Aussie accent, revealing that I was an American fan.

No more than a few seconds after I received my change did another amazing thing happen: I was introduced to none other than Peter Wynn himself! The girl behind the register was so impressed by my fandom of footy, that she insisted I meet the man behind the store. Of course, being a Rabbitohs fan, albeit a newcomer to the world of footy, I didn't know much about him at the time; I wouldn't know what to say other than what an amazing store he had. This rather tall gent with his shaven head looked so much like Midnight Oil's Peter Garrett; I was almost tempted to compliment him on his music career! He was a really friendly bloke who was only too happy to introduce himself to me.

When he saw all my Rabbitohs swag, the former Parramatta captain attempted to make an eel out of me. Alas, his attempts were futile, as this Bunny would not be swayed. Nonetheless, he was kind enough to autograph a poster for me with the message that read, "*To Jared, it's NEVER too late to be an Eel! PS... Rabbitohs are fine!*" He also threw in a free coffee mug with the inscription, "*To Jared, You Scored! Peter Wynn 2013. PS...Be an EEL!*" Boy, when it comes to team love, I will definitely give it up for him. But I'm sorry, Mr. Wynn; this New Yorker is not wearing any other colors! Nonetheless, he was still kind enough to pose for a photo with me and even do a pose where he pointed to his own name in the storefront. What a ham! Now I know why footy players are held in such high regard Down Under. They aren't just heroes on the field, but off the field as well. They are both approachable and rather casual with their fans; something that I believe is lost on American sports fans. Maybe it is all the pampering and spoiling we have done to them, but it just so damn refreshing to meet someone who is not just one of Australia's greatest footy players, but also a really nice guy! Peter Wynn, however, wasn't the only footy star I was fortunate to meet in person. In fact, I learned that being an American Rabbitohs fan among the professionals has its great advantages...

PART III:

Hope And Heartbreak

CHAPTER 18
The Rabbit and the Falcon

SEPTEMBER 13, 2013

It had been one week since my inaugural visit to ANZ Stadium, where I had seen my very first rugby league match between the South Sydney Rabbitohs and the Sydney Roosters. It was the deciding Minor Premiership, and the atmosphere had been nothing short of electric. Sadly, the match did not go the way I had wanted it to, and I had had to endure a lengthy train ride back to Town Hall station filled with smug Chooks fans who kept giving me and my Rabbitohs friends the business. And by that, I mean reminding us that we hadn't won a Premiership since 1971. Not cool, Roosters! Suffice it to say, I was sort of licking my wounds and silently weeping. Of course, I was determined to not let it damper my vacation; I had just experienced one of the greatest spectacles in sports! Still, I needed closure. I just needed to see the mighty red and green kick ass! I just didn't want to go home without seeing the Rabbitohs win in person!

Unfortunately, I was, however, without a ticket. Here's where I learned just how unbelievable kind the red and green fans truly are. One of my favorite fans was Michelle Booth, who was in charge of procuring tickets for members in The Burrow; she had reserved a ticket for me for the playoff round. Little did I know that my Rabbitohs/Giants friend, Bill Gotsis, had also managed to score a ticket to the first qualifying match for me as well! Talk about having my back! During the train ride from Lidcombe to Olympic Park, I was doing everything I could to psyche myself up for this September showdown. Survivor's *Eye of the Tiger* and Eminem's *Lose Yourself* blasted into my ears from my iPod; nothing like some inspirational music to pump you up. The train was filled with eager Souths fans that were stoked to see their Bunnies redeem themselves against the purple powerhouse known as the Melbourne Storm, who by the way, were, at the time, the defending premiers from 2012.

Once the train pulled into Olympic Park, I made my way through the station, and toward The Brewery to meet up with Bill. That's when I spotted a TV camera and a man with a microphone. Not wasting a second, I unraveled my poster in order to get their attention. The two men from Channel 7 saw my poster, and it was at that moment I got my fifteen minutes of fame! Or rather, less than five minutes of camera time. The two men interviewed me and were indeed surprised, if not speechless, to see an American at such a match, let alone one with a passion for the red and green. I managed to make it through the interview without stammering or fainting, and before I knew it, I was more famous Down Under than I was in America. If everyone at the first game was psyched to have met me, imagine what they would say after they saw me on the evening news.

Over at The Brewery, I managed to run into my old Twitter and Facebook fans instead. Bill flagged me down and before you could say, "Cheers, mate!" we buried our thirsty faces in a couple of cold ones. I offered to pay Bill for the drinks, but he insisted that it was on him. To say that these Australian Bunnies are among the kindest group of fans is an understatement! I received a shirt off a guy's back, several beers, and a free ticket! I'm just gonna say it: Rabbitohs fans are the best! I spent a good portion of my time there shaking hands with the fans. Inside the Brewery, I met the faces of many Twitter and Facebook followers. It was astounding how many of them recognized me because of my posters. So many wanted to have a beer with me and have a photo op with me.

In between sips and snapping pics, I was in for another big surprise. One of my friends alerted me that Rabbitohs great Mario Fenech was over by the ticket windows doing an interview. Not wanting to miss this opportunity, I grabbed my poster as I struggled to control my heart rate. Mario Fenech is a big celebrity among the Rabbitohs. As the former captain of the team from 1986 to 1990, he led the team to their last minor Premiership in 1989, and is considered by many Aussies to be one of the greatest rugby league players, ever. He is known as the "Maltese Falcon" in that he is of Maltese decent; a native of Valleta. And like the Maltese Falcon of cinema, Souths fans will tell you he is the stuff dreams are made of! Well, providing you're a Bunnies fan; if you're a Roosters fan, then he is in your nightmares!

Mario Fenech, a native of Malta, spent his childhood in the Botany region of Sydney. During those young years, he was a South Sydney youth champion from the Mascot Juniors team. Fenech's career spanned from 1981 to 1995, and he played for the South Sydney Rabbitohs for all but five of those years. He was a strong runner from dummy half and given his style and size, almost always attracted a number of defenders intent on stopping his progress. Since retiring from football, Fenech has worked tirelessly with the South Sydney Football Club, has been a regular contributor on The Footy Show, and has written books about his days on the field.

Trying hard not to blush, or curl my feet, or do anything cliché that people do when they're shy, I took a deep breath as I bravely approached the Maltese Falcon. I had been following him on Twitter for months before my arrival, and I had received a few shout-outs from him, including ones where I posted pictures of my poster. I had first gotten to know the famed former Souths captain not from the NRL but from an episode of Anthony Bourdain's *No Reservations* in which the Travel Channel bad boy paid a visit to Sydney. One of the things he did during the episode was attend a Rabbitohs game at ANZ Stadium with Fenech by his side. It was the one time I could remember in which the Rabbitohs received a fair amount of publicity on one of the highest rated travel shows on cable; I would have loved that episode even more had the Bunnies defeated the Roosters in that episode.

I stepped forward, mustering every ounce of courage I could. It is often said that one should not meet their heroes in person, for fear that they will be disappointed. That would not be the case that evening, as Mr. Fenech recognized me from my Rabbitohs poster from Twitter; he was most pleased to meet me. I quite honored to shake his hand, and he must have felt the same; to meet a big Bunnies fan who had come from so far away to see a match of such caliber. After all the pleasantries, I graciously asked him to sign my poster, to which he gleefully obliged! The ink wasn't even dry by the time he and I were posing for pictures, courtesy of my Rabbitohs friends. In all my life, I've never caught a foul ball at a baseball game, never been invited into the locker rooms, and never sat courtside at a basketball game. But now, I can add my encounter with the Maltese Falcon to my list of sports greats!

CHAPTER 19:
Two Happy Bunnies
(First Half of the 2013 Qualifying Round)

I thought I had seen Bill Gotsis' red and green-ness at the Roosters game a week ago, but this game was where he didn't just show his colors, he bled them! Hell, anymore a fan, and he could have morphed into Reggie! Actually, I'm still working on that.

Before we headed into ANZ Stadium, we had a few minutes for beer and tucker. Mario, Bill's cousin, brought us a bounty of McDonalds, or as they say Down Under, "Maccas!" We stuffed our faces and managed a few more beers in between bites of Big Mac. Mario was asking me about Sydney, specifically what I had seen so far since I had arrived. In an attempt to impress my Aussie friends, I made some interesting comparisons between American building magnate Robert Moses and Australia's Dr. Joseph Bradfield. I was merely making an astute observation about how Bradfield presided over the construction of Australia's most iconic bridge as Moses oversaw the construction of New York's many highways and bridges over the course of his long career. To hear an American make this comparison, let alone know who Bradfield was, made Bill and Mario laugh so hard, they practically laughed up their food!

Bill and I took our seats; the emcee announced the opening lineup for the Storm as Led Zeppelin's "Kashmir" blared over the stadium. As I would make return trips to the Rabbitohs over the years, it seems that this tune is commonly played down here, much like when the New York Yankees play the "Imperial March" from *Star Wars* as the visiting team's lineup is announced. "Glory Glory to South Sydney" began playing;

Bill and I stood up and hummed the opening drumbeat. I fumbled with my camcorder to get a clear shot of the team tunnel from the other side of the field. Sure enough, Reggie stormed the field and the 21,063 fans in attendance that night cheered and screamed as if they were seeing The Beatles playing on the Ed Sullivan Show. Well, my screams were the loudest!

The game was underway as Jeff Lima got tackled at the 15-meter line, followed by a tackle to Luke Burgess at the 20-meter line, then Jeff Lima again at 28-meter, and then a pass to Sam Burgess which resulted in him getting tackled at the 40-meter line. A punt on 4th tackle gave the ball to Melbourne's Billy Slater. Bad luck would have it as Melbourne was awarded a penalty thanks to a shoulder charge; they would restart at their 45-meter line. We would have to wait another ninety seconds before we regained control. A close call came at around 6:16 seconds into the first half when the Storm punted the ball high on 5th tackle, as it looked like it would be caught inside the end zone. However, my prediction was half-right; Nathan Merritt intercepted the possible Storm try, thus saving South Sydney from being down first. About sixty seconds later, South Sydney would get its first lucky break in a big way.

After a brief surge from the Rabbitohs, Adam Reynolds punted the ball on 5th tackle, which was caught Billy Slater. Justin O'Neil would then lose the ball on their 20-meter line, giving the Rabbitohs a chance to get within striking distance of a try. Sure enough, Reynolds passed the dropped ball to Dylan Farrell and he carried it into the end zone for the first try of the match! A converted kick by Reynolds would put the Rabbitohs ahead 6-0.

As the first half wore on, I began asking Bill, or as I would later refer to him that night, my "Rabbitohs sensei," about some of the finer points of rugby league. Specifically, all the little similarities and differences between American football and Australian rugby league. Things like downs versus tackles, having what are called restarts instead of safeties, and how rugby league is more like American football than rugby union. Bill's knowledge was never-ending; if it weren't for the game, I could have spent the entire night talking to him about every nuance of footy.

At around nineteen and a half minutes into the first half, we caught a break when we were awarded a penalty; we restarted the play from thirty meters inside the Storm's zone. Sam Burgess was tackled inside the 10-meter line. A pass to Ben Te'o resulted in him getting tackled inside the 5-meter line. Just when it looked like we would get another try, we were awarded a penalty after Isaac Luke was held while being tackled. The Rabbitohs opted for a field goal, and at the twenty-second minute, Adam Reynolds put it through the uprights, putting us ahead 8–0.

At twenty-three minutes into the game, the Storm regained the ball and began charging up the field again. Luckily for us, the men in purple fumbled the ball; a scrum was awarded to the Rabbitohs. Shortly after the scrum formation, a differential penalty was awarded to the Rabbitohs; a restart from inside Melbourne's 20-meter line came next. First, George Burgess was tackled inside the 5-meter line, then Greg Inglis was pushed back inside the 10-meter line, but then another penalty was awarded to the Rabbitohs; it was the fifth penalty in five minutes. Continuing our run toward the end zone, Sam Burgess got the ball but was tackled inside the 3-meter line. After getting up, Sammie passed the ball to Jeff Lima, who easily carried it across the line for the Rabbitohs' second try. A converted kick from Reynolds put us up 14–0. Suffice it to say, Bill and I were feeling pretty amazing!

At around the twenty-eighth minute, the Storm gained a scrum after the ball went out of bounds when Reynolds wildly punted it on 5th tackle. For the next few minutes, Bill and I would have to endure a little stress as Melbourne would have possession for almost the rest of the first half. Roy Asotasi was put on report for an illegal tackle to the neck; this brought the Storm just thirty meters away from the end zone. At the thirtieth minute, Nathan Merritt dove on the ball in the end zone, which forced a line dropout; it was the second one of the night. Melbourne's Stephen O'Neil looked like he would give the Storm its first try when he was inside the 1-meter line on 3rd tackle.

Bill and I held our breath until the instant replay went up on the jumbotron. The replay showed Dylan Farrell just barely catching the ball before Stephen O'Neil was able to put pressure on it in the end zone. The ruling was NO TRY, and the Rabbitohs fans cheered as they all gasped a collective sigh of relief. The play, however, would restart from inside the 10-meter line. At the thirty-fourth minute, the Storm were awarded a penalty after the Souths were caught holding down a tackle for too long. At the thirty-fifth minute, the same thing happened when Adam Reynolds was accused of holding down too long. These were the kind of mistakes that made half of us grit our teeth with frustration, while the other half of us held our heads in our hands in confusion. Two consecutive holding tackles on us?

Thankfully, at around the thirty-sixth minute, Souths defense would kick in as they would deny the Storm another try at the 1-meter line yet again! However, the Storm, on their 5th tackle, would punt the ball; the fate of a possible try hung in the air. John Sutton was there to knock the ball out of the way. Toward the end of tense first half, Sutton would attempt a drop goal, but missed the uprights. Just before the siren sounded at the fortieth minute, Cameron Smith, captain of the Storm, would attempt a penalty goal kick for two points after a penalty was awarded to them. The kick veered off to the side as we finished the first half 14–0. I just hoped we could keep this lead going into the second half; I could not bear a second consecutive loss.

I Traveled Over 10,000 Miles for my Very First Game!

I'm Red, White, and Blue on the Outside. But, I Bleed Red & Green for South Sydney Rabbitohs!

A pregame drink with my new bunny mates at The Royal Oak pub.
Here, I am welcomed into the Warren.

From clockwise: Tanya Atkinson, Joe Mancusi, Wendy Celarc, and Brigitte Weiss.

NRL football signed by the 2013 Rabbitohs squad.

The Rabbitohs Warrior. Watch as he holds aloft his mighty sword to sever the Rooster's head.

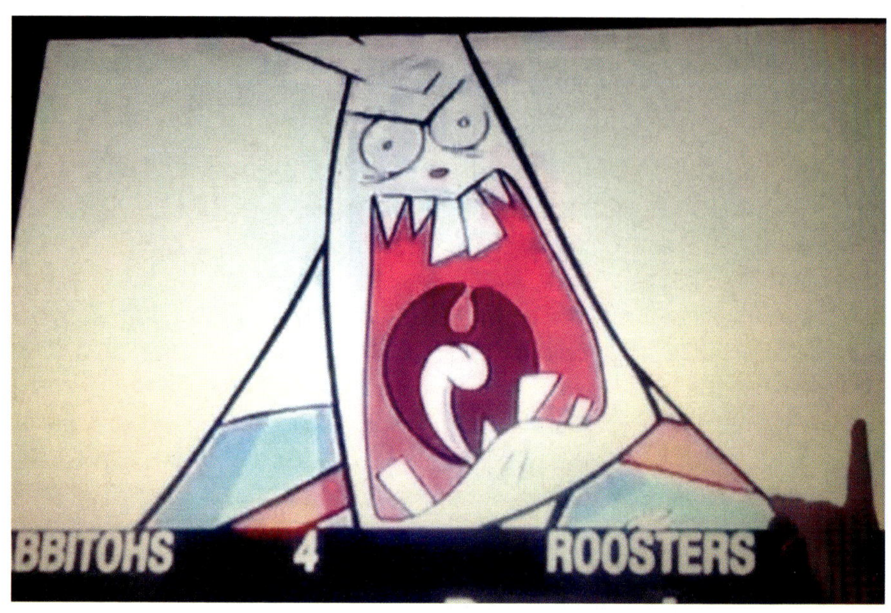

"Death to the Roosters! Vengeance, my Bunny brethren! Glory Glory to South Sydney!"

First try of the game is rewarded with one angry bunny!

Reggie Rabbit leads The Burrow with a cowbell during the Minor Premiership.

The historic Redfern Oval, the former stadium and current training grounds of the Rabbitohs.

Upper left (Tanya Atkinson & Brigitte Weiss), lower left (Brian "Ed" Rabbitoh), right half (Souths Juniors)

The many residential homes along the Hawkesbury, both on land and on water.

Hawkesbury River's beaches, Parsley Bay, Hawkesbury River Marina, and Dangar Island wharf.

Dolcissimo's in Haberfields: The Little Italy of Sydney.

My two new Aussie friends: Daniel (he's the human!) and Turbo (he's the rabbit!).

Jamison Valley Railway: The world's steepest railway.

Scenic World's famous Skytram as it sails over Jamison Valley.

The Three Sisters (from left to right): Meehni (922m), Wimlah (918m), Gunnedoo (906m).

Leather, get'yer leather right here! The best leather and uggs in Bullaburra.

Me with Mario Fenech, the Maltese Falcon of the Rabbitohs.

The Bunny from NYC and the Eel of Parramatta. I certainly scored here! Good on ya, Peter!

Are these not the two happiest and most proud Rabbitohs fans you have ever seen?!

My first Rabbitohs selfie! Me with Souths superstar, Jason "Clarky" Clark. Good on ya, mate!

Here in the wilds of Redfern, we see the majestic South Sydney Rabbitohs in their natural habitat.

Reggie Rabbit greets his adoring fanbase during the qualifying match against Melbourne.

Traveling from Lidcombe to ANZ Stadium? No, just two Bunnies on their way to see the Giants!

I made it into the pages of Rugby League Weekly! Am I the first American Rabbitoh to do so?!

My newest converts to the Rabbitohs red and green army! They're rabbit breeders, but they're Rabbitohs fans now! Me with the members of the Long Island American Rabbit Breeders Association.

The newest member of the Gotsis family! A Bunny brother from another mother...

Only a Rabbitohs fan could love a rabbit this much!

Kate Richardson and I posing with Reggie Rabbit at the Australian NYC after a Souths win!

Look at all those shiny rabbit trophies. Those are the kind of awards befitting only a Rabbitoh!

For the front side of my 2014 poster, I had the decency to convert into metric!

For the reverse side of my 2014 poster, I decided to tell the world who I really am on the inside!

This American is proudly representing the Rabbitohs on behalf of the team and all USA fans!

From counterclockwise: Statue of Liberty, Brooklyn Bridge, Nathan's Famous, and Coney Island

Eat your heart out, Playboy Bunnies! They got nothing on these Bunny gals from Down Under!

A photo op with Australia's biggest Bunny! Another important rite of passage as a Souths fan! Photograph is courtesy of Elizabeth Brown.

Today, I consider myself the luckiest Souths fan on the face of the Earth! Good on ya, Reggie! Photographs are courtesy of Elizabeth Brown and Jared Schnabl.

My red and green Australian Bunny family! They may be loud and a little drunk, but I love'em! Clockwise, upper left: (Dingo MacNaughton, Ursulla Whiteley & Brigitte Weiss, Michelle Booth, and Will Gotsis.

The look of shock on the fans in The Burrow after the close loss to the Roosters. Oh, the agony!

Which one is the Australian? Which one is the American? You decide!

Me with Greg Inglis (upper left), Adam Reynolds (lower right), and Sam Burgess (far right).

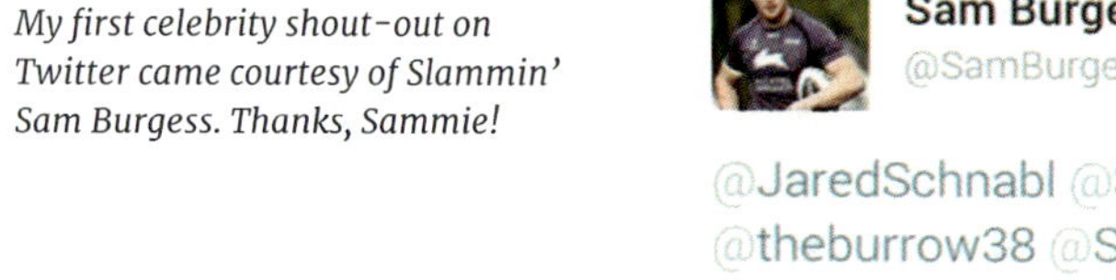

My first celebrity shout-out on Twitter came courtesy of Slammin' Sam Burgess. Thanks, Sammie!

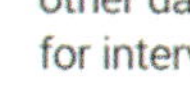

Me with Coach Michael "Madge" Maguire (left), Jason "Clarky" Clark (upper right), and Jeremy "Jezza" Monahan (lower right).

Me with Sock Tighe, hardcore Rabbitohs fan I met on Facebook. He recognized me in Redfern!

The entrance to the Waratah Trail from Berowra train station. Don't be bothered by the graffiti.

The scenery along the Waratah Trail in Kuring-Gai National Park near Berowra.

A Bunny in Berowra! Notice the hive-like structure in the tree (lower right)?

Aussie schoolchildren heading home. And no, I didn't step back in time to the early 20th century!

Going counter clockwise: Me with Paul Selmes, Me with Vicki Hayes, Me with Paul Selmes and Brigitte Weiss, and Me with Rabbitohs on the brain!

Top row: All painted up for the big game. Lower left: bar hopping with the Bunnies at the Cricketer Arms Hotel on Foveaux Street. Lower right: Me with Tammie Saunders Kemp.

This enthusiastic Souths fan owns one of the best Italian restaurants in all of Sydney!

Live, from Sydney, Australia, it's the Cracca and Macca Show! Staring Cracca and Macca!

Me with Kellie Bishop (left) and Tammy Saunders Kemp (right). Two lovely ladies of the Souths.

Me celebrating with Lorraine Carpenter (left and lower right) and Janet Hill (upper right).

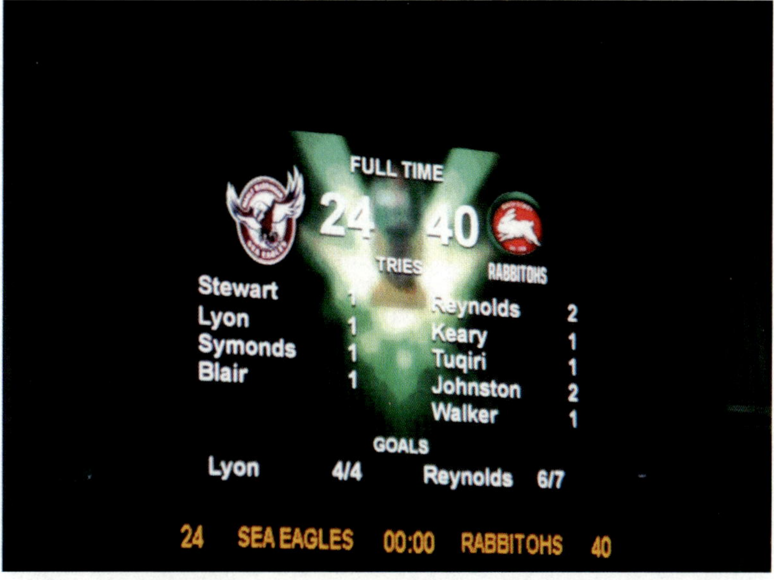

Game, set, and match! The final score was Bunnies 40, Sea Eagles 24. Bunnies beat Manly!

Me shaking hands, er, paws with South Sydney's biggest and most famous bunny!

Reggie Rabbit dancing and flexing his muscles for his devoted red and green fanbase.

Me at 2014 Oz Comic-con! On the left half, I am being photobombed by a giant Eevee. On the right half, I am trying to not blink as I am being photobombed by the dreaded weeping angels!

Wondabyne Station. I finally made it! Best of all, I found an unguarded tinny!

A lone Bunny wanders along the trail above Wondabyne. This is my little hideaway in Australia.

The many views of Brisbane Waters National Park from Wondabyne. Notice the log steps?

My new tattooed mate Frank, sharing a love of Midnight Oil and AC/DC.

My combination compass/whistle. Don't leave home without it! What a way to catch a train!

Me bidding farewell to my favorite Aussie family, the Gotsis. Till we meet again, mates!

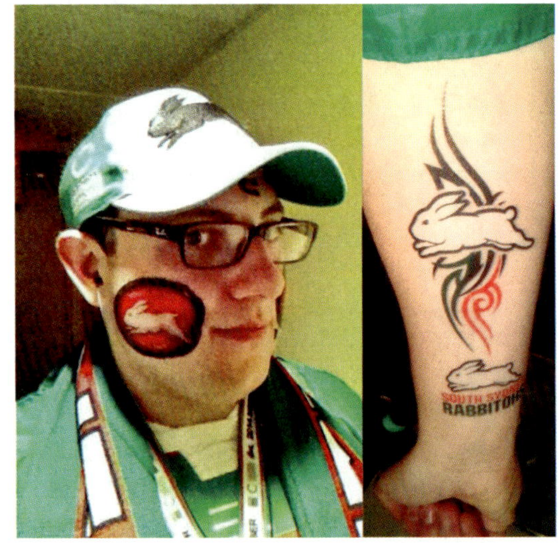

An American Souths supporter is dressed to kill. My face and arms are inked up for the game!

The look of tension on an anxious Souths fan after the score was evened up at 6–6 in the 2nd half.

Me with Tom Cawte, Rabbitohs under-11's alumni, fan, and Aussie native from Long Island.

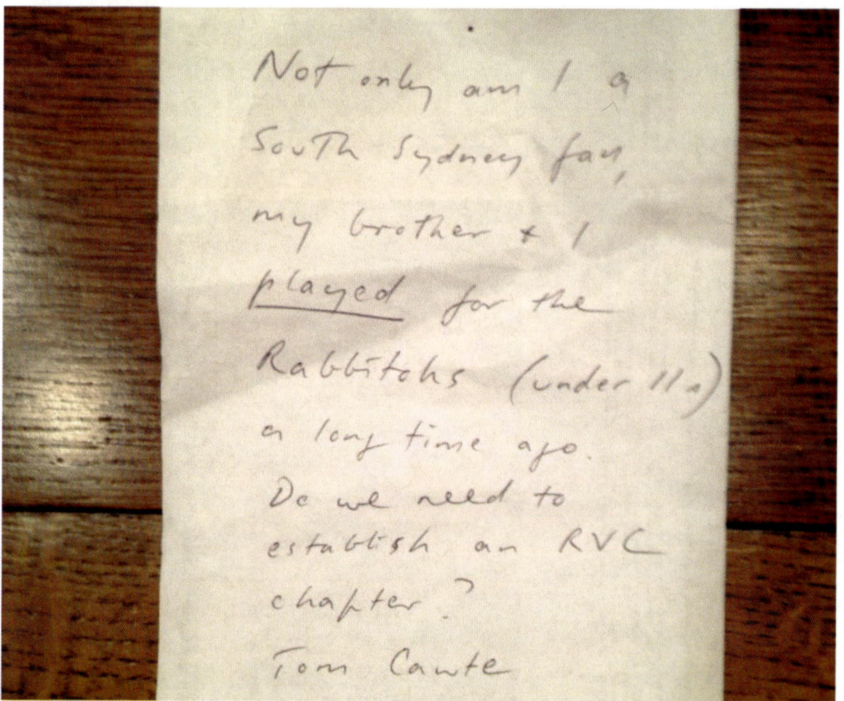

Not only am I a
South Sydney fan,
my brother & I
played for the
Rabbitohs (under 11s)
a long time ago.
Do we need to
establish an RVC
chapter?
Tom Cawte

Apparently, the Rabbitohs fan base is alive and well in Rockville Centre, NY! Heck, who knew?!

Three proud Bunnies celebrate a Premiership victory at sunrise in the confines of The Australian.

The coolest Rabbitohs decal artwork, courtesy of Sam Aretem of Bankstown. They're so beautiful, I don't know if I can peel them off.

Me with former Nickelodeon game show host, comedian, and future Souths fan, Phil Moore.

Me with legendary voice-actor extraordinaire and future Souths fan, Billy West, the man whose voice reigned supreme at Nickelodeon for many years.

The most adorable, fluffiest, long-eared Rabbitohs fan in the world!

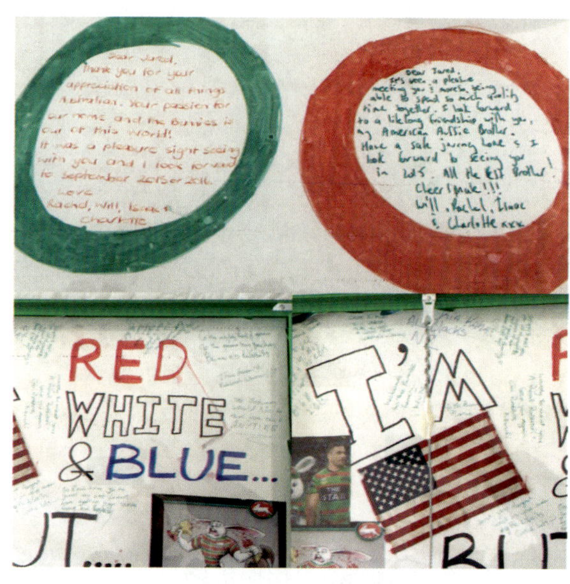

Here's a collection of signatures from all the wonderful Bunnies of South Sydney!

My high school yearbook never saw this many heartfelt signatures!

Don't worry, my Bunny Brethren. This Bunny from the Big Apple will return...

I got the 2014 Rabbitohs to sign my poster! Thank you, Bunnies!

CHAPTER 20
Two VERY Happy Bunnies
(The Second Half the 2013 Qualifying Round)

The score was looking rather promising as we approached the second half. Forgive me if I sound a bit repetitive from my earlier sentiments, but I was rather desperate to see a Souths victory! I guess I had not yet gotten over seeing those dang Chooks rob us of both a win and the Minor Premiership. Bill could tell I was nervous from the look of concentration on my face and from the way I was pacing around the seating bay. He offered to buy me a beer; how could I say no?! Bill just looked at me and assured me that we were going to win this. From the way we were narrowly stopping the Storm in the end zone from our offensive line, it was enough to get me to sit down and enjoy the game.

The second half began with a big kick from Bryson Goodwin. A few seconds later, Melbourne's Cooper Cronk punted the ball on 4th tackle, but it went out of bounds which gave a scrum to the Rabbitohs. Greg Inglis got hold of the ball but went down on 1st tackle; Jason Clark was next to go down on 2nd tackle; George Burgess after that on 3rd tackle; Sam Burgess went down on 4th tackle; Chris McQueen went down on 5th tackle; Adam Reynolds then punted it before 6th tackle. A few seconds later, the Storm were called for holding the ball too long on 6th tackle; the Rabbitohs regained possession.

For most of the second half, Bill and I sat through a series of scrums and punts so brutal, I worried whether or not the players could keep track of how many had occurred. Midway through the second half, Reggie Rabbit was making his rounds on our half of the stadium. Knowing I wouldn't have another chance to meet him, I rushed as fast as I could down the aisle toward the edge of the field. Unlike the Meadowlands, where even those in the first row were about ten feet above the ground, what was nice about being at ANZ Stadium was that you were no more than a few inches from the ground. In other words, you could step over the small steel fence and feel the grass between your toes. When you go to a footy match Down Under, you are really close to the action! Also, how could Reggie greet his adoring fans? I hopped down to the first row and crouched down so as not to obstruct the view of the game.

I saw Reggie approach our section and my heart began to thump. I had brought my poster with me to the game in the hopes that he would either autograph it or pose for a photo with it and me. Just before he finished posing for a photo with some kids, some fan—a woman—yelled at me to get down. I had just gotten up for a second because my legs and knees were getting sore from all the crouching. Either I was going to stand my ground and remain firm in my hopes of meeting South Sydney's biggest player while running the risk of angering a footy fan, or slink back and avoid some embarrassing imbroglio. I went with the latter as I am admittedly a timid individual around highly active sports fans. In hindsight, it was an unwise decision, as I saw Reggie walking in the opposite direction.

Knowing it was now or never, I flagged Reggie down and he came back to the edge of our section. I took a deep breath and unraveled my poster and showed him both sides. He looked up and gave two thumbs up! He then approached the section and I reached out to shake his hand. Not only did I get a handshake, but I also scored a bonus fist bump. For that short, yet sweet two seconds when my hands met with his furry paws, I felt time slow down. I couldn't believe it had really happened. It felt surreal to be quite honest. I don't mean to sound mushy, but it was one the greatest moments, ever! Could this night get any better? I was about to find out that, yes! It was about to get even better.

I happily made it back to my seat where I showed Bill a few quick pics I had snapped of Reggie from my phone. For the most part, the next few minutes were a bit uneventful. That would change around the fifty-third minute when Bryson Goodwin caught a punted ball from the Storm, but unfortunately dropped it which resulted in a knock on, thanks to Dylan Farrell. The Storm were given a penalty, which was followed by a scrum, which resulted in Billy Slater carrying the ball in for Melbourne's first try. Cameron Smith converted the kick and Melbourne made it onto the scoreboard, 14–6.

The crowd let out an unhappy moan which was followed by a resounding "BOO!" from most of The Burrow; so much for a shutout. After finally getting control back from the Storm, the Bunnies went right back to work. At the sixtieth minute, John Sutton passed the ball to Ben Te'o, who passed it to Adam Reynolds, who passed to Dylan Farrell. Farrell punted the ball, but it bounced out of the end zone, which resulted in a touchback; the Storm would get to restart their play. A nail-biting moment came when Melbourne's Chris Chambers attempted to kick the ball into the end zone and run toward it for a try, but Bryson Goodwin dove on top of it, which forced a line dropout for Souths.

At the sixty-third moment, Cooper Cronk kicked the ball in from five meters and Billy Slater caught the bounce for a try for Melbourne. Just when I thought that the tide was turning for the Storm in a humiliating way for the Bunnies, a small glimmer of hope came when the refs called out "NO TRY"; they went to the instant replay to see if the play was legit. The footy gods smiled on the red and green faithful when the refs decided that the try was no good as Chambers interfered with Souths by bumping to Nathan Merritt prior to Slater's catch. Slater's try was denied and the Bunnies maintained an eight-point lead.

This close call made everyone in the Burrow let out a collective "Whew!" but it awoke something within the team. The inner angry Bunny that had remained dormant for quite some time was about to unleashed. You might say the spirits of Bigwig, Reggie, and Bunnymund were about to be unleashed. Just before the sixty-fifth minute, the Storm forced a line dropout, which allowed the Bunnies to restart their play. A minute later, just before the sixty-sixth minute, the Bunnies kicked the ball out of the end zone, which resulted in a line dropout; the Bunnies would restart the play from their 45-meter line. John Sutton passed the ball to Adam Reynolds, but was tackled. On 3rd tackle, Reynolds handed it off to Greg Inglis, who passed it to Isaac Luke. Isaac Luke, or "Bully" as he is known by the fans, extended his arm with the ball in his hand over the line and put the ball down for a try! Although the ball popped out of his hand, it landed over the end zone just in time for it to count. In that glorious moment, every last red and green rabbit in ANZ Stadium stood up and screamed their lungs out! The Burrow exploded out of their seats in a heartbeat; the amount of happiness contained in that one try score could not be measured!

Luckily, I had my camcorder on to witness The Burrow at their most uninhibited. Bill, being the die-hard Bunnies fan he is, didn't disappoint! He leapt out of his seat, put his arms up, jumped on top of his chair, and screamed his throat sore! It was like he was a kid again; the only difference between him and the other kids cheering at the game was that he was the biggest kid there! And because the try was made by Isaac Luke, I got in touch with my inner Warren Smith and shouted "*Luke for the Line,*" mimicking his famed call from 2012. The try was counted and Adam Reynolds successfully converted it for two more points; the Rabbitohs went up 20-6.

Around the sixty-eighth minute, the Storm kicked off but managed to intercept the ball, giving them control. For the next few minutes, they'd go on quite a tear; I just hoped we wouldn't find a way to blow this nice lead we had going. Still, the Bunnies would have to play some tough defense. Sadly, the Storm got as far as inside our 5-meter line. We almost managed to intercept the ball, but the Storm knocked it out of the way, resulting in a knock-on. The Storm suffered an injury when Cecil Whangarea landed on his head, which resulted in him being wheeled out of the game on a stretcher. Moments later, the Storm would restart their play. Cooper Cronk would pass to wingman Will Chambers, who would get the ball across the line for a try. A groan erupted from The Burrow in response from this, but we breathed a slight sigh of relief when Cameron Smith failed to convert the try; the score remained at 20–10 in favor of the Souths.

With less than five minutes to go in the half, the Storm would get one last chance at a last-minute upset when Will Chambers would make an impressive run after catching a pass from Cooper Cronk. Fortunately for the Souths, he was brought down inside our 20-meter line. The Rabbitohs regained the ball and as the clocked ticked down, The Burrow all got up and began singing our sweet song of victory, "Botany Road," named after the long thoroughfare in the South Sydney suburb of Botany, which was sung to the tune of John Denver's "Take Me Home, Country Road."

"Botany Road
Take me home
To the place, I belong
Back to Redfern
South of Sydney
Take me home, Botany Road."

We counted down the final seconds in unison: "*5...4...3...2...1... WE WON!*" And there it was: my first Rabbitohs victory. And what a win it was! Bill and I hugged each other so hard, I think I head our spines crack. We must have high-fived everyone in The Burrow; our palms were so sore, they probably stayed red for days. Moments later, the entire team along with Reggie stepped out onto the field to shake hands with their opponents and wave to the fans in triumph. I stood up on my seat and saluted the boys in red and green for their victory over Melbourne. I didn't move from my seat until I watched the entire team and Reggie disappear into the tunnel. I remained on top of my seat, waving my hand, while everyone else in The Burrow slowly began shuffling out of the bay and out of the stadium.

Sadly, it was time to leave the hallowed grounds. Deep down, I did not want to leave. This was one of the most exciting sporting matches I had ever been to and I wanted to remember every last bit of it before heading back out. I took a deep breath and with a heavy sigh, Bill and I headed outside the stadium. I wasn't just a footy fan after that game. I was an Australian Bunny Rabbit, and proud of it! I just hoped that this win was a sign that the Bunnies would finally end their four-decade-long drought for a Grand Final win.

CHAPTER 21
Rabbitohs in the Rain

SEPTEMBER 16, 2013

The morning of the sixteenth of September was a wet and rainy one. Even when the sky is gray and the ground is wet, Sydney still looks lovely. Not wanting to be cooped up for the day, I borrowed an umbrella from the hotel and ventured out. Following my Rabbitohs instinct, I made my way to the Redfern Oval. Unlike the first time where I needed a taxi, I headed by train and by foot now that I knew where to go. I was hoping to perhaps catch a glimpse of the Bunnies doing some training for the upcoming semi-finals. It was a long-shot, even in the rainiest of weather. Little did I know that I was in for an unforgettable experience. I was about to have another South Sydney rite-of-passage. I was about to meet the legendary Bunnies, in person!

After finishing off a hot sandwich and iced tea at the adjacent Park Café, I glanced with my own two eyes the mighty South Sydney Rabbitohs in person! Like with most celebrity sightings, the Rabbitohs players looked much taller in person. I stood in the wind and rain with my rental umbrella, nervously watching the Bunny boys stretch and tackle. I had seen them put an upset on Melbourne just a few nights ago, and now here I was, seeing them train in person. I saw the Burgess Brothers on the opposite end of the field running laps, back and forth, up and down the oval. I saw Nathan Merritt practice kicks and Greg Inglis stretching. And for the record, the kicks that these guys were doing were so high, they could easily give the Radio City Rockettes a run for their money!

By the time they started pulling in the tackling dummies and water coolers, I knew practice was ending. And I knew that now would be a most opportune time to introduce myself as the loveable, yet loyal fan from America. *I wonder if any of them would recognize me from either Twitter or Facebook. Oh, man, am I scared! Make your move, idiot*! I said to myself as I saw the team heading down into the locker rooms. It wasn't easy, as I could feel my toes curling up into my feet, not to mention I could hear my heart beating like a drum solo in a Rush song. It was even harder because I did not have my iconic poster with me; I couldn't bring it in the rain, now could I? After blowing the chance to introduce myself to Merritt and Sam Burgess, I knew it was now or never. I saw Rabbitohs hooker Jason Clark grabbing a few items, at which point I walked up to him and said, "Great game on Friday, mate!" To which Clark responded, "Thanks, mate!" Acknowledgments aside, I then finally blurted out, "I came all this way from America!" I said with a burst of pride, trying hard not to stutter.

"Really, mate? No way!" Clark responded with a raised eyebrow. Now that I had his attention, I went right into my brief story of how I had come from Long Island and wound up in the world of both footy and the Bunnies. He seemed so genuinely interested in this nervous, yet enthusiastic long-distance fan. I mean, for someone who came over 10,000 miles to see the Rabbitohs, he just had to hear me pour my heart out. Meanwhile, in the back of my head, I couldn't help but think about how awesome this moment felt. I mean, I had never caught a foul ball at a game; I could never get close enough to major league players without being tackled by thuggish security guards, and I don't even think courtside seats at an NBA game could feel this intimate. These guys felt so genuinely nice—not to mention they were huge, in both size and generousness! Talk about being humble. Not wanting to keep Mr. Clark away from the team (after all, they had games to play!), I politely asked him for a photo. He just smiled, looked into my iPhone, and gave me my most memorable selfie! It wouldn't be the last one, however.

My one regret was that I didn't gather enough courage to ask Mr. Clark if I could come on down into the locker room. With the team safely under the oval, sheltered from the falling rain, I knew my time there was done. As I shuffled off to Redfern station, I couldn't help but stare at the way the rain just gently dripped off the leaves so elegantly. Not to mention the sweet smell of eucalyptus and frangipani filled the wet air with a fragrance so enticing. It may have been raining in Redfern, but it was a sunny day in my mind!

CHAPTER 22

A Swan Song in Chinatown

SEPTEMBER 21, 2013:

My last day in Sydney of 2013 was a day of mixed emotions. I was awash in sadness; my appetite was weak and I pondered if I were to ever come back. I spent most of my last morning wandering around Darling Harbour taking a last look at all the ships and stores that had been the view from my hotel window for more than two weeks. The first time I had come to Sydney, I had also felt sadness on my last day after my two-week journey throughout the country. This time around, I was feeling even sadder, probably because of all the friends I had made from footy and all the new places I visited, I felt as if I was going to leave a piece of myself behind. I didn't come here as a tourist, but as sports fan. But I was going to leave not just as a footy fan, but has an honorary Australian Bunny Rabbit! I only wished I had a little more time. Alas, all good things must come to an end. I had spent the afternoon cramming everything into my suitcase. I had bought so many Rabbitohs gifts that I had to buy an additional suitcase just for my red and green swag. I couldn't leave, however, without saying goodbye to my Bunny family.

To properly send me off, the Gotsis family took me for one last meal in the city that I had grown to love over the last sixteen days. They picked a rather lovely Chinese restaurant in Chinatown called Golden Century. The restaurant featured every cliché aspect of a classic Chinese restaurant; Lazy Susans, round tables, a menu that featured almost as much text as an encyclopedia, and giant fish tanks filled with lobsters, just ripe for the picking! Bill ordered me up a Chinese beer, while Rachel and I split some hot tea. I watched as Isaac practically ate his way through my entire entree of spring rolls. One thing was for sure: he certainly wasn't picky about picking food off of my plate! The only thing he liked more than his food was someone else's food. Namely, mine! For our main course, there was a rather modest banquet of noodles, peppered beef, honey-battered chicken, squid, shrimp chips, fried rice, and tea. What was cool was that I ate noodles out of a small bowl that looked like a candy dish or sugar bowl.

Once the bill was paid and Charlotte wiped every last bit of yum cha off her cute face, the Gotsis family walked me back to my hotel. The look on Charlotte's face was truly priceless. Back at my hotel, we took a couple of photos together. It as if I was a part of their family. It was if I was their adopted Bunny brother!

I promised to keep in touch as they bid me farewell. I am so fortunate to have met and befriended this family. What began as a friendship over the Giants and the Rabbitohs had blossomed into something, well, to quote Blinky Bill: "*Extraordinary!*" Do you know what else was extraordinary? The fact that I squeezed every last piece of Rabbitohs gear into both suitcases along with my clothes and computer was a miracle! And the next morning, I comically dragged both enormous totes down Sussex Street to a line of waiting taxis. How I ever managed to drag those into the airport, let alone get them back to New York is anybody's guess. Now I just had to deal with the banality of being back in New York. Once you've explored the Blue Mountains, hung around with Rabbitohs fans, driven through Wollongong, and scaled the Sydney Harbour Bridge, everything else just seems mundane.

CHAPTER 23
Heartbreak at Dawn

SEPTEMBER 27, 2013:

It was 4:15 in the morning on the East Coast of the United States. I had been back home from Australia for less than a week when I pulled up to the Rockville Centre train station parking lot. I came dressed in my Rabbitohs jersey, cape, flag, and socks. This was the day of the much anticipated semi-final bout between the Rabbitohs and the Manly Sea Eagles. The winner of this match would play either the Roosters or the Knights in the Grand Final. For this must-see match, I headed into New York to see the game live at The Australian NYC. I nervously awaited the next train into Penn Station. On the way over, I posted a selfie to Facebook to alert my Bunny brethren that there was one die-hard Yank who was wide awake for this crucial match.

You see, since the Rabbitohs hadn't been in a Grand Final match since 1971, let alone won a title since that year, this was huge for us Bunnies. After seeing the team in person and watching them clobber Melbourne, I was really riding high on this feeling. You might say that I was building my hopes and aspirations up for this game. The train slowly pulled into Penn Station around 5:00 a.m. The game had just started only a few minutes earlier, so I dashed the five-and-a-half blocks across Herald Square to reach The Australian.

By the time I entered the bar, about seven minutes had passed; I had just missed a try made by John Sutton but caught an instant replay on the TV. Luckily, I saw Adam Reynolds convert the kick; the score was 8-0 in favor of Souths. Just before I arrived, the first two points came courtesy of a penalty goal made by Reynolds. In spite of the magnitude of the game, the bar was barely half full; only a few dozen people were there. I was too nervous to stand and watch so I plopped down on the stairs that led up to the upstairs seating area and stared at the wall of TVs over the bar. At around the twelve-minute mark, Nathan Merritt made a great try which was followed up by a perfect conversion by Reynolds; Souths would go up 14–0. Even though we were less than fifteen minutes into the game, I was feeling comfortable knowing we had a two-try and penalty goal advantage to sit on. Still, fourteen points wouldn't last long and I knew overconfidence could be a greater threat than any injury. At the twenty-minute mark, Manly retaliated when Brett Stewart would give the team their first try and follow it up with a conversion by Jamie Lyon. I tried to shake it off and told myself that one try would not derail our hopes, let alone our confidence. Before I could blink, the first half was over and the score was Rabbitohs 14, Manly 6. If we could just keep up our defense and find a way to keep penetrating Manly's line, it looked like the Rabbitohs would finally end their semi-final dry spell.

Just before the second half began, I copped an orange juice from Annie, The Australian's bartender. "You look awfully nervous, mate. You look like you're about to faint!" she said with a small laugh, obviously trying to loosen me up. In spite of her candor, the score told no lie; we only had an eight-point lead. I would feel better if we were to score at least two more tries, both converted. Sadly, that is not what I would receive that morning. Instead, for the next forty minutes, I would be treated to a barrage of ugly plays, sloppy defense, and an onslaught of goons in maroon. The second half would play out, in the eyes of a Souths fan, like a snuff film.

Not five minutes into the second half, and Matt Ballin delivered a try which was followed by Jamie Lyon converting the sucker. Our lead was cut to two points. My stomach began to churn with this uneasy feeling. I tried hard to not let it shake my confidence and I went right back to having my eyes glued to the TV. I just sat, frustrated, watching the Bunnies struggle to put the ball over the line. Their defense, however, was even worse. Instead of watching big Bunnies throw their weight around and halt the Manly offense, I watched helplessly as the red and green army flailed around the field, missing the ball carrier. I saw them dive for their legs, but miss them; it was as if Manly's offense could foresee each move.

At the fifty-eighth minute, Jamie Lyon made both the try and the conversion, thus giving Manly their first lead with a score of 18–14 over Souths. Now it was time for my Bunnies to play real defense. Unfortunately, I couldn't even ask for adequate defense. Four minutes later at the sixty-second minute, David Williams gave Manly yet another try as well as another conversion by Lyon; Manly increased their lead to 24–14 over Souths. All I could do at this point was hope and pray that the Rabbitohs would somehow pull off another two tries in a minute miracle like they did against the Roosters back in 2012. If it happened once, it could happen again, right?

Time, however, was not on our side as I continued to watch in sheer agony as the Bunnies blew more chances to score. With ten minutes left in the game, I grew frustrated at the TV; my frustration quickly subsided and turned to melancholy as I saw Manly score one more try courtesy of Tom Symonds. And of course, it had to be converted by none other than Lyon. Finally, I snapped. I could bear no more of this grotesque humiliation. Since there was no towel to throw in, I picked myself up from the staircase and slowly trudged out the door just as the sun was coming up. I felt a tad disrespectful walking out on my Bunnies like this, but I wasn't going to stick around and watch Manly have the last laugh as the Souths would yet again miss out on a chance to return to the Grand Final.

Turns out that just after I flew the coop, the Souths would score one last try (perhaps a pity try from Manly) courtesy of Dylan Walker and a converted goal by Reynolds. Game, set, and match: Manly Sea Eagles over Souths, 30–20. I was so heartbroken; I didn't even acknowledge Annie or any of the other bartenders on my way out. In the back of my mind, I tried to make sense of this tragedy. One the one hand, I felt like South Sydney should have won that match; they were favorites going into it, after all. They finished second on the ladder, had a stellar line-up, and everyone, whether they were a fan or not, was looking forward to seeing them in the Grand Final. But I have seen from American sports how everyone banking on you to win it all can give you a swollen head and can lead to overconfidence, which can be worse than an injured player.

On the other hand, Manly being touted as the underdog must have given them the edge. Teams who don't get picked to be favorites thrive on that kind of attention and they really unleashed that on the field and hit South Sydney where it hurt most: on the scoreboard. The defeat wasn't the only thing that hurt the Rabbitohs, however. The morning before the match, coach Michael Maguire's mother passed away and the entire team and fan base grieved. First, we lost Sofia Gallico, and then Madge's mother. Heartbreak must have been a theme with this club this past season. Time heals all wounds, and time, mind you, would be an invaluable ally; in due time, the Souths would have their moment of glory.

The train ride home hurt. After my inaugural season watching every Souths game all year, it all came crashing down. I completely lost my appetite for the next few days. The only thing that could console me was some wise words from my other favorite Australian rabbit, Bunnymund: "Hope is the most powerful thing alive. It never dies, it never stops, and it never leaves you alone." Fortunately, hope for me would come sooner than I expected...

CHAPTER 24
The Rabbit Whisperers of Long Island

Getting Americans into rugby (sorry again, I meant, league!) wouldn't be an easy gambit. Americans are incredibly picky about sports and are extremely proud of their own bread-and-butter athleticism. We are a country that worships baseball, football, wrestling, and any other sport that emphasizes both masculinity and individuality. Maybe that is why we are so apoplectic about soccer whenever the World Cup occurs every four years. There is so much animosity, especially on the political right about how "un-American" watching soccer is, let alone caring about it. But really, it is just a not-so subtle throwing up of the middle finger to every other country that is not us. We see soccer as "foreign," mostly because we are so damn patriotic, but really, we just love to hate anyone who is the "other."

While I may be mildly into soccer, the Rabbitohs inspired me to get really into the brutal ballet of rugby. Still, I could only imagine how impossible it would be to convince even a small number of people in America to care even an iota for Australia's national pastime. I, however, would not be deterred. Thinking outside the box, I realized that maybe there'd be another way to appeal the red and green army to Yanks. Since their logo was a rabbit, maybe it would have an effect on people who liked rabbits, specifically rabbit breeders and/or pet rabbit owners. My first non-Rabbitohs rabbit friend was Terrie Adams from North Carolina. Much like the majority of my Aussie mates, she was someone I found via Facebook. Since I had grown fond of South Sydney, I had also developed a fondness for rabbits. I had never owned a pet before, but seeing so many rabbit pics on Facebook made me want one very much.

Terrie and I chatted a lot; I asked her many questions regarding pet rabbit care, breeds, nutrition, health, and such. And she was more than happy to answer my rabbit-related queries. Eventually, I told her about this group of players from Sydney and bragged endlessly about how a legendary sports team had a rabbit as their symbol. While she may not have been made into a footy fan, she was most impressed. That's when she told me about how I could meet up with other rabbit breeders in my neck of the woods in New York. She informed me of ARBA, or the American Rabbit Breeders Association and how they had chapters and organizations in each state. If I was going to spread the word of South Sydney, this was definitely a brilliant strategy. That is how I got in touch with Carol Doukas from Ronkonkoma, a large town in central Long Island. She informed me via Facebook that the Long Island-based group met every month on the grounds of the 4-H Club at the Suffolk County Farm in the small town of Yaphank.

When the day of the meeting came, I grabbed almost every piece of Rabbitohs gear I had in my house, loaded them into my car, and made the forty-six-mile journey. It sure wasn't easy; the town of Yaphank is small and not well illuminated. Once I found the farm, I spent nearly half an hour driving up and down the main driveway trying to find the correct farmhouse with lights on. By the time I found the meeting, it had just ended. I stumbled in, red in the face, but Carol rushed up to greet me. She apologized for the confusion, and still welcomed me in. There was a smattering of cake and coffee. There were mostly women who looked to me in their late forties through sixties, and they had even brought their rabbit cages and a few bunnies with them.

Sadly, I didn't have the time to unveil my Rabbitohs bounty. Carol told me that I would have to wait until the next meeting in a month. And just like that, before I could blink, it was another month. This time, I came just a few minutes early. To grease the wheels a bit, I brought a cake with me. And since it was a meeting for rabbit breeders, I brought the only appropriate dessert I could think of: a carrot cake.

Although ARBA was technically for rabbit breeders, Carol informed me that non-owners were welcome if they were interested in rabbit ownership. Truthfully, I was there with ulterior motives: to spread the word of the Bunnies! After sitting through a bit of business from the ladies on the panel, I stood up in front of the room and presented my assortment of red and green wares. Like a traveling salesman with his caravan of goods, I spun fantastic tales of the gigantic red and green rabbit who is the heart and soul of Australia, or so I said. I went into complete and vivid detail of the team's history, its logo, the fans, and how this team, in my opinion, made me a fan of rabbits. I hoped by the end of my Australian tales that I would convert some of these rabbit fans into Rabbitohs fans.

Before I knew it, I was turning up to almost every monthly meeting. What began as a way to spread the word of the Rabbitohs soon snowballed into a friendship with these ladies whose knowledge of rabbits was unending. Not to mention, I became rather fond of their long-eared companions. One such member I grew fond of was Su Ruckduschel, a rabbit breeder and farmer from Ronkonkoma. She ran a rabbitry, a shelter for rabbits out of her home, and her seasonal farm stand in the nearby town of Hauppauge. To say that she was knowledgeable about rabbits would be a huge understatement; this woman was practically part human, part bunny!

These monthly meetups with the so-called "Rabbit Whisperers" didn't erase the humiliating loss to Manly from my mind, but I did make some cool, new friends and gained a greater appreciation for the animal from which South Sydney gets its name. Not to mention I also developed a taste for kale, which I learned rabbits prefer over carrots.

CHAPTER 25
Two Bunnies in the Meadowlands

Being away from Sydney long enough made me miss being around the Rabbitohs fans. Having been to my first two footy matches in Australia, it made me realize how out of shape football fans in America truly are. Not to mention we don't have the same level of energy rugby fans do Down Under. As the fall season of 2013 rolled on, I headed to see the New York Giants in the Meadowlands in East Rutherford, New Jersey, just across the Hudson River from New York City. My family has been season ticket holders for more than forty seasons, and going to see the Giants is sort of a tradition for my family. I had always loved going to see the boys in big blue play, but ever since I got back from seeing the Rabbitohs, watching football in person just seemed dull all of a sudden.

The Burrow was on their feet most of the time; half of them were singing and half of them were drinking. I had never seen a more jovial lot in professional sports. The crowd at the Giants game was, well, distracted to say the least. Some fans were on their phones, some had their faces buried in either nachos or a hot dog, and some were too busy shouting profanities at opposing fans. Sure, the Rabbitohs fans were not shy about having a salty tongue, but when they cursed, it was delightful! Well, having an Aussie accent and using old Aussie slang may have had something to do with it. I did, however, make it a habit to wear as much Souths gear to the game as I could. I became a red-and-green beacon in a sea of blue jerseys. I wore the colors proudly as I watched the game from the ten-yard line. I still wished my friend Bill could join me for this all-American spectacle. I would, however, get my chance to have a fellow Bunny join me in New Jersey for some gridiron action.

NOVEMBER 18, 2013:

Callum Bushby was a Souths fan on vacation in New York that I had met at The Australian NYC during the State of Origins over the summer. When he returned to New York in November, I reconnected with him. I took him on a tour of New York, visiting the Brooklyn Bridge, getting lost in the subways, teaching him how to properly swipe a MetroCard, and apologizing for the freezing weather. For a special treat, I took him out to lunch in Rockville Centre in Long Island. I introduced my Rabbitohs friend to something Aussies don't get enough of: coal-oven pizza. We ordered up a pie with a smoky smell that tickled our noses. It was drenched in ricotta, pepperoni, and onions. Halfway through the pie, Callum attempted to tear off a slice but it fell off the table and crashed to the floor.

We finished off our day by driving to the seaside town of Long Beach. One place he wanted to see was Asbury Park on the Jersey Shore since he was a big fan of Bruce Springsteen. Had there been more time, I would have been thrilled to take him aboard the New Jersey transit and head down the shore. However, we gladly settled on Long Beach since the town had a boardwalk and he wanted to see if there was any leftover damage from Hurricane Sandy, which had devastated much of the American northeast in 2012. Actually, it wasn't a total loss. I did manage to squeeze in a bit of New Jersey by taking him to Liberty State Park in Jersey City so he could see one of the best views of Manhattan.

NOVEMBER 24, 2013:

With only a few days left before he had to head back to Sydney, I offered Callum an extra ticket to join me for an afternoon of football at the Meadowlands. It was a big game:

the New York Giants versus the Dallas Cowboys. If Callum was going to be introduced to his first NFL game, he couldn't do better than two of the most famous teams in football. During the train ride over from Secaucus Junction, we were dressed in our Souths gear as if we were traveling by train from Lidcombe to ANZ Stadium.

The game was an exciting one. We definitely stuck out in our Bunny duds in a sea of blue-and-white jerseys. For a while, it felt great to have a real Rabbitohs fan cheering next to me. Dallas began with a touchdown; not the appropriate introduction to a Giants game I wanted Callum to see. Luckily, around the second half, the Giants would make a comeback, making the score 24–21 in favor of Dallas. It was a close game, but sadly, Dallas held on to their lead, resulting in a loss for New York as well as a loss for Callum's first football game. Still, he left pretty stoked, as did I. It just felt so good to have a Rabbitohs fan by my side in my neck of the woods.

CHAPTER 26
Two Long Distance Dedications

It had now been a month since I had returned to the States; I couldn't shake off the feeling of seeing my Bunnies lose in the semi-final. We were so close, and after such an exciting season, this was a tremendous letdown. Deep down, there was this part of me that wanted to put away all my red and green gear and sulk until next season. But I just couldn't do that. I couldn't stay mad at someone forever, let alone for the next four to five months. It's just that this season was kind of my unofficial introduction to the Rabbitohs, in that I didn't miss a game, I became invested in all the players, all the teams, and not to mention I made my long trip Down Under to my first two matches.

This should have been our season to dominate, but it was not meant to be. And to add insult to injury, our hated rivals from the Eastern Suburbs, the Sydney Roosters, won the Grand Final. Bad enough they beat us for the Minor Premiership, and now they had to take the big prize? God certainly works in very mysterious and often twisted ways. I was reminded how Cubs and Brooklyn Dodgers fans would always say to themselves, "Wait Til' Next Year!" Next year couldn't come fast enough. I didn't think there was anything that could cheer me up. Until I saw what was posted online...

OCTOBER 10, 2013:

When I first discovered *Rugby League Weekly* in Sydney, I took it on face value as the footy equivalent of *Sports Illustrated*. During my stay, I bought up copies and began pawing through the pages and studied which teams were hot and which teams were not. And if there was a copy that had the Rabbitohs on it, it was mine! But after the loss to Manly, I was in no mood to read it. And thankfully, I was a long way away from any available copies. When the issue featuring the 2013 championship Roosters (ugh!) made the stands, one of my Twitter followers, Tanya Atkinson from Brisbane, tweeted me a picture of one of the pictures from the magazine. I couldn't believe my own two eyes when I saw who made the page:

It was too good to be true. Just a few weeks ago, I was just another American fan of some sports team from Australia who was wandering aimlessly on Twitter looking for common ground with other fans. Now, I was a rather well-known American fan of the greatest Australian team who managed to make a small name for himself amongst a small demographic 10,000 miles away. Not too shabby!

DECEMBER 8, 2013:

My twenty-eighth birthday came with one hell of a present. My friend Bill was doing ground announcing for a soccer match in Australia. When he wasn't working behind a desk, Bill Gotsis put his pipes to good use on the air; he did on-air play-by-play commentary for the Western Sydney Wanderers, a professional soccer team from Parramatta. Before I left Sydney, I asked Bill if there was any way I could listen in on a soccer match that he was broadcasting on the radio. He gave me the link to a station called 2GLF in Sydney. And it just so happened that the Wanderers had a match against the Melbourne-based Heart on the 8th of December, my birthday!

Bill tweeted to me that he was doing a live broadcast of that match and that he'd give me a birthday shout-out on the air during halftime. I knew the time difference would be great, but I didn't care. Around 2:00 in the morning, I sat quietly in my basement with all the lights turned off. I clicked on the link for

2GLF's station feed, hit the play button, and I soon heard Bill and the rest of the crew broadcasting the Wanderers match. I patiently waited on the edge of my seat for my name to come up. When halftime came, I pulled out a digital Dictaphone and recorded the sound of the match from the speakers of my laptop. I just had to hear if this was going to be for real. The crew announced that they had just come back from a commercial and recapped the score at 1–1. At precisely 2:38 a.m., Eastern Standard Time, one of the guys on the horn said, "… couple of shout-outs, especially got a couple of listeners over in New York City of all places!" My ears and eyes lit up when Bill hit the mic and said, "Yeah, one of my best mates, Jared Schnabl, is staying up to the wee hours of the morning listening to us. It is 2:38 a.m. in Rockville Centre, New York. Jared, a big shout-out to you from here in Sydney, mate. It's almost your birthday, so, a big happy birthday from Australia, mate!"

My face was awash in what may have been the biggest grin I had in a long time! It was arguably the best birthday present I had gotten in years. But Bill wasn't finished yet. A few minutes later, one of the guys in the booth was talking about the weather and segued into how freezing cold it was in New York, then mentioned the Meadowlands, as if he was setting Bill up for a shout-out. "Yeah, I promised Jared I'd get to MetLife Stadium sometime soon. He's awake and smiling and he said he's just tweeted in." One of the announcers then chimed in with his two cents about how if he was going to see a football game in America, he'd pick Lambeau Field in Green Bay. Humph! By the end of the match, I was just about to pick myself up and sign off, but I was hoping for one last shout-out from Bill. Sure enough, when Bill was signing off to his listeners from Parramatta Stadium, he proudly announced, "Jared—it's almost four o'clock in the morning in New York and he is still listening. He's our longest listener today, so have a great birthday for tomorrow. Be sure and spread the word, mate!" The last word of the broadcast belonged to one of Bill's cohorts who said, "Burnsie, do we have the ability to ship a hat or a bumper sticker over to New York? No? No? Are you sure about that?"

It was so worth staying up past four a.m. for that present! For my twelfth birthday, I took my friends in the sixth grade to a New York Rangers game at Madison Square Garden in the skybox where I had my name spelled out on the jumbotron over the rink. And as much I loved seeing my name in lights over the world's most famous arena in front of thousands of die-hard hockey fans, hearing my name over the radio in Sydney by my closest Rabbitohs friend just may have topped that! The motto of the Western Sydney Wanderers is "Who do we sing for?!" After that broadcast, consider me one of those singers! But I'm a Souths fan first. Always.

PART IV:
The Year Of The Rabbit

CHAPTER 27
My Flemish Friend

Since my introduction to the Rabbit Whisperers of Long Island, I had become something of a regular visitor to Su's Rabbitry at her home in Ronkonkoma. You might say that I had become quite fond of her long-eared denizens. None more was I fond of than her largest Flemish giant, Mr. Bubba, whom I had affectionately renamed Reggie. Su had over a hundred bunnies from all walks of life. Dogs and cats, apparently, weren't the only ones with several breeds. Her long-eared friends came in all sorts of shapes and sizes. Reggie was something special.

I had long admired him from afar as he sat quietly in his cage. Whenever I'd show up, I would watch him scarf down a giant leaf of kale. Right next to her back gate, Su kept a huge box of kale, which I later learned rabbits love. Carrots, admittedly, they do like, when it is once in a while. Kale, however, was their veggie of choice. I would show up and bring Su some extra kale stalks from the supermarket. I'd help her feed her lot and watch as they would adorably nibble away at the dark roughage. They were so nuts for this stuff that they even convinced me to start eating it.

One day, as I was feeding Reggie, Su asked me if I wanted to hold him. I immediately said "Yes!" while trying to hide the fact that I was blushing. She flipped the top off of his hutch and scooped him up from his big, fluffy behind. She taught me that the proper way to hold a rabbit was by keeping one hand on the rear, just below the tail, and covering the back with the other hand, as if I was gently cradling it. I did just that, and before I knew it, I was holding a Flemish giant in my arms. As the massive rabbit stretched his paws and sank into my arms, I stared back at his twitching nose and hazel-colored eyes. I felt my heart a flutter and a big smile washed over my face. I hadn't felt this way about an animal, since, well, actually never. The only other creature I loved was a St. Bernard that was walked by a dog walker I knew from Manhattan. I would see the two of them at least once a week and I would be in awe of just how huge and gentle that gigantic pooch was. Reggie had a little of that big dog in him. Then again, Flemish giants are sort of the St. Bernards of the rabbit world.

As I held Reggie in my arms, all warm and snuggly, I began telling him stories. Of course, being the Souths fan I was, I told him stories about the Rabbitohs. Once, I spun the story of how John Sattler broke his jaw in the 1970 Grand Final. I told him the uplifting story of how the Rabbitohs were re-introduced into the NRL. And, I told him the amazing story of how I met Reggie Rabbit at ANZ Stadium and why I named him after Australia's biggest Bunny. Every time I'd show up to Su's Rabbitry, or as I affectionately called it, "The Warren," I'd wear my Rabbitohs jersey and scarf, scoop up Reggie, and tell him stories about my time in Australia among the red and green army. Of course, I would spare him the story of the origin of the Rabbitohs' name. I didn't want to traumatize the little fella!

As I made more trips to Su's, we became good friends and I would always ask her questions about rabbits; how to take care of them, their diet, grooming, and so forth. In exchange for her knowledge and friendship, I would give her pieces of my Rabbitohs collection to add to her warren. She had as many rabbit-themed knick-knacks as I did Rabbitohs and Australia paraphernalia. From that point on, visiting her rabbitry became one of my favorite things, knowing my Flemish friend would be there. And deep down, beneath his fluffy exterior, beat the heart of a new fan of the Rabbitohs! I can't quite possibly put into words just how much I adore this big bunny. For a long time, Reggie and Su's rabbitry was sort of my own little secret.

Now that I had Su and a few of the LI-ARBA members rooting for the Rabbitohs, it was time for me to take my Souths fandom to the next level. And come the thaw of winter and the beginning of spring, I'd get my chance. But first things first: the 2014 Rabbitohs season was on the horizon. Our season for redemption was underway. Our long journey to our 21st Premiership was about to begin.

CHAPTER 28
The Road to 21 Begins...

The 2014 NRL season was underway. The Bunnies began their season on March 6th, appropriately enough, against our hated rivals, the Roosters. Oddly enough, it was on a Thursday night at ANZ Stadium. According to footy fans, Thursday night games were sort of an insult in that they were played on a school night, so not a lot of kids would be at the game. As such, Thursday night games were considered ratings purgatory for home viewers.

Despite the scheduling, we won our first match by crushing the Roosters 28–8 in front of thousands of happy red and green fans. Unfortunately, our next couple of matches gave us a total reversal of fortune when we lost three consecutive matches; first to Manly 14–12, then to Wests Tigers 25–16, and finally to Canberra 30–18. The Canberra match was so bad; we were trailing 0–22 at halftime. I was in Key West, Florida on the eve of that game and had no way of tuning in other than reading the Twitter feed one tweet at a time. Reading the plays and results was too much to take. It took a scornful press, an angry fan base, and a fired up Michael Maguire to snap our losing streak.

On April 6th, a 26–6 victory over the St. George Illawarra Dragons silenced the critics and gave us another reason to believe in the Bunnies. During that match, John Sutton, who had been named captain of the Bunnies for the 2014 season, made his 212th first-grade game. We followed that up with an 18–2 win over Penrith, in which Nathan Merritt made his 145th first- grade career try at Sportingbet Stadium after five consecutive matches of being scoreless. Truly, this was going to be an exciting season of footy.

Around the start of the season, I made a new friend at The Australian. Her name was Kate Richardson. And like me, she was a born-and-bred Bunnies fan. On game days, I would see her at the bar, mostly with her boyfriend, now fiancé, Rowan. It was so good to have some company while watching the Rabbitohs. One can only sit alone at the bar in red and green before he is jonesing for like-minded Souths fans to corroborate with. To talk about the team while analyzing the game with someone every week made each game something to look forward to. And the fact that Kate and Rowan were both living in New York made it all the better.

Kate was in the States to study for the bar exam and become a lawyer. She already had a license to practice law from Australia, but she needed to retake the bar in America. And while she was always putting her nose to the grindstone, she'd always be there on game day watching the red and green. Later on, I had learned one more reason why Kate was such a diehard Bunnies fan. Her last name, Richardson, was no coincidence, as she was the niece of Shane "Richo" Richardson, the CEO of the Rabbitohs.

Whenever we'd watch the Bunnies play and they'd score a try, I'd jump up from my barstool and wave my giant Rabbitohs flag in triumph. You might say that I was trying very hard to bring the energy and joy of The Burrow to The Australian all by myself. Having Kate and Rowan sitting at the bar with me made it a lot better. Well, you might say I looked forward to each game as I felt a bit homesick for the sights and sounds of a footy match. All that was missing was the jumbotron and Reggie. Ah, well.

Six rounds into the 2014 season and I felt much better about the team after those three consecutive losses. The Rabbitohs were starting to come together as a team worthy of a Premiership. I also got a kick out of seeing Jason Clark play, even more so whenever he'd score. Maybe it was because he was so nice to me at the Oval and made me feel so welcome; he was someone I enjoyed rooting for on game day. Whenever he scored or drove the ball down the field, dodging the defense, I would applaud until my hands were red and sore!

CHAPTER 29
Bunnies in Bethpage

APRIL 11, 2014:

While the Bunnies were battling their way up the NRL ladder, I was busy climbing an actual ladder inside a barn. Ten thousand miles from Redfern, I was on the grounds of the Old Bethpage Restoration Village, an outdoor museum in the town of Bethpage in Long Island. It was the day of the 2014 LIRBA (Long Island Rabbit Breeders Association) Rabbit Breeders Show. It was basically a dog show, but with bunnies instead. Several of my friends from the LIRBA meetings in Yaphank were there to show off their rabbits for the judges. While they set up shop on one side of the barn, I was setting up shop on the other side. I, however, wasn't here to show off actual rabbits, but the Rabbitohs. Since this event would play host to rabbit breeders, owners, and enthusiasts, I figured that this would be the ideal place to promote a team nicknamed "The Bunnies." If ever there was a chance to create new fans, this would be the place. I may have seemed opportunistic, but that was the point. I wanted people living in my part of the world to discover this team.

Half of my day at the show was spent sitting behind my own makeshift table hawking as much Souths gear as possible while trying to politely corral any showgoers with my amazing stories of the team, its history, and its logo. I had my South Sydney showcase set up right by the entrance so I would ensure I'd get as any people as possible. I would greet new visitors and surprise them by tossing them my Rabbitohs ball or greet them by waving my Rabbitohs flag. I was no salesman, but I used every trick in the book. When that failed, I brought out my secret weapon: Reggie! Su managed to bring almost her whole bunny brood to Bethpage, including my favorite Flemish giant.

With my Souths jersey on, I scooped him up and trolled the floors, bunny in arms. Breeders in attendance would be drawn at first to the big ball of fluff in my arms as they "oohed" and "aahed" at him with adoring eyes. As they petted him, I would tell them about my jersey and how there is a professional sports team with a rabbit as their mascot. It certainly made them feel better, if not tougher, for being fans of what was otherwise a cute animal. It was sort of the same bizarre appeal that drew me to the club in the first place. That plus rugby is a cool sport. For a few hours, I felt like a missionary spreading the word of an Australian rabbit.

By the end of the convention, I didn't manage to procure any new members, let alone sell them membership. I did, however, set out to spread the word of the Bunnies and I felt like I had done a pretty damn good job. It was my own little contribution to giving South Sydney some much-needed advertisement far away from The Burrow. Well, that plus spending time with Reggie.

CHAPTER 30
Driving Miss Rachael

APRIL 25, 2014:

Just one week after the crushing one-point loss to the Doggies during the annual Good Friday match in which Canterbury won on a drop kick from Trent Hodkinson, giving them a 15–14 win over the Souths, we were looking to rebound in a big way. On the day of the ANZAC match from Suncorp Stadium in Brisbane, we gave it to the Broncos in a big way. During the first half, an amazing try by none other than Greg Inglis became one of the most talked about plays of the year among footy fans. He scooped up a wayward ball from Ben Barba in the fourteenth minute, leaving the Broncos defense in his wake. Inglis picked up the ball and just kept going—and going and going, like a gigantic Energizer bunny, wearing red and green of course! He nearly tripped just a few meters from the try line but completed one of the most amazing runs in Rabbitohs history.

In addition to Inglis' try, it was also the debut of rookie winger Alex Johnston but it was also the unexpected end of Nathan Merritt's illustrious career with Souths. The remainder of Merritt's season would be played with the North Sydney Bears. The Rabbitohs would go on to beat Brisbane 28–26, but this game that I saw at The Australian was where I was introduced to Rachael Roberts.

APRIL 27, 2014:

Rachael was a visiting model and Rabbitohs fan from Penrith who had come to New York to do modeling work and some sightseeing on the side. Like so many others before that came into The Australian, she too was fascinated by my love for the Bunnies and my knowledge of both the team and Australia. I had offered to show her the sights and sounds of the Big Apple, and she happily obliged. And what began as a friendly sightseeing venture turned into sort of an adventure between two new friends. We went to have lunch at Katz's Deli on New York's Lower East Side. And there is nothing more satisfying than a mountain of corned beef, pastrami, pickles, and matzo ball soup. It's what we New Yorkers call Jewish penicillin! Dishes like these are hard to come by Down Under, so it seemed only fitting to introduce her to the finest New York eats. One funny moment came when she ordered a knish and asked the waiter in her Aussie accent if they had a broccoli (*brock-coh-lie*) one; it was pretty funny the way she pronounced it. It was also a funny moment when I taught her how to say such Yiddish sayings like "mishpoche" and "mehshuggehnah." If you want a good laugh, teach an Aussie how to speak Yiddish or Hebrew. How Hollywood hasn't tried to create a Jewish "fish-out-of-water" story set in Australia is beyond me; it's a premise just waiting to happen.

After lunch, we headed into Brooklyn to the neighborhood of DUMBO to stroll across The Brooklyn Bridge. The weather, unfortunately, was just lousy. It was April, and the rain and wind made it feel more like early February. Still, we made it across 131-year-old structure effortlessly. Our adventures continued at the Statue of Liberty where we continued to defy mother nature's bad day over New York. It was so cold and windy, you'd think a snowstorm was brewing over the city. Still, we managed a nice trip. When we broke for lunch, Racheal's one moment of disappointment came when we learned the snack bar didn't have any soup. It was so cold, it was something she was hoping for even more than a statue souvenir. We also entertained a security guard at the boat dock when he asked us about our Rabbitohs gear. We even hit up the Museum of Natural History and a few spots in Central Park to round out the day.

Actually, my favorite moment came right before the tour started. When I went to pick her up at her friend's place, she invited me in for a spot of tea and some vegemite on toast. It was here where she taught me how to properly apply the savory spread. Instead of slathering it on like you would with Nutella or peanut butter, you put a dab on each toast triangle and a spoonful of butter. It was more palatable this way. Still strong for my American taste buds, but slightly better than glopping it on. Months later, I would see Hugh Jackman teaching Jimmy Fallon this same tactic on The Tonight Show. Great minds do think alike!

As for the modeling side of her stint in New York, when she learned off my love of Souths, not to mention saw pics of my many Rabbitohs gear, she humbly requested to borrow some of the items for a photo shoot. Seeing this as another opportunity to spread the Souths love in America, I happily accepted her proposal and delivered to her a small set of scarfs, capes, and a Rabbitohs football.

MAY 4TH, 2014:

Continuing our adventures throughout the Big Apple, Rachael and I hit up Coney Island. While Aussies have their own playground in the form of Luna Park in North Sydney, there is no substitute for the original. We took an exciting ride on the Cyclone where we got a case of whiplash from the dips. Or perhaps we just got motion sickness. Then, we did lunch at Nathan's Famous. You can't come to this city and not taste the most famous hot dog in New York. We continued with a relaxing stroll up the boardwalk while talking about Rachael's modeling, my fascination with Australia, and I even spun a story about the legendary Brooklyn Dodgers, which led to a discussion over whether or not there were some parallels with the Bunnies and "dem Bums." Just before our tour of Brooklyn wrapped up, Racheal showed me her Rabbitohs model shots on Facebook. I'm no model or fashion expert, but I have to say, why doesn't Elle MacPherson ever model wearing the red and green?! In short, it meant they were awesome! It looked like she was trying out for the Rabbitohs cheerleading squad, which the team used to have years ago. Who needs Playboy Bunnies when you have South Sydney Bunnies?!

MAY 6TH, 2014:

For Racheal's last week in New York, she wanted to get some serious shopping done. But having visited almost every pricy retail joint in the city, this called for a road trip. I had mentioned that there was an outlet mall on Long Island with several high-end retailers. I saw this as an opportunity to show her my backyard of Long Island. I would be a long trip, however. Our destination was the Tangers Outlet in the town of Riverhead, about ninety miles east of Manhattan. First, we headed into Rockville Centre to pick up my car and we sped off. I was tempted to show her around the island, but we were running on a tight schedule that day. Racheal needed to get back to New York by the early evening and, unfortunately, had almost no time for sightseeing. Still, the car ride was a fun one as we talked about our favorite Aussie rock bands. The best part came when I rigged up my iPod to play my Midnight Oil playlist through the car stereo. It felt so good to belt out our favorite socially/politically conscious Aussie band with a friend. I had never met another person who rocked out to the Earth and Sun and Moon album!

Once in Riverhead, we, as the old saying went, shopped till we dropped. I have to say, I look terrible in a pair of thigh highs and high heels! We even made a pit stop to the Harley-Davidson Motorcycle store near the mall where Racheal had to pick up a piece of Harley memorabilia. After all, when in American, you gotta ride the hog, or at the very least, grab a piece of hog swag.

On the way back, eyeballing the clock on my dashboard, we had a few minutes to check out one sight. I took her to my collegiate alma mater, Stony Brook, just long enough for some photo ops on the main quadrangle. A funny thing happened on the way back to the Long Island Expressway. With Mother's Day approaching, Racheal was in need of a greeting card to send to her mom. With no Hallmark card store in sight, we pulled into a 7-Eleven where she found an oversized greeting card. On the card ride back, whenever I stopped at a red light, I watched her fumble with the enormous card as she attempted to sign it. Quite frankly, it was one of the funniest things I had ever seen.

As we made our way to the Rockville Centre train station, Racheal and I ran up the escalator to the platform, shopping bags and giant card in tow. Luckily, she made the train with less than two minutes before it arrived. We bid each other a heartfelt goodbye and she thanked me for showing her around New York and Long Island. I told her that if I was ever in Penrith, I'd love a tour of her neck of the woods. But I am not putting on a Panthers jumper!

CHAPTER 31
Summer of Red and Green

The Rabbitohs' 2014 season rolled on like a giant rabbit about to step on every last opponent. On May 26th, round 11, I watched from afar as the Rabbitohs shut out the Cronulla Sharks 18–0 in front of a rain-soaked crowd at Remondis Stadium in the Sutherland Shire. Two days later on the 28th, the first of three State of Origins games occurred with New South Wales claiming a narrow victory over Queensland with a 12–8 win. It was a big deal for the fans in turquoise, as they had not won a State of Origins series against the fans in maroon for years. Less than a month later, they would do just that with a 6–4 win over the maroons.

JUNE 14, 2014:

The happiest moment of 2014 came on a sunny day in Chicago when my little sister Jenny was about to wedded to her tall and handsome beau, Leland Brewster. It seemed so surreal to be in the presence of something so beautiful; I never thought it would happen so soon. Everyone from the Schnabl family and the Brewster family had gathered at the University Club in Chicago for the event; there was so much pride bursting from everyone, you would think an explosion was imminent. At the reception, family members and friends all took turns taking the stage on the dance floor to give speeches and a toast to the happy couple.

A few days earlier, I had begged my mom and my sister to allow me to give a speech at the wedding. Knowing I'd face a wrathful family if I began talking about the Rabbitohs,

I promised to keep it footy free and only focus on Jenny and Leland. I gave a funny, yet touching speech about how I had reacted to the news that I'd have the tallest man in Lake Forest for an in-law. I managed to hold back tears as I miraculously made it through without stuttering or getting bum-rushed off the stage. Just before closing the speech, I grabbed a flute of champagne, gulped it down, and right at the moment when thunderous applause deafened the ballroom, I shouted into the microphone, "*AND GO RABBITOHS!*"

Thankfully, half the crowd laughed as I left the floor. Everyone told me I gave a touching speech; to be honest, I was just freeballing it. I merely said what was in my heart. My heart was, on this day, reserved for my sister and Leland. But a small piece of it had to give a shout-out for the team. And speaking of the team, just a day before the wedding, the Rabbitohs defeated the Wests Tigers 32–10 which resulted in the Souths' fourth straight win. Mazel Tov to Jenny, Leland, and the Bunnies!

AUGUST 3, 2014:

The Rabbitohs' recent routings of both Parramatta and Canberra were indeed satisfying. It felt like we couldn't ask for a better win, at least not since our round 9 thrashing of Gold Coast where we won 40–18 over the Titans. Then came our match against Newcastle up in Cairns. Last time we played them at ANZ in 2013, we won the match as a tribute to Charlie Gallico (Reggie Rabbit) after his wife Sofia passed away in a come-from-behind win. How could we top an unforgettable moment like that, especially after he was hoisted on the shoulders of the team?

Enter Alex Johnston. We had only seen small moments from this rookie earlier in the year and were waiting for him to make a statement. At Barlow Park up in tropical North Queensland, just a stone's throw from the Great Barrier Reef, we Bunnies were introduced to Alex Johnston, the fastest Bunny in Australia. Granted, he had made his debut earlier that year, but this was the match where we saw just what this rookie sensation was capable of. I was at my summer home in The Hamptons for this match but couldn't find the game on any channel. Desperate not to miss the game, especially since it was on earlier than normal matches for the New York time zone, I was forced to read the live Twitter feed of the game. I was in bed with my iPad waiting for the word "TRY" in full caps as I anticipated each play. And boy, did the Rabbitohs not disappoint! It was just one try and another, after another! And almost every joyous tweet involved Alex Johnston. It was almost as if each play involved him getting the ball down the field and across the end zone. His three consecutive tries reminded me of Reggie Jackson's three home runs in the 1977 World Series. The game ended with a lopsided 50–10 win over the Knights and I went to bed around 3:40 a.m. with a giant smile on my face that stayed on past sunrise. When I found footage of the game on the Internet and saw how fast Alex Johnston ran, I thought to myself, *Australia has found its own Usain Bolt!* It makes sense that Johnston would be fit for this team. As Bunnymund once said, "Ooh, you don't wanna race a rabbit, mate!"

AUGUST 8, 2014:

Our next match against Manly would be a big one, and not just because it would be set on the hallowed ground of the Sydney Cricket Ground (SCG), one of the oldest and most beautiful stadiums in Australia. After losing to them in a close match in round 2, not to mention still feeling the bitter sting of defeat from the 2013 semi-final, I was dying to see the Bunnies give it to those goons in maroon. Unfortunately, I had someone breathing down my neck for this game. Matty Astil, owner of The Australian, came from the footy world as a lower-grade player for both Manly and Newtown. Suffice it to say, he was no fan of South Sydney. I decided to make a wager with him: If Souths won, he'd buy me a drink. If Manly won the game, I'd have to pay double for my booze and admit that Manly was awesome to Matty's face.

The Rabbitohs must have heard this deal with the devil and went to work in a one-sided win over the Sea Eagles at the SCG. A 23–4 win sealed the deal as well a cold Cooper's and Jack and Diet for the win. As they say, to the victor go the spoils. And boy, were those spoils refreshing! Thankfully, Matty and I were both gracious in defeat and victory respectively. I lifted my beer toward the TV as I saluted the Bunnies in their big win.

CHAPTER 32
The Rabbit Returns

SEPTEMBER 4, 2014:

It was around 6:00 in the morning and I had just awoken from what felt like an eternal nap. I was on a Qantas flight from Los Angeles to Sydney. Luckily for me, I was only a few minutes from the ground; my flight was hovering about 1,000 feet above the city. I was so close that I was able to spot the CityRail from high above as the plane made its final descent into Kingsford-Smith Airport.

After collecting my bags and clearing customs (and I learned that the customs agents down there are quite friendly when you tell them that you are there for the footy and you're an American), I hopped on the train and headed for Town Hall station. It was a rather gray and dreary morning; the sky was overcast, there was rain, and it was unusually chilly, even for Sydney. My favorite moment of the commute came when the train pulled into Circular Quay. I stood up from my seat and saw the magnificent Opera House from the tracks. Even in the rain on a dreary morning, that oh-so-familiar Aussie tableau still looks magnificent.

After just a few minutes, I arrived at Town Hall where I dragged my luggage out of the QVB; I looked pretty comical as fumbled with my suitcases like someone who had just arrived at Ellis Island after a lengthy voyage. Luckily, the Four Points Hotel was a short walk away just toward the waterfront at Darling Harbour. Right when I stepped through the automatic doors, I was greeted by a voice saying, "*You again?!*" which came from behind the concierge desk. It was Peter, a familiar face that I remembered from my earlier visit in 2013. I had somehow, in just a year's time span, become a familiar face around the hotel. I must have made an impression on them because after I checked in, I had my room upgraded at no extra charge; I had booked a city-view room, but they gave me a harbour-view room instead! Being an American Souths fan who loves Australia really does have its advantages, indeed!

I was still reeling from the jetlag, but I was too excited to sleep. I had arrived in Sydney for the epic Round 26 rematch against the Sydney Roosters. In spite of the euphoria from last year's match, which was my first footy match ever, I was still mad as hell at the Roosters for robbing the Bunnies of the Minor Premiership. This was a do-or-die match for the Souths. Just a week before my arrival, I was up late watching the live broadcast of the Panthers versus Sea Eagles match in Amagansett at my summer home. The two teams were both jockeying for the top spot, with Manly leading Penrith but trailing the Roosters on the ladder. If Penrith could beat Manly, it would bode well for the Souths, as we would have a little insurance under our belts; a win by Penrith meant we could lose to the Roosters and still get the top spot on the ladder provided that Manly would lose the next week as well. Alas, it did not go that way. I watched helplessly at 3:00 a.m. as I saw Manly narrowly defeat Penrith, which put the Bunnies in a precarious situation. I was so mad at the Panthers' narrow defeat, I nearly screamed out loud, almost waking my cousins up! If ever there was a moment to redeem ourselves from last year, this would be it!

Just three and a half hours before kickoff, I waited outside the hotel on Sussex Street for a friend. Before my arrival, I had promised a friend that he could drive me to the game. That red and green cabbie was Joseph Gal from The Oaks. Just before his arrival, I got another amazing surprise in the form of a surprise fan. A tall man coming out of the hotel approached me and asked, "Mate, are you Jared Schnabl?" I said yes, pretending that I knew him. He told me that he was Kate Richardson's father. He happily told me that he had heard about me from his daughter back in New York; apparently, Kate must have told him to keep an eye out for Jared at the Four Points. He was so pleased to shake my hand; he told me that it was an honor to meet someone so passionately dedicated to the Rabbitohs. Suddenly, I remembered why I had missed this place so much! Not ten hours in Australia and already, my name was spreading.

Shortly after my newest Aussie fan took off, I was introduced to Joseph Gal. Sporting a Rabbitohs members jacket, he happily welcomed me back to Sydney and then we headed down Sussex Street to his Jeep; I knew it was his when I saw his Rabbitohs red and green vanity plate on the back. He presented me with an amazing gift in his back seat; a box of goodies, as Joseph told me. It was a cardboard box inside a milk crate that was full of Rabbitohs gear! There were stickers, pennants, advertisements, flags, face paint, and a set of trading cards. And just for good measure, he presented me with a bottle of Australian Shiraz, vintage 2010. First the fans bought me beer at the game and now wine?

We were off to Allianz Stadium for the game. Rather than heading by train from Lidcombe to ANZ Stadium at Olympic Park, Allianz Stadium was not within walking distance of any train station. Well, a bit of a hike from Central Station, but it was too dark and wet to tread. It turns out that there was a lot of traffic on the way. A *lot* of traffic. It felt like forever sitting in a row of cars. Just like being back at the Meadowlands, it was like waiting in gridlock on the New Jersey Turnpike when you're just a stone's throw from the stadium.

We pulled up to Allianz Stadium and parked the Jeep on the grass along with most of the cars. No fancy garages here, just pull'em up on the green and you're done. I have to say that it was a very impressive venue. Allianz Stadium, built in 1988, is also known as the Sydney Football Stadium or just SBS for short. It sits in Moore Park just off of ANZAC Parade, a large thoroughfare, and it is the premier venue for soccer, rugby league, and rugby union in the city. The SBS sits next door to another iconic Australian venue, the Sydney Cricket Grounds, or SCG.

I had never seen a cricket stadium before; I tried to get a good peek through the gates as Joseph and I marched from the Jeep to Allianz. In typical English fashion, I saw picket fences and beautiful wrought iron fixtures that made it look like something out of the turn of the century. The rain was finally starting to ease as Joseph and I approached the main gates at Allianz. I, however, was not so thrilled to see the marquee for the venue. Since this was the Roosters' home stadium, my eyes were treated to a smattering of Roosters flags and banners strewn about all over the entrance. I could hear the "Imperial March" from *Star Wars* echoing in my head, as I knew I was deep in enemy territory. It felt like the time I went to a Red Sox versus Yankees game at Fenway Park in Boston. It wasn't such a thrill to see all the Roosters merchandise being bandied about, I must say. After passing through the turnstiles with Joseph, we made our way to our seats. Back to our beloved Burrow.

CHAPTER 33

The Biggest Bunny in Australia

(First Half of Round 26—2014)

The Burrow for Round 26 was sitting in the end zone of the SBS. It felt like being at a high school reunion, only with a better-looking bunch. Everyone was there from Dingo and Kylie MacNaughton (the ones who gifted me with my F**k the Roosters shirt), Brigitte Weiss, Michelle Booth, Ursulla Whiteley and her husband Darren, and every last one of their adoring faces welcoming me back with such a hearty hug. With all the handshakes and hugs I had from the moment I arrived, it reminded me of the scene in *Goodfellas* where Henry Hill and Karen are married and she is introduced to every one of Henry's mobster buddies and associates inside the wedding reception. There was the line where she says, "It was like he had two families. By the time I finished meeting everybody, I felt like I was drunk." That's kind of how I felt being reunited with my red and green family. It was like I had a second family and I wasn't even drunk. Well, I would be soon.

As I finished shaking hands with all the familiar faces, it was time to bring out the big guns. I pulled my two newest posters for 2014 out of a cardboard tube and unraveled them for The Burrow in all their red and green glory. *For the front side of my 2014 poster, I had the decency to convert into metric!*

One thing was missing: autographs! Within a few seconds, I had a small collection of autographs from several Burrow members. I was saving space on the front side for members of the team. Since this was a Roosters home game, there would be no opening drumbeat to "Glory Glory to South Sydney," which was sort of a letdown, for me at least. The moment I knew it was game time was when the Bunnies erupted out of the team tunnel led by our long-eared leader, Reggie Rabbit. I jumped up and down like a kid on Christmas morning; it was wonderful to see this famous face from Down Under once again. He ran right past the Roosters cheerleaders as some of them looked like they were slyly shaking their pom-poms for him. I don't blame them! But at the peak of my euphoria, the Roosters fan tried to douse our joy by angrily booing our Bunny. I watched Reggie trot up to the "Chook-pen" (nice name for a fan section, by the way!) and give it to those red, white, and blue flag wavers.

We in The Burrow retaliated with a deafening chant of, "*You know we still hate the Roosters! Still hate the Roosters!*" The louder we sang, the more faint the booing from the Chookies got, at least that's what it sounded like to us. I grabbed my posters and my camera and ran down the bay to an empty aisle of seats so I could get a better view of the game and players.

I watched the opening kick sail across the field and the game was underway. While the Rabbitohs and the Roosters duked it out near the end zone in the first few sets of tackles, I noticed something bigger coming my way. Reggie was making his usual rounds on the edge of the field with fans and damned if I was going to miss this golden opportunity. The moment he came over to the Burrow's bay, I nervously began fumbling with posters and my camera. Thankfully, I managed to compose myself; I took a deep breath and pulled myself in for a hug and said to Reggie, "*Hey, Reggie! G'day, mate! All the way from New York, my friend. I came all the way just for this!*" My heart raced as my face was flushed red with joy. I thought my slight handshake and fist bump from the qualifying round last year was something, but this could not have gone any better! For the few seconds I was with Reggie, time seemed to stand still.

CHAPTER 34

We STILL Hate the Roosters

(Second Half of Round 26—2014)

Meeting Reggie up close and personal was indeed a magical moment; a rite of passage for any newcomer to the Rabbitohs family. I thought my brief handshake and fist bump with him last year at ANZ Stadium was a surreal moment. This moment at Allianz made me feel lighter than air as I gravitated back to my seat behind the goal posts. Once I got back to my seat, however, I was brought back to down to reality. The first half of the game lacked the same pizzazz I had seen a year ago when we were ahead 12–10 at the half. We could only muster a measly penalty goal from Isaac Luke after waiting twenty-six minutes; the score at halftime this year was 8–2. Our defense may have done a good job keeping them at bay, but our offensive line seemed to be absent. I just wanted so badly to see the Bunnies score a try from only a few meters from where I was standing in the bay. Sadly, I'd have to settle for a distant penalty kick.

The second half began rather ominously when Kirisome Auva'a was sin-binned just two minutes into the second half. As if that wasn't bad enough, the Roosters went ahead and scored three unanswered tries in just ten minutes. Each try was like a knife in my heart, not to mention having to watch those damn flags from the Chook-pen wave over and over with each score. Before I could blink, the Souths were down 2–22. I was determined to stick it out to the bitter end; my loyalty would eventually be rewarded.

With fifteen minutes left to go, I was hoping for a second-half comeback like I had come to expect from watching the Souths. The Rabbitohs didn't disappoint as they made three consecutive tries. The score, with less than a minute to go, was 18–22. When I saw the score, only one thing went through my mind: Round 19 from 2012. The Rabbitohs were down 12–22 against the Roosters at Allianz Stadium with less than two minutes to play. Against all odds and logic, they made two miraculous tries to beat the Roosters 24–22 in one of the most memorable and shocking wins in Rabbitohs history, and possibly even in the history of sports! The score was 18–22 with less than a minute to go when Warren Smith lost his mind up in the announcer's booth as Adam Reynolds fell into the end zone with the game-winning try and then the game-winning conversion.

Now, it was two years later, and we in The Burrow thought we were on the verge of seeing history repeat itself. Could we be treated to a second stunning upset by usurping the Roosters? Well, one key factor was missing: Adam Reynolds. Our star kicker was absent from the field after being forced to sit out the match thanks to a penalty from the previous match against Canterbury. In spite of that, everyone was on their feet for this final minute. Everyone was either screaming their lungs out or they were too scared to cheer as if they had become superstitious. We watched from the other side of the field as the Bunnies struggled to find an opening in the Roosters' defense. Finally, with only a few seconds to go and on fifth tackle, a long bomb kick flew up and our Minor Premiership fate hung in the air. I could just hear Warren Smith's call echoing in my head during this slow-motion second the ball was in the air.

But, alas, John Sutton narrowly missed grounding the ball just meters from the end zone for the possible match winner. And right on cue, together, almost everyone in The Burrow let out a collective, "*Aw, Shit!*" The final score was Roosters over Rabbitohs, 22–18. Our comeback was denied. We ended the season with a third place on the ladder and the Roosters, once again, claiming the top spot, the Minor Premiership, and the $100,000 prize to boot. If this is what Souths fans are accustomed to feeling like every year, how long before I am numb to this?

In spite of the loss, we left Allianz Stadium with a sense of hope for the playoffs. For those last fifteen minutes, we had those Roosters on the ropes and we put up one hell of a fight. We were salivating at the thought of hopefully revisiting them should the circumstances of the postseason allow us a rematch. We were not, however, over the loss so quickly. As we shuffled our feet toward the exits, we chanted our signature rebuttal, "Ya know we still hate the Roosters! Still hate the Roosters!" Ya know what? They can have their top spot on the ladder. They can have their prize money. But that money can't buy what we had our eyes on. Oh, and it can't buy a die-hard fan-base that can hold their heads up high after that close call. It only made us want to get back on the field and play again.

CHAPTER 35
Dinner in Schofields

SEPTEMBER 6, 2014:

It was so wonderful to see my good friend Bill in The Burrow during the game. I was, however, really looking forward to seeing his family again. In the tradition of going to a friend's house for dinner, I made a date to see the Gotsis' in their neck of the woods, in the town of Schofields out in the Western Suburbs of Sydney. Rather than bring over booze or Tupperware, I caught the next train from Town Hall to Schofields.

If there is one thing I do love about Sydney, it's that it is a very transit-friendly city where getting where you want is as easy as hopping on and off the train. It really is a place that definitely caters to the New Yorkers as well as the Angelinos, in that the former has easy access to the train while the latter feels at home with both the beaches and the highways. Riding the CityRail felt just like the Long Island Railroad, only with a cleaner interior and a slightly cheaper fare. The scenery felt just like being back in Long Island; the further the train got out to the suburbs, the more the towns starting looking like I was back in Suffolk County, just with the cars on the other side of the road. That's something I tend to look for whenever I travel abroad. I try to look for the foreign equivalent of what I would normally see in Long Island. It tells me that no matter where in the world I am, we're not so different.

Outside the Schofields train station, a white Mazda SUV pulled up and lo and behold, my favorite Rabbitohs family was there! Of course, me wearing a Rabbitohs polo shirt and holding several gift bags certainly helped them locate me in the crowd. The kids sat in the back seat with Bill and Rachel was behind the wheel as we sped off in search of dinner. I wasted no time unleashing my first gift on the family: a tin of cookies from my favorite bakery in Long Island. I stashed these rare treats in my backpack and somehow, they managed to barely survive the long and bumpy flight. Until the family could come to Long Island, I wanted to give them a taste of what would be awaiting them overseas. I insisted they save the pink dot cookies for last, as those were my favorite.

We made our way to a little shopping center off the main road right near a KFC and Macca's. A KFC, a McDonalds, and a mini-mall; so far, still felt like Long Island. We happened upon a casual Italian joint called Millone's. Isaac was rather appropriately dressed for dinner; he was wearing a Rabbitohs jersey. It was like he was anticipating my arrival! I presented him his gift, a wooden train in the shape of a New York City subway car. That way, he'd be the coolest kid in the neighborhood! For Bill, I whipped out his gift, a New York Giants coach's shirt, similar to the one Tom Coughlin would wear at practice and during press conferences. Like a kid on Christmas morning, he wasted no time throwing it on while at the table.

With my Rabbitohs shirt and his Giants shirt, we started posing for photos as Rachel tried to contain her laughter. It was like we had switched bodies and the American was wearing the Aussie shirt and vice versa. It was like we were brothers that were separated at birth and we were reunited. Were we a bit dorky? Maybe. Were we proud to sport our team colors? You bet! As the waitress came over to take our order, Bill bragged to the staff about his unique friend. Rachel looked like she wanted to bury her head for a second, but she looked like was secretly enjoying watching her husband really enjoy that new shirt.

The food was, in my opinion, quite satisfying. As far as I was concerned, it was comfort food, Italian style—a salad consisting of rocket, a long leafy vegetable, and a bowl of spaghetti in meat sauce. *Mangia*, mate! The best was watching Isaac down a bowl of spaghetti with his hands, or as I refer to it, the proper way! After posing for a few more photos with the kids outside the joint, we headed toward the home of the Gotsis family. On the way over, Bill and Rachel gave a brief tour of Schofields, which included a visit to this big shopping center; an upscale outlet mall would be a more accurate description. Why take me shopping after dinner? Actually, Bill wanted to show me this colorful fountain in the middle of the mall because it was the spot where he proposed to Rachel. Ah, romance! I felt rather honored that Bill and Rachel would share this happy memory with me.

Seeing Schofields was one of my favorite parts of the trip because it introduced me to suburbia, Down Under. As I have said before, finding places around the world that bare similarities to home sweet home is one of my favorite things to do whenever I travel far and abroad. The neighborhood where the Gotsis' lived looked very similar to any suburb in Long Island. In fact, I would go so far as to say it was a Levittown-esque place where almost every home looked identical just like the assembly-line manufactured homes that popped up all over Long Island during the post-war era. Almost all the houses were one story tall. Bill and Rachel explained that the style is the norm among most Australian houses, as most Aussies choose practicality over style. Not to mention they are easier to clean and maintain. But what they lack in size on the outside, they make up for on the inside and the backyard. In true Aussie fashion, they had a Hills Hoist and barbecue in the backyard. If it was daytime and I was much younger, I'd be swinging on that laundry carousel like it was the greatest ride in the world!

Once inside, the Gotsis' had two surprises waiting for me. First, Isaac presented me with a gift bag of Rabbitohs merchandise, adorably referring to me as "Uncle Jah-wid." I know that I was already knee-deep in red and green bunnies, but Rabbitohs items are like Lays potato chips: you can't have just one! My favorite item was a beach towel with Reggie on the front. It only made we want to go back to Bondi beach even sooner. And while I was aware that the beach is technically in Roosters territory, I was going to spread out that rabbit on the beach as if to say, "*Chookies be damned!*" There was also a smaller Rabbitohs beach towel for kids that came complete with a built-in hood for drying wet hair. A beach towel that you wore like a poncho and dried your hair? Man, those Aussies are brilliant!

After rummaging through my red and green gifts, Bill and I spread out on the couch and enjoyed the night's entertainment: *The Sam Burgess Story* on DVD. This must-have autobiographical documentary is found in the DVD library of every Rabbitohs fan throughout Australia. It showcases Sam Burgess' talents from his humble beginnings in England on the Bradford Bulls league club, to his stint on the English national union team, to his glorious arrival in Redfern. It also takes an in-depth look at his family life, his brothers, his lovely mom, Jules Burgess, and the tragic loss of his father.

As Bill and I sat quietly and watched the evolution of one of the greatest footy players alive, it made me love the Rabbitohs even more. This was a young athlete who came more than halfway around the world to play for one of the oldest and most winning clubs. Throughout the entire piece, he demonstrated a love for the game, his family, and the fans. He appeared to be a young man who was tough on the outside, but a wonderful bloke on the inside. I'll bet if I were to meet him at the Redfern Oval, he would be tickled pink to learn an American came all this way for the Souths, not to mention he would be a really nice guy.

Once the credits began to roll, it was time for me to roll out of there. While Rachel was putting the kids to bed, Isaac and Charlotte each gave me a good night kiss before heading off to dreamland. Rather than catch the next train from Schofields to Town Hall, Bill volunteered to drive me back to the Four Points. I bid Rachel and the kids farewell and Bill and I hit the road. On the way back, Bill was asking me how I knew so much. He said that he had never met another person who was as "learned" and "cultured" as I; that I seemed to know the answer to any sort of question. I could say the same thing about his savvy knowledge for the Giants.

CHAPTER 36
Deep in the Warren of Redfern

SEPTEMBER 8, 2014:

One year earlier, on a rainy afternoon at the Redfern Oval, I had the good fortune of meeting Jason Clark, face to face. To me, it was one of the coolest moments of my life. Little did I know that that fortunate happenstance would be but a precursor to what would come only a year later. In life, they say that it is not what you know, but who you know. My friendship with Kate Richardson, along with some emails and repetitive tweets on Twitter had allowed me to get into contact with the media department. It was through the magic of email that I was introduced to Jeremy Monahan, one of the head bigwigs in charge of the Media Department at the Rabbitohs' headquarters. Actually, I was also introduced to him via a podcast called the Sports Geek in which he was interviewed. This was such a rare treat, and not just because I found a piece of Rabbitohs-related media on iTunes.

In this thirty-three-minute-long interview, Monahan sat down for a one-on-one with host Sean Callanan. In it, Monahan talked about the club and how they managed to utilize new technology in social media within the organization. It was an interesting insight into a part of the Rabbitohs I was previously unaware of. According to Monahan, the Rabbitohs were light years behind other clubs when it came to reaching out to new members and communicating with the press. It was almost like they were using typewriters when other clubs were using computers. And the years in which they were absent from the NRL competition didn't help much either.

However, in the last five to six years (at the time of the podcast interview), the Rabbitohs have learned the importance of how social media can broaden their fan base and increase membership status, which is one of the biggest goals within the organization. During the long flight over, I listened to the interview as a way of studying this figurehead of importance within Redfern. Following him on Twitter didn't hurt either.

The night before my interview, I was too nervous to eat; I was afraid I'd get a stomachache or worse. I couldn't even sleep; my eyes were wide open and I was reciting all the possible questions I'd be asking the team. I got up bright and early; I threw myself out of bed minutes before my alarm clock went off. I showered, shaved, threw on a suit and tie, and grabbed my poster. If I was heading to Redfern Oval, I certainly couldn't miss out on adding Rabbitohs autographs to my artwork. My friend, Michelle Booth, had told me over the phone that the team would be having a practice session there that afternoon.

As I approached Chalmers Street, I felt like it was the day of the most important meeting of my life. This was a chance for an American to present himself to the higher echelons of one of Australia's biggest sports clubs. This was a meeting that I thought to myself would be the first step in my joining of this amazing organization and its motley assortment. Sure enough, I saw my friends having a late brunch at the Park Café on Chalmers as well as the boys in red and green moving and up down the field. It was then I spotted Jason Clark himself, walking alongside the iron fence along the edge of the field. Would he remember me from last year? I had spoken to him on Twitter all year long, congratulating him on each game. Just like last year, I took deep breath and blurted out, "G'day Clarky!" as if I was one of the locals, so casual in my announcement.

"Jared! Hey, mate. Welcome back!" he said, which stopped me in my tracks.

I couldn't believe it. After nearly a year of being away from the Oval, he still remembered me. One of the NRL's best players, a favorite celebrity among the Rabbitohs' constituency, and he didn't forget! In America, a famous athlete would be with a fan, in one ear and out the other; business as usual in the world of being a celebrity athlete. These boys in red and green, however, were different. They weren't just guys you saw on TV who played professionally in front of millions—they were members, if not friends, within the community. The Brooklyn Dodgers, for example, lived in the neighborhood during their heyday at Ebbets Field in Flatbush. They lived in apartments and brownstones next door to Mr. and Mrs. John Q. Public and even worked in blue-collar jobs in the city when they weren't on the diamond. This was such a stark contrast to the pampered and privileged world of the celebrity-obsessed country that America is today. Both countries do love their star athletes, but here was a place where the fans and the players co-mingled harmoniously and the players returned the love back.

I wasted no time making my way down to the field and introducing myself to the players. Last year, I was so nervous that I barely worked up enough courage to say hello to anyone. This year, I was flush with confidence and determined not to stay quiet while the players played. I spotted the big man himself: Greg Inglis. He was even bigger in person than I could have imagined; any taller and he could have been Kareem Abdul-Jabbar with an Australian accent and a beard. He was most polite and seemed flattered to know that an American had come all that way to see the Rabbitohs. I asked if I could get a photo with him and his autograph for my poster. He happily posed for a photo and loved my red and green artwork. And just like that, the mighty GI added his ink to my Bunnies poster. But I was only getting started.

Next came the Burgess Brothers. Specifically, the one they

call “Slammin’” Sam Burgess. There he was, in the flesh. I had seen him in person the year before in the rain at the Oval but blew the chance to introduce myself. Not this time. I walked up to him and introduced myself as the biggest Bunnies fan from New York. Much like how I got Jason Clark’s attention, it worked. Sam was delighted to shake my hand. He was just delightful and very friendly, not to mention he was much bigger in person; those shoulders of his could support scaffolding. I was determined to introduce myself to him, not just because he was one of the best footy players in Australia, if not the world. I wanted to meet him because this was going to be his last season with the Souths.

Earlier in the season, Sam Burgess announced that he was going back to his native England for three seasons of play with the Bath Spa Rugby Club; not only was he heading to the other side of the world, he was switching codes from rugby league to rugby union. A lot of us in the Rabbitohs community thought he was doing this move to prepare himself for a spot on the English national team for the 2015 Rugby World Cup in his native England. It would be awesome to see a member of the Burgess Brothers help his team and country win a World Cup and hoist the Webb Ellis Cup in front of the world. On the other hand, no one in the Rabbitohs community could fathom the idea of losing one of our greatest players to union code, much less a team on the other side of the planet.

When it was confirmed that 2014 would be his swan song year in Redfern, we knew that this had to be the year the Rabbitohs had to win a premiership; a wonderful player like Sam Burgess deserved to go out with a big win, especially after we were cruelly denied a premiership a year ago. I told Sam that I was a big fan but I was not about to beg him to stay. I merely wished him the best of luck at Bath and told him that he was an amazing player. Deep down, I was stunned that he was going to play, out of all the clubs in England, for Bath

Spa. Back in April 2000, my family took a trip to England and we made a day trip from London to Bath. We passed by the famed stadium known as the Recreation Oval or "The Rec" and that is where I was first introduced to the sport of rugby. I even brought home a pair of Bath rugby jerseys from my trip.

Well, at least it would give me something to look forward to come 2015. Sam happily posed for a photo and added his ink to my artwork. Once more, he also complemented me on my suit and tie. I told him that I had a meeting with the staff inside the HQ; I bashfully told him that I had aspirations to join the staff at Redfern. He wished me good luck with my endeavors and high-fived me. And if you doubt the kind words of this wonderful player, he later sent out a tweet of our photo, with him praising me for my long-distance fan dedication and my suit. I could definitely confirm that he was as sincerely awesome as he was in that documentary I had seen at Bill's house. Actually, I don't know if words can do him justice.

One of the best moments came when I had asked Sam Burgess to autograph my poster; he asked what football team I rooted for. I answered "Giants!" with the same level of enthusiasm that I give when people ask me about the Rabbitohs. At that moment, like Pavlov's dog, all the players began shouting their favorite NFL team. It was like I had turned on a switch. Suddenly, these Aussie blokes revealed a side that I didn't know about them. I always figured myself an American on the inside, an Australian Bunny on the outside. These enormous Aussies (The Burgess Brothers being British) seemed to be hardcore American sports fans on the inside. I wouldn't be surprised if they all started fighting over which baseball team is the worst or which beer tastes the best with nachos. You know what? We're not that different! Professional sports are, indeed, the great uniter of all nations.

One more big name I had the good fortune of meeting was kicker extraordinaire, Adam Reynolds. I excitedly shook his hand and congratulated him for his astounding try from the memorable round 19 match in 2012. I told him how that come-from-behind win was one of the main reasons I became a Souths fan and why I came all this way from New York. Like a nervous schoolgirl or an overly excited nerd, I repeatedly thanked him for being both an amazing player and also for scoring that try, not to mention wishing him luck in the qualifying round against Manly.

Just before the clock struck four, I scurried up inside the headquarters on Chalmers Street. Just behind a desk inside the gift shop were the offices where all of the Rabbitohs business took place. I felt like I was in some amazing waiting room about to be called into the most important meeting of my life. Before I knew it, I was escorted behind the desk and entered the offices of the South Sydney Football Club. It might have looked ordinary, but with each step I took, I held my breath. Next to getting access to the locker rooms in the shed or being invited to the homes of players, this was considered quite the forbidden territory in the footy world. I was brought into this small meeting room; a small boardroom, if you will. Three members of the Rabbitohs Media Department joined me: Jeremy "Jezza" Monahan, whom I was already familiar with, Tom Skolarikis, and Chris Beavon. What followed was a ninety-minute interview in which, and pardon my French, they picked my brains and I spilled my guts.

I practically poured my heart out over how much I loved the team, the fans, the game, Reggie, and why it was one of my favorite things about Australia. After all, why else would I spend more than fifteen hours on a plane to come here? I also brought up some suggestions on how to make their website more efficient as well as how to market the team more overseas. I understood that rugby, especially in America, has but a limited appeal. After all, every four years when the World Cup comes along, one only needs to turn on Fox News to see how apoplectic we are toward soccer, let alone anything that appears "un-American." Of course, we Americans love violence through contact sports with a side of uber-machismo; rugby seems to deliver all that and then some and yet, we casually ignore it.

I practically came close to begging the boys in the meeting room to start advertising the team as well as the rest of the NRL to the USA. I thought it seemed like a doable gambit, considering there is a wide swath of Americans who enjoy soccer; I pointed to such demographics like expats, anyone from Latin America, as well as the rare audience of Americans who love to argue who is better: Manchester United or Liverpool? Rugby, to me, deserved some media attention in the home of the free. Tom did, however, tell me about the time the Rabbitohs played an exhibition match in Jacksonville, Florida back in 2008. I had learned about this match not too long ago and I had to ask how the hell the Rabbitohs played a game in, of all places in America, Jacksonville? Well, it was because of connections made through Russell Crowe, who knew someone who owned the stadium and was able to get a game between the Bunnies and the Americans. Well, I just hoped a game at the Meadowlands in New Jersey wasn't too far off; America needed to be introduced to the likes of the Burgess Brothers, GI, and Reggie!

Although Russell Crowe was absent from this meeting, I did ask them if they could tell him to do more to promote the Bunnies in America. After all, Spike Lee has been a New York Knicks devotee for years and he is always courtside, as is Jack Nicholson for the Los Angeles Lakers. Every major sports team has a celebrity face and I felt Crowe should use his Hollywood swagger to make the Bunnies big in America. I will give him some credit for mentioning the team on the occasional late-night show, as well as several photo ops where he bestows his Rabbitohs gear on his fellow A-list chums. I do wish, however, he would do more to promote them.

Meanwhile, I told them the story of how I came across the team in Alice Springs and how I did my part in spreading the gospel of the Bunnies throughout New York and Long Island. They seemed to laugh at the prospect of that story; my discovery of their team happened completely by chance in the middle of nowhere. I also praised them for doing the unthinkable: making the bunny rabbit into a kick-ass animal and in a country that historically has hated rabbits. And yes, we all agreed on one thing from that story on how the Rabbitohs got their name: Australians do indeed have a wacky sense of humor!

Throughout the meeting, they seemed so impressed with my knowledge and passion for the team; one of them thought I was an Australian pretending to be American! They asked me things like what they do well with their website and what they could do better. For a while, I felt a little out of my element discussing business terms, but I just did what I do best: talk about the Bunnies! Somewhere in the back of my mind, I felt like I could be a legitimate member of the team someday, and not just a fan. And that is when I asked them if there was anything I could do for this team while I was in Sydney. That's when Tom, Jezza, and Chris gave me the opportunity to contribute to an article for the Souths website. It would be a story-like article that would introduce me to the red and green fan base as a "proud US Rabbitoh" along with me meeting the team and being at the first qualifying match against Manly. It would be a piece that would capture the joy and camaraderie that the "Rabbitohs family" is known for as told by a Long Islander. They did, however, give me explicit guidelines to adhere to, as dictated by none other than Michael Maguire.

There would be no trashing of anyone on the opposing team, no talking our boys up, no bragging about how we were going to win this year's premiership, and like all journalists, get all the names and facts straight. This was it! I was about to get my feet wet, as a freelancer no less. Still, this was the chance I had been waiting for. I may not have been a footy expert, but I was going to give them the best damn article about how much this American loves the Bunnies. I got them to autograph my poster, we shook hands, and I was on my way back to my hotel to hit the keyboard. Although it would have been awesome had Rusty and Reggie joined us in the board room, the meeting couldn't have gone better! And for a brief moment, I got a look at a place where I hopefully would be working one day.

Suddenly, my leisurely trip to Sydney became a business trip. And don't you just love it when you can mix business with pleasure?!

SEPTEMBER 9, 2014:

Before I knew it, I was on the next train from Town Hall to Redfern. I was hard at work on my article, but I still needed some input. Luckily, Michelle Booth had told me that the team was practicing that day. Another chance to see more of team and hopefully, Madge. I was no more than about 100 yards from the station when some bloke in a parked car listening to his stereo at full blast called me out.

"Hey, mate. Uh, by any chance, your name wouldn't happen to Jared, would it?" he asked me in a pleasant manner. Stunned, I calmly answered back, "Yes, I am. You mean Jared Schnabl?" I asked, attempting to confirm this question.

"Yeah, Jared Schnabl, is it? It *is* you!" he said, his voice going from polite to enthusiastic. He introduced himself as Sock Tighe. For a minute, I wasn't sure how to answer him, as I had never met this man before. He said that he was Sock Tighe from Facebook; he spelled out his name and that's when I knew who he was. His last name was pronounced "*tie* or *ty*," rather than "Tiggy," which I had expected; I recognized him at that moment because it was one of the most hard-to-pronounce names on Facebook. We both had a good laugh about our last names. I told him that most people in my life either misspell my last name or make fun of it in the meanest way.

He asked me where I was off to. I told him that I was on my way to the Redfern Oval, not just to see the team practice, but for a meeting at the Media Department inside headquarters on Chalmers Street. He wished me the best of luck and said that he was a big fan of my Rabbitohs photos on Facebook as well as my travel blog. I'd be lying if I said that I was blushing from my chance encounter with Sock. He gave my poster a quick signature and posed for a photo with me before I continued my walk toward Chalmers Street. Once again, it was just another fortunate Rabbitohs-related happenstance with the red and green fanbase. It seemed that this was becoming so common, that I was becoming the most famous American Rabbitohs fan in Australia. Then again, what other American spends his time in Sydney not on the beach but hanging around the Redfern Oval?

At the Oval, it was the usual sight of fans with their eyes glued to the players as they ran circles around the field and stretched their legs into the air. I waited patiently for my chance to say hi to the players, especially Clarky. Sure enough, as the team's practice wound down and the players began collecting their gear, I made my way to the edge of the field where I saw him greeting the fan base. And right on cue, he greeted me with a loud "G'day!"

It was then that I saw the coach himself, Mr. Michael Maguire saying hello to the fans behind the guardrail at the field; it was now or never. I'd be lying if I said I wasn't nervous. After all, one of my clearest memories of Madge was when he flipped his lid at the team during halftime of the round 25 match against the Wests Tigers. That was the match where we were losing to an otherwise adequate team and I saw Madge just blow his top! Thankfully, we came from behind to win, not to mention we had all four Burgess Brothers' playing on the field for that unforgettable match. Still, I hoped Clarky or some of the other Bunnies had told him about me. Making my way up to him with the same nervousness and tenacity I had with the team before, I approached him from behind.

"Mr. Maguire. G'day. I'm Jared Schnabl, big fan from New York. I came all this way to Sydney just for this," I said, with each word trailing out, remarkably, without a single stutter.

"Oh, G'day. Oh yeah, I think I may have heard about you. I've heard of you on Twitter, I think," he said in such a friendly way. My eyebrows raised in an instant. Did Michael Maguire just admit out loud that he knew me? I hurried to unravel my poster, perhaps as a way to fully tell if this was why he knew me from Twitter. "Oh wow! Yeah, I think I saw this on our Twitter page. Yeah, that is a beauty, mate! You really captured the best moments of the team on that artpiece." Yup, my ears weren't deceiving me.

I told him that one reason why I was fond of him was that he reminded me of my high school varsity sports coach, Jeff Weiss. During my high school years at Lawrence Woodmere Academy, I played on the varsity boys' soccer and basketball teams. Jeff Weiss was my coach and he led us to an undefeated soccer season, several league basketball championships, and a state basketball championship. He was a tough, yet enigmatic leader. He was someone who knew how to get fired up before, during, and even after the match. He was someone who knew how to get real mad whenever our team played terribly. Much like when Maguire blew his top during the Round 25 match against the Wests back in 2013, Coach Weiss would angrily tell us to turn in our jerseys whenever we blew a game or even if we won but got lucky in the end.

Maguire's love of the game and his talks with his team reminded me so much of my time in the locker room whenever Coach Weiss would talk to us before and after the match. Perhaps I felt nostalgic for the varsity team whenever the cameras caught Madge in the sheds giving the Bunnies a pep talk. I knew that Madge didn't know who Jeff Weiss was, but I said to his face that he really captured the essence of a man who really cared about the game and was not going to mince words whenever his team played terribly; I even mentioned his Round 25 meltdown.

"Oh yeah, I remember that! I didn't think I was that mad. When I saw myself on TV from that game, I was actually laughing at myself!" he said with a chuckle.

"Yeah, I loved that, with all due respect. If it weren't for that comeback win and all four of the Burgess Brothers on the field, that would have been the most famous moment from the match," I replied.

After I explained how I discovered the Bunnies in Alice Springs and how I was doing my part to influence the team overseas, I asked if he could add his signature to my poster. He happily obliged. I must say, in spite of the intimidation he gives to his players, he was most gentlemanly and very friendly. To say that he is an amazing individual would be but an understatement. I might say that he has sort of a Vince Lombardi or Herb Brooks approach to coaching. Okay, maybe that is a bit of a stretch, but his love of the game and his wins are not artificial in any way. And if he can win a premiership for the red and green, he, in this fan's opinion, can take his place among those coaching greats. Besides that, he is a man who loves footy, just like the fans.

CHAPTER 37
Bunny in Berowra

SEPTEMBER 11, 2014:

A train ride into the bush on a sunny day was a splendid idea. But I wasn't headed toward the Hawkesbury or the Blue Mountains. I was headed toward the bush in the town of Berowra. Just forty miles north of Sydney on the way to the Hawkesbury, this small town was the gateway to Mount Kuring-gai and Kuring-gai Chase National Park, one of Australia's most beautiful natural reserves. In the 1960s, this verdant paradise became famous for being the filming spot for one of Australia's most beloved television shows, *Skippy, the Bush Kangaroo*. Americans, for a short time in the late 60s and early 70s were exposed to this Australian version of Lassie. I myself had seen a handful of reruns and was utterly delighted by the many adventures of the titular marsupial. Perhaps I might be fortunate enough to meet a descendant of Australia's most famous TV 'roo.

The train slowly pulled into Berowra station, which was located just between two highways: the B83 (the Pacific Highway) and the M1 (Pacific Motorway) and both were opposite from a vast valley separating the mountain range where Kuring-gai Chase was located. It was at this station that I learned yet again why I love taking the train in Sydney. Much like how the station at the Hawkesbury River puts you at the river's edge and how Town Hall puts you in the middle of the city, many stations out near the country could put you in the heart of nature without having to hitchhike a ride into nowhere or climb up and down a mountain. One minute you are in the thrust of a busy metropolis, and in less than an hour, you are smack-dab in the middle of an unspoiled forest.

That is what it was like hiking into Kuring-gai Chase from Berowra. It started with a short walk from the station across a dusty bridge over the highway and toward a green signpost leading to a path called the Waratah Trail, named after the colorful flower. This was where my adventure in Berowra would truly begin. Once I passed through this signpost and onto the trail, it would be like Alice jumping down the rabbit hole and into Wonderland. In a matter of seconds, I was surrounded by a whole new world. It suddenly turned eerily quiet. Well, for a few minutes until I heard the passing sound of cars on the highway. Still, it was pretty surreal. But you know what else what surreal? The fact that I was hiking this path all by myself! I mean, here I was, thousands of miles from home, in a part of Australia I had never been to before, and I'm blazing a trail like I'm Lewis and Clark on the hunt for the Northwest Passage.

There was this big rock underneath what looked like a pine tree, an unusual arboretum to be found in Australia. I climbed atop the rock; a risky gambit as it was at the edge of a small cliff. The view atop, however, was almost too beautiful for words. The mountain tops and rolling hills looked so perfect with their curvatures, and the sounds of birds singing could be heard from every chasm and corner of the valley. In a corner of my eye, I spotted a small body of water called Cowan Creek, which empties into the Hawkesbury upstream. I took a deep breath and felt my heart racing as I was treated to such a remarkable tableau of nature. Alas, I couldn't take too long to enjoy the scenery from this vantage point. There was still more of this valley to explore.

My descent into Kuring-gai continued as I hiked slowly and precariously down the trail. Feeling the ambiance, I began singing Midnight Oil's "In the Valley," as it was the perfect song to match the feeling of my new surroundings. It felt so good that I broke out in goosebumps and I could hear my heart beating again. Maybe it is only the kind of feeling one truly gets when they connect with the great outdoors. The distance sound of cars and trains gave me a bit of comfort, however, to know that I wasn't totally stranded and that I could hear my way out of the bush. Not to mention the path was clearly marked. But just in case daylight was running out on me, I brought a headlight with me to guide my way out. The trail kept descending downwards into the valley. The longer I walked, the quieter it got. At a certain point, the roar of the freeway and train tracks got fainter and fainter and the only sounds I could hear were the birds, the wind, and the crunching of my sneakers against the ground. Furthermore, there was no one else around. I hadn't run into another person since I stepped off the train.

I wanted to turn back and head uphill, but something in me just told me to keep walking down. Down the trail, down the rabbit hole. The only sound that followed me throughout the bush was the loose change that jangled endlessly from the moment I stepped off the train. At times, it distracted me a bit from the scenery and in hindsight, it wasn't so wise to have stuffed my pocket with so many coins. In my defense, however, I had those coins jangling as sort of a reminder to keep myself together. In case I was feeling lost or felt like I was getting nervous, I would pat my pocket and feel those coins. Sort of like a bell around a cat, so to speak. Still, better safe than sorry.

As the trail kept going down into the valley, I stopped to check my watch. I hadn't realized how much time had passed. Afraid that I'd be stranded in Berowra, I made a 180 and dashed back up the trail. It didn't even occur to me how far I had hiked until I made my way back up the trail. Like an outdoorsman, however, I knew I was heading up the right way when I passed by numerous rocks and trees that I recognized; the indentations and unique shapes were hard to miss and stuck out like a sore thumb. I only wished my outdoor education and gym teacher could have been there to see me ace that trail!

By the time I made it back up to the sign and entrance to the Berowra Track, I saw the motorway and the train station in the distance. It was a reassuring sign that I was no longer off the beaten path, but it was rather bittersweet to bid farewell to such an idyllic part of the bush. The train slowly pulled into the station only a few minutes later and I made my way back to Town Hall. I just couldn't take my eyes off the scenery; I was hoping the train would slow down a bit so I could get a better look at the moving mountains and verdant valleys. The Long Island Railroad and New Jersey Transit had nothing on this commute! I thought that the bush was the most interesting thing that I had seen all day, until my train began picking up passengers.

Starting around Wahroonga station and continuing all the way to Town Hall, I saw dozens of children heading home from school. Only they weren't on some old, yellow bus, but rather commuting like every other grown-up on the CityRail. But that's not what piqued my interest. They were all wearing matching school uniforms in the tradition of British boarding schools. The Aussies, throughout history, have borrowed many traditions from their British ancestors like a common love of sports, food, architecture, and government. In fact, almost everything except for weather and dental hygiene! One thing noticeable throughout the country was how their schools mirrored their educational practices, which included a rigid dress code.

They were all quite elegant with their suit jackets emblazoned with the crest of the school or academy they attended. It almost reminded me of the matching robes worn by students at Hogwarts in *Harry Potter*. Or perhaps the students all did some work on the side modeling for Brooks Brothers.

Some weren't even carrying backpacks, but fancy briefcases instead. But the one article of clothing that raised my eyebrows were how some wore matching hats, specifically straw boaters that looked like they just auditioned for *The Music Man* or just stepped out of a nifty nineties tableau. It was one of the most peculiar and adorable images I had ever seen.

I knew Australia practiced a strict dress code for students, but I didn't know it extended to hats, much less for teenage students. I had seen young schoolchildren, about six to nine years of age wearing those large floppy hats commonly seen on rangers in the Outback to shield harsh sunlight, but seeing those cute hats on the heads of teenage boys was hilarious to say the least. Of course, from an American's perspective, it did seem humorous, but I say that in an endearing way. I expected one of them to approach me on the train and start talking about forming a marching band!

CHAPTER 38
Bar Hopping and Bunny Hopping

SEPTEMBER 12, 2014:

With the loss of round 26 as well as the Minor Premiership well in the past, we Bunnies were ready and raring for a win. We had a full lineup, not to mention Adam Reynolds was back on the team after he had been sat out the previous week. I was busy prepping myself in my hotel room. I painted my face, grabbed my poster and my camcorder, and rushed out the door, bound for Central Station. Since we finished third on the ladder that season, we would not have homefield advantage at ANZ Stadium like last year when we finished second; teams who finish first, second, fifth, or sixth on the ladder of eight get a home game in the first round of playoffs.

We were up against the Manly Sea Eagles and it would take place on the Roosters' terrain at Allianz Stadium at Moore Park. This was due to the fact that Manly's home stadium of Brookvale Oval, albeit a historic park, did not accommodate a crowd under NRL playoff standards. I had heard that many Manly fans were a bit peeved that they were forced to make a long commute to Moore Park. Hopefully, that would just mean more Bunnies than Eagles in the stands.

Central was the closest stop to Allianz, but I had plans before the game. I had several hours to kill and I planned on killing a few brain cells with my Bunny brethren over some cold ones. Tucked away on a corner adjacent to the train tracks at Central was the Aurora Hotel on Elizabeth Street where I was to rendezvous. I made my way upstairs to this sports bar; in Australia that meant that this was a place where you could legally gamble on sports matches on TV. I saw my red and green family members grazing and toasting to tonight's game. Brigitte and Michelle from the Chalmers Café were there, along with some newcomers that I recognized from Facebook. There was Paul Selmes, this jovial cue ball who was really excited to see me; he told me how he recognized me from Facebook and that it was a privilege to meet me. There was also Vicki Hayes, who had on an eye-catching Rabbitohs jersey that was done up in an Aboriginal dreamtime motif.

After we talked, laughed, and chugged a few beers, we gathered everyone up and marched out the door toward Moore Park. It was on this day that I was introduced to a beloved pregame tradition within the footy fandom: the pub crawl (aka bar-hopping). In America, before the start of a football game, tailgating is our national pastime. In an episode of *The Simpsons* called "Any Given Sundance," Homer explains to his family as they park their cars outside a football stadium that they aren't there to watch the game but are there just for the tailgating. He lovingly explains how there is nothing more American than eating burnt meat in a grey, drizzly parking lot while watching overly paid professional athletes exercise. Ah, America!

Since my family are season ticket holders for the New York Giants, we have had front row seats to this American spectacle. The sight of jockish men tossing beanbags while holding a beer and juggling a burnt sausage, tossing a miniature football while dodging SUV's, and setting up camping supplies while scraping a hibachi is a sight all too familiar with how the world seems to perceive the average American football fan. I don't mind the frivolity, but since tailgating means driving to the game, it usually means waiting in traffic, then looking for a parking space, and thus running the risk of missing the big game. Thank God the Meadowlands built a train station or most of my recent football memories would have been made sitting on an exit ramp on the New Jersey Turnpike.

All in all, tailgating seems to be more mockable than enviable. In Australia, however, their pre-game ritual is a bit different. Every fan meets up with their fellow fans at their favorite bar for some drinks and also sees who else will show up. Once everyone has had their fill, everyone in a close-knit group marches off to another nearby bar in search of more booze and more friends to join in their growing band of merry men. You walk into a bar, preferably one that has an outdoor dining area where you can stretch your legs and commiserate loudly, and start your imbibing all over again. You repeat this process with more booze and more fans you collect on the way to the game. It begs the question why so many Aussie fans aren't totally hammered by the time they're inside the stadium. In this fan's opinion, these Aussie footy fans have quite the high tolerance for alcohol. They can down five or six cans of Tooheys or Carlton Draught and still carry on an intelligent conversation while keeping track of the game. All I can say is thank God for carpools and public transportation. Still, being a part of this parade of lovable drunks in red and green felt like quite an honor for a newcomer.

Not to sound like someone who wanted to be the center of attention, but whenever one of my friends would introduce me to a couple of random strangers as the sole Yank who came all this way for the Rabbitohs, I felt like the most important person in the room. It also was a great excuse to add more autographs to my posters. This Australian tradition may not have had barbeques and beanbags, but it did feel a whole lot more social since you were kind of required to participate in interacting with each other. No one was plopped down in some cheap folding chair while spilling relish on their jeans. Everyone here was singing, drinking, and practicing cursing for their game. I have to say, this pre-game tradition was awesome! I don't mean to sound cliché, but beer somehow tastes better when you're enjoying it with close friends.

CHAPTER 39

The Cracca and Macca Show

(First Half of the 2014 Qualifying Round)

The climax of my pub crawl came at the Captain Cook Hotel, which was around the corner from Moore Park in the Paddington neighborhood near Flinders Street and ANZAC Parade. According to all my Bunny friends, this was one of the most popular pubs in the city and a favorite haunt for all footy goers heading to Allianz for a game. Although it was a stone's throw from the Roosters' turf, it was not uncommon to see Souths fans frequent this establishment, especially when the two played each other. When we entered the place, it was packed! It was loud and crowded, but everyone seemed to be in such high spirits. And the nice thing was that since we had Allianz Stadium all to ourselves that night, the bar was awash in red and green, save for a few Manly fans in maroon.

We ventured to the rear of the pub where I saw a small stage reserved for a live band along with concert posters that were slowly peeling off the wall. It felt a little bit like CBGB's, only without the mosh pits and mohawks. It was the perfect mix of classic rock paraphernalia and footy fans under one happy roof. It was here that I was introduced to a few more ladies of the Souths, like Kellie Bishop, Tammie Saunders Kemp, and Lorraine Carpenter Psomas. I found them under a whole lot of red and green balloons throwing back a few beers. Right away, each of them told me that they had only heard about me on social media and were only too happy to shake my hand.

Just as we were finishing up inside the Captain Cook, it was here that I was introduced to two of the most lovable footy fans that I have ever had the pleasure of befriending:

Cracca and Macca. Yeah, you heard me. Cracca, also known as Matthew "Wooly" Woolston (yup, two nicknames!) and his friend Macca were these two affable Rabbitohs fans who whooped and hollered from the moment I met them inside the Captain Cook Hotel. While some of the other fans decided to kill a bit more time inside over beer, I headed with Cracca and Macca across the street to Allianz. With my camcorder pointed at them, I began documenting their antics; I especially loved how they pronounced Long Island as "*Long Oy-land!*" with that great accent.

Those two were like a couple of kids getting ready for the big game; they would not stop smiling all night long and cheered every moment they could. Afterwards, I broke away from the new dynamic duo and I took my camcorder around the edge of Allianz Stadium to explore the pre-game festivities. After an entire afternoon of pub crawling and immersing myself in Australian pre-game rituals, I finally found a near identical American-style tailgate going on right outside. Instead of a massive parking lot where concrete and asphalt stretched from here to next Friday, it was mostly all grass and dirt. In fact, almost all cars were parked on the grass like it was the county fair. Where I was, outdoor electric heaters and patio umbrellas popped up like daisies.

I managed to find some barbeque but it didn't come from the trunk of someone's SUV. It did, however, come from a small tent kiosk that dished out meat and beer. It was a fairly decent burger, but not something I would call amazing. Maybe this is why when it comes to tailgating, Aussies are amazing at the pub crawl and Americans are better with hibachi meats and cornhole.

With our stomachs full of booze and a little bit of meat, it was game time! I practically ran through those turnstiles with my poster in tow as we prepared ourselves for this momentous night. After that close-call loss against the Roosters, we were even hungrier for a win tonight, even if it was on the Roosters' home turf, or in this case, the Sea Eagles' turf, as it was a home game for them. Prior to the match, Minor premiers Roosters surprisingly lost to fourth-placed Penrith in a stunning upset. Because of this result, a Rabbitohs versus Roosters Grand Final could not come to fruition; so much for an historic showdown.

The bottom four teams were, in decreasing order, North Queensland Cowboys with 32 points, Melbourne Storm with 32 points, Canterbury-Bankstown Bulldogs with 30 points, and Brisbane Broncos with 30 points. The only two teams representing Queensland both bowed out early, which was something of a mixed blessing for me. On the one hand, it was a relief to not have to face the powerhouse of Johnathan Thurston, a man who had been a thorn in the side of the Rabbitohs, as we had not beaten them since last season when they beat us 27–10 at ANZ in Round 10. On the other hand, we'd have to wait until next season to finally get some closure if we wanted to beat the boys from Townsville. Suffice it to say, it was going to be a very interesting post-season. Anyway, back to the game at Allianz.

The Burrow was seated just halfway to the 10-meter line. I met another proud Bunnies supporter named Lorraine Carpenter Psomas, whom I also recognized from Facebook. She presented me with a gift of a red and green flag with the word *Believe* written on it. Next to Lorraine, I ran into my dear cabbie friend from The Oaks, Joseph Gal. I was a little embarrassed that I didn't recognize him right off the bat since his outfit was different and I wasn't even drunk yet. Nonetheless, we had a good laugh as he was very happy to see me.

After player lineups were announced over the jumbotron, it was game time! "Glory Glory to South Sydney" echoed over the loudspeaker as every Rabbitohs fan stood up and sung. With my camcorder aimed toward the tunnel, I saw our dear

Reggie Rabbit excitedly lead our boys in red and green into battle. What better way to get psyched up for an epic match than by having a gigantic bunny lead out the biggest arsenal of athletes on Earth? Just another typical day in the life of a Souths fan! Our cheers were interrupted when the Manly boys in maroon marched out and were met with an ear-splitting "*Boo*!" And to think that this was supposed to be a Manly home game. At least it meant that there were far more Souths fans in Moore Park that evening. Greg Inglis kicked off the evening with a beautiful kick across the field and into the arms of Manly's Breton Lawrence.

The first exciting moment came about two and half minutes into the game when Isaac Luke handed the ball to Adam Reynolds, then Reynolds kicked it to Lote Tuquri on 5th tackle. Unfortunately, there was no try as Manly regained control. From that point on, it was a seesaw battle for control. While the Sea Eagles and the Bunnies duked it out, I was busy commiserating with my favorite big Bunny. I saw Reggie Rabbit was making his rounds around the edge of Allianz, meeting and greeting his loyal fanbase. My heart skipped a beat and I grabbed my poster and, well, bunny-hopped down to the edge were I saw my gargantuan Australian friend shaking paws with the anklebiters; I even saw him dancing, shuffling his cleats and shaking his tail. I was hoping that he would remember me from a week earlier from the Roosters game. I mean, Jason Clark remembered me after a year, so surely Reggie would remember the sole Yank after a week? Sure enough, he pointed to my poster and came right over to me. We had a hug and exchanged quite the handshake; it felt like it went on for hours.

At the seventh minute, we got an early scare when Brett Stewart went in for a try as it looked like Greg Inglis attempted to bat the ball away, but the play went up to the video ref for further review. On the instant replay, Inglis managed to kick the ball out of the way before Stewart could land his hand on the ball, thus giving the Bunnies a line dropout. No try was awarded and we Bunnies regained the ball. At the ninth minute, the crowd roared when Dylan Walker ran more than twenty meters untouched at high speed just before getting tackled inside the 40-meter line. At nine minutes, fifty seconds, Adam Reynolds punted the ball on 5th tackle to Lote Tuquri, hoping he'd catch it and deliver a try. Instead, it bounced out of his arms and into the arms of Dylan Walker. Walker kicked toward the try line and Adam Reynolds beat Brett Stewart to give the Bunnies the first try of the game, and managed to convert his own try as well. Bunnies were up 6–0.

At sixteen minutes in, Dylan Walker handed the ball off to Kirisome Auva'a and he made an amazing sprint from the Bunnies' 20-meter line to the Manly 20-meter line. It would be the start of one of the best drives of the game. Shortly after getting tackled, Auva'a, in a moment of hesitation thinking he was legitimately tackled, froze for a moment. The ref, however, let the ball play on. Auva'a lobbed the ball to Isaac Luke, who then lobbed it to Adam Reynolds, who lobbed it to Sam Burgess, who then gave it to Lote Tuquri, who got tackled just five meters out from the line. On 3rd tackle, Tuquri rolled it back to Sam Burgess, who gave it to Reynolds, and completed the play by kicking it over the line. Luke Keary dove on top of the ball for the second Souths try after an amazing drive. Reynolds converted the try and the Bunnies were up 12–0.

Just after twenty-one minutes, Lote Tuquri handed off the ball to Greg Inglis and Inglis would go on an amazing sprint from the Bunnies' 20-meter line to the Manly 20-meter line, mimicking the same run Auva'a had just five minutes earlier. Inglis brushed off a near tackle from Anthony Watmeau but was eventually brought down just eighteen meters away from the line. Luke Keary handed the ball off to Dylan Walker, who got tackled just ten meters shy of the line from Steve Mattai at the twenty-second minute of play. Unfortunately, Walker would succumb to a leg injury, thus stopping play temporarily.

The clock was reset to 21:43. George Burgess passed the ball to Isaac Luke, who gave the ball to John Sutton, who lobbed the ball over to Greg Inglis, who handed it off to Alex Johnston who went in for the try. The Rabbitohs celebration was short-lived, however, when upon further review, the ball just slipped out of Johnston's grip before putting pressure on it. His presumptive eighteenth try in his sixteenth game as a Bunny was denied and a knock-on in goal was called. An enormous groan echoed from The Burrow in spite of the damning evidence of Johnston's botched try.

With Manly regaining the ball, the Bunnies went back to work on defense. Luckily, we would have a chance to redeem ourselves at the twenty-sixth minute. Adam Reynolds punted the ball on 5th tackle; the ball went good and high as everyone in The Burrow held their breath collectively. In the corner of the field, Lote Tuquri stood square under the football as he leapt into the air, caught the bugger, and put it down just a few inches over the line for another great Rabbitohs try which elicited a massive roar from every Bunny in The Burrow. In just a split second of his try, I was sandwiched in a hug between Lorraine and Brigitte. Reynolds quickly converted the try and the Bunnies went up 18–0.

At the thirty-first minute, Greg Inglis gave us a bit of a scare when he received a dangerous tackle from Anthony Watmaugh and Jamie Lyon. Thankfully, he managed to brush it off and both Manly players were put on report. The last thing we needed when things were going so well for us was for our biggest Bunny to get seriously injured. Around the thirty-third minute, the Rabbitohs were awarded a scrum feed after Manly dropped a punted ball. We would restart with a scrum from inside Manly's 10-meter line; we could taste another try. Luke Keary passed the ball to Lote Tuquri, who was brought down on the 10-meter line for a first tackle. Thomas Burgess got the second tackle from inside the 5-meter line. It was a collaborative team effort which resulted in Alex Johnston getting a pass from inside the left corner and easily running in for another Souths try! Though Reynolds missed his first conversion, it was wonderful twenty-two-point lead we had at the thirty-fifth minute. Shortly afterwards, the halftime siren wailed at we Bunnies looked at the scoreboard and smiled. We had a rather comfortable lead and Manly was scoreless. Things were definitely looking up for us.

Just before the end of the first half, I made another Bunny friend when this tall bloke with silvery hair noticed my non-Aussie accent. He asked if I was American, and I told him that I was from New York. He was so jazzed that he broke out laughing hysterically as if he had just been tickled. He only got even happier when I told him that it was my fourth Souths game and that I was an enormous fan. My new friend told me that he owned a small Italian restaurant in downtown Sydney near the Australian Museum called Bill and Toni's; he told that I must come for a visit as his guest. As if getting a personal invite to a restaurant from an enthusiastic Souths fan wasn't amazing enough, he whipped out his cell phone and dialed his wife. He insisted that I talk to her; he just couldn't believe that there was an American fan of the Rabbitohs sitting next to him that was more decked out in gear than he was. It was like he had befriended a rare creature and he wanted to show me off to his friends and family, even if it was over the phone.

I honestly didn't know what to say other than "G'day!" and "Go Bunnies!" I am amazed I was able to carry on a conversation given the level of cheering and noise emulating from every corner of the stadium. It was such a surreal moment, it seemed to whiz by me in such a blur. He shook my hand and posed for a photo with me. And just like that, I had added another Bunny to my already growing warren of Souths fans!

CHAPTER 40
Victory for Bailon
(The Second Half of the Qualifying Round)

I would be remiss if I did not bring up a rather somber and grim bit of news that occurred inside the Captain Cook Hotel just a few hours before kickoff. When I came over to the table where Kellie and Tammy where seated, I noticed that several Rabbitohs fans were all wearing black armbands like they were at a funeral. Everyone had told me that a few days earlier the Rabbitohs family had lost one of their most devoted and youngest fans. Bailon Johnson, a four- year-old from Tamworth had succumbed to neuroblastoma cancer after a fifteen-month battle. The news had pierced the heart of not just the community of Tamworth, but the Rabbitohs fanbase was grieving too, with thousands of tributes pouring in across social media.

It was one of the saddest moments for everyone in the red and green army and at a time when spirits where very high around playoff season. Bailon was a Rabbitohs fanatic, attending many games over the course of two years and meeting many of his idols in person.

Kellie gave me an armband to wear around my jersey. Actually, we didn't really have armbands so we just wrapped some black electrical tape crudely around the sleeves of our jerseys. Still, it was a somber moment for all us. In addition to the "armbands," the fans were distributing some laminated cards featuring little Bailon that we were to hold up during the beginning of the match. It was the saddest moment of my trip. Suddenly, the close loss that the Rabbitohs had to the Roosters a week ago became just an afterthought. My head was so full of emotion from that news, but I managed to put on a straight face and be stoic. In fact, just a few months earlier, my family had lost one of our oldest uncles and I usually feel it thrust upon me in a room full of grieving people to be the stoic one. I am always there to comfort those who need it, despite my own tears.

I went to the bar and got a bottle of Tooheys. I came back and proposed a toast; a toast to not only the Rabbitohs defeating Manly and winning our 21st premiership, but dedicating that we would win tonight's game for little Bailon as well as his parents, Randy and Renee. The team themselves donned black armbands and Isaac Luke even emblazoned the name "Bailon" on his wrist in a moving tribute. Souths players have vowed to use Bailon's positive attitude in adversity as an inspiration. Despite the sadness emanating from almost every fan, it was yet another reminder of just how close-knit the Rabbitohs are with their fans. With most professional sports teams, they'd probably leave their prayers and thoughts via Twitter or during an interview. With the Rabbitohs, however, they went to such lengths to give this sweet little Bunny a proper salute.

Donning armbands and leaving heartfelt tweets were just the tip of the iceberg. The team donated autographed jerseys and banners for his funeral. They even wrote his name on their wrists underneath their armbands. The Rabbitohs, both the team and the fans, even the office bigwigs behind the scenes, are all family. They look out for one another. When one fan celebrates, they all celebrate. And when one fan or family grieves, they share their sorrows and tears. I always thought these fans were amazing because of how devoted they were to the team and how much fun they were to be around. Seeing them come together for this one young fan was beyond wonderful. This was an extended family that wore their team colors and their feelings literally on their sleeves; a passionate base that looked out for another and beyond their community.

The team wasn't the only role models; the fans were as well. If only there were more Australian Bunny Rabbits in this world.

And now, the second half of the 2014 Souths qualifying match was already in progress...

The scoreboard pretty much said it all. Four consecutive tries with only one missed conversion. A comfortable twenty-two-point lead and we were playing with a full, stacked deck of Bunnies. But we all knew it was still too early to celebrate. As I learned the hard way from last year's gruesome defeat in the semi-final against Manly, one must never sit on a lead, no matter how ahead you are. Also, we needed to make sure our defense would stop Manly at all costs. I didn't even want to see a single offensive player in maroon get more than halfway up the field. Maybe we couldn't avenge our loss to the Roosters that night, but we could sure as hell give Manly another good drubbing. Sure, we had beaten them earlier in the season next door at the SCG, but this match wasn't just to advance and get a bye, but for our dearly departed anklebiter, Bailon.

Reggie led the boys out to kick off the second half. And boy, did we begin the half in a big way when none other than our golden-footed Adam Reynolds scored a try when he beat Manly's fullback Brett Stewart to the ball inside Manly's zone, resulting in a quick try for the Bunnies at the forty-second minute. Reynolds managed to convert his own try and every last fan in The Burrow screamed their lungs out. Right on cue, I was screaming "Reynolds! Reynolds!" mimicking Warren Smith's illustrious call from 2012. In fact, in a Pavlovian response that I am now accustomed to, whenever Reynolds scores a try, I can't help but channel Warren Smith in a jubilant fashion. We were not two minutes into the second half and Reynolds notched the Rabbitohs' lead 28–0. His conversion was most impressive; it went unimaginably high, putting pressure on Manly. Reynolds, I believe, is sort of our good luck charm. Kind of like a lucky rabbit's foot. And wouldn't you know it? He is our star kicker and we seem to jell better when he is in the lineup. It felt so good having him back on the field after his absence from last week, indeed.

Ten minutes later at the fifty-second minute, Dylan Walker scored near the posts, fighting his way through would-be defenders to score near the right upright, pulling off an impressive, yet forceful try. A conversion from Reynolds put the Bunnies up 34–0. From the press box, commentator Phil Gould said after Walker's try: "They can do what they like at the moment—inside, outside, up the middle. They are rag-dolling them."

As quickly as you could say, "dummy half!" a brilliant pass to Alex Johnston within two minutes put him in the clear. Running with such blistering speed as he maneuvered his way past the Manly defense, which at this point was rendered moot, he placed his try in the corner of the try line. Watching him run with that ball, it was like the team knew he was going to put it in just the right spot. You know how in a game of billiards, someone will say "8-ball in the corner pocket?" Well, with Alex Johnston, it's more like "AJ, number 2, in the corner try zone." Like clockwork, it was something he had been doing almost all season, at least since he joined the team.

The fans, at this point, were downright delirious, if not ecstatic. The TV cameras cut away to Russell Crowe's personal box and announcer Ray Warren said, "The Gladiator's happy. All of South Sydney is happy!" Although I wasn't sitting next to the Academy-award winning actor, I zoomed in on him using my camcorder. I managed to catch a glimpse of him pumping his fists in the air and jumping up and down. Any happier and he could have broken out into song or started dancing. As for me, that is just what I did with all my mates in The Burrow. I was hugging Lorraine and Kellie so hard that I swung them into the air. As a matter of fact, they hugged me so hard, they almost did the same! Reynolds converted AJ's try and the Bunnies went up a crushing 40–0! The scoreboard said just that, and I was sober as judge.

With the lead so massive, I began to get rather comfortable. I no longer felt nervous watching the game. I was even feeling, dare I say, a bit overconfident. And apparently, so were the Rabbitohs. The second half is usually where the Bunnies unleash hell on their opponents, as I have witnessed ever since I started watching. About a few minutes after Johnston's speedy try, the Bunnies began to get a little too comfortable and started to let their guard down. At the sixty-fourth minute, Brett Stewart delivered Manly's first try of the match, followed by a converted kick. We all shrugged it off and considered it a sympathy try. Just four minutes later, Jamie Lyon converted his own try and suddenly, we Souths fans began to feel wary. We weren't anticipating a loss; there were only twelve minutes left to play and an upset was highly unlikely. Still, two consecutive tries in less than five minutes after a juggernaut performance by the Souths was a brief slap in the face.

Well, we got another slap in the face at the seventy-fifth minute when Tom Symonds scored and Lyon converted another Manly try. Now we were wondering if the Rabbitohs had either gotten bored or their overconfidence had gotten the best of them. I didn't want to say that it was starting to look like last year's tragic semi-final game where we lost 30–20, but some of us looked like we were having flashbacks to that fateful night. Well, at the seventy-ninth minute, you would think we would put our foot down and lock this game up. Unfortunately, Cheyse Blair scored the last try for Manly followed by, you guessed it, another converted try by Jamie Lyon. That didn't stop us from getting on our feet and bellowing "Botany Road" with every ounce of strength we could summon. Just hearing that sweet siren song of the Bunnies took our minds off those four terrible tries in spite of what the scoreboard said.

The final siren rang, at long last, and we screamed in delight and fell into an orgy of hugs and fists pumping in the air. The celebration and almost one-sided victory wasn't enough to keep the Rabbitohs safe from the wrath of Madge. After the game, Michael Maguire was apparently filthy in the shed, giving his players a verbal beat-down. In spite of the win, a team as good as the Souths does not allow four consecutive tries from the opposing side, no matter how far ahead you are. I'm glad I wasn't there to see the ruckus inside the sheds, but I could only imagine what it must have been like. I flashed back to when Maguire nearly lost it after round 25 in 2013 when all four Burgess Brothers played against the Wests Tigers and to when I was on the varsity basketball team in high school. I saw so many parallels between my coach and Maguire, but it only solidified my respect for Madge. A guy who gets that fired up at his team for being that careless in the second half in spite of a crushing win is a man who cares not just about winning, but the game itself.

With a win under our belt and a bye week coming up for us, it was time to head home. For me, that meant a long walk back to Sussex Street. I gave every last fan in The Burrow a hug and hoped that we'd run into each other again, and hopefully before I left Sydney. As I headed out of Allianz and toward Central Station, I passed by the Cricketer Arms Hotel on Foveaux Street, one of the many pubs my Bunnies and I popped into during our pub crawl. There was a party going on and there were a substantial number of Souths fans inside celebrating the big win. Think of it as sort of an after-party for the Bunnies.

The hotel might have had the name cricket in the marquee, but inside it was noisier than a soccer match. I could barely hear a thing, let alone a thought in my head. Then again, my head was already pumping from the screaming inside Allianz. I made my way to the bar and ordered a bottle of Tooheys and a bag of Walkers when I bumped into some footy fans toasting the recent victory. I joined in their toast and it was then they heard my American accent. Right then and there, I worked my charm on the merry lot of Aussies and it wasn't long before they were buying me another beer and I was barely halfway through my first Tooheys! Oh, and they even comped me two more bags of Walkers! I'm starting to think that Australians might just be the friendliest people in the world! All I have to do is be a devotee of footy, preferably the Souths, and I never have to pay for a drink! If I move to Sydney, I won't have to allocate money for booze or chips!

I got back to my hotel just after midnight. I was drunk on both victory and beer. To me, this had been a perfect night. It was, dare I say, magical. In just one evening, I had more to drink than I could possible remember, and luckily, I wasn't even sick. I made a whole new mess of friends, including the proprietor of an Italian restaurant! I got to shake hands and fist bump Reggie, not to mention the Bunnies crushed Manly in spectacular fashion! It was such an amazing game, I was even willing to overlook those four tries by Manly, albeit Madge sure wasn't gonna. But best of all, on behalf of Bailon Johnson and his family, whom we all came to rally around for this important game, we won this one just for him. Sleep peacefully, little anklebiter.

CHAPTER 41
The Nerdy Bunny

SEPTEMBER 14, 2014:

One of my favorite words in the English language is serendipity. It is a term first coined by a British politician and art historian named Horace Walpole in 1754. It is the act of finding the wonderful when you least expect it; a "fortunate happenstance" or "pleasant surprise" if you will. And like many moments throughout life, some of the best things tend to happen when you least expect it.

Much like my discovery of the Rabbitohs in Alice Springs, this serendipitous moment happened on my train ride back from my walkabout in Berowra just two days earlier. I had found an old newspaper next to my foot with a color photograph of three people dressed as Superman, Batman, and Spiderman. What caught my eye, however, was that it was an advertisement for Oz Comic-con, which is the largest annual comic-book convention in Australia. And what a coincidence that it was set to take place in just three days.

I was already occupied by the Souths game against Manly and I thought that there was no better capper to an epic footy match than an epic gathering of my fellow nerds. Rabbitohs fans and comic-con geeks are not as different as I had thought. Both are devotees of a certain subculture and wear their pride on their sleeves and then some. One thing is for sure: they look out for their fellow brethren and everyone around is a friend. Well, at least until you get into a heated argument over which Rabbitohs player is the greatest, or in this case, which version of Doctor Who was the coolest and which 80s cartoon character did you have a massive crush on?

I was fortunate to learn that I did not need a ticket weeks ahead of schedule; I could just show up at the ticket window on opening day and pay the premium to carouse the floor. I was unfortunate, however, to not have a costume with me. To show up at comic-con with no outfit whatsoever is quite taboo. The one person at the convention who is not dressed as their favorite character is seen as the real odd one out. Naturally, I knew just what to wear: my Rabbitohs gear. I would be in attendance as Reggie Rabbit's American counterpart!

After a short walk from the Four Points Hotel across Pyrmont Bridge, I caught the next ferry for Glebe Island with a horde of nerds; a ship of fools were we! While it was smaller than the more famous comic-con in San Diego and New York, it did not disappoint. For starters, the outfits were amazing; they ran the gamut from playful, to laughable, to realistic, to even risqué. I saw one congoer who went as Princess Peach, but in drag. Another congoer combined Pokémon with what looked like a either a cocktail dress or a fur suit. Of course, having visited Anthrocon, the largest gathering of fur suiters in the world, the people here were gonna have to step up their game! Suddenly, I realized my Rabbitohs outfit would be lost in the shuffle among the anime and video game cosplayers. Still, it felt great to be around some of my favorite people!

When Americans think of Australia, "nerd" is not a term associated with this great country. In fact, it is not something we tend to use in the same sentence, let alone the same breath. Geek, dork, fanboy, fangirl, or any other cliché term for the stereotypical nerd isn't something we think Australia has any of. The image of the Aussie, in the minds of Americans who have been brought up with the likes of the rugged Crocodile Dundee, the dashing Errol Flynn, the gorgeous Olivia Newton-John, the hot model that is Elle MacPherson, and the bad-ass rock stars of AC/DC, Americans tend to fetishize Australians as rough, tough individuals who embody both masculinity and toughness from a male perspective, or beauty and hotness from the female perspective. And you can't conjure those images if someone is all brains and no brawns. Maybe this all still comes from the fact that we still can't stop associating Australians with being related to convicts, which is where we get the "tough guy" image from. You might say we have something of a perverse admiration for a country that started off as a penal colony and wound up with beautiful beaches, surfer girls, and Hugh Jackman.

Then again, we Americans worship the concept of masculinity and toughness as if we're worried about being judged by everyone. And yet, my few hours inside Oz Comic-con surrounded by hundreds, if not thousands, of hardcore nerds blew that silly stereotype right out of the water. In fact, in recent years, Australia has made great contributions to the nerd universe. Comedians like Rove McManus and Jim Jeffries have made their mark on the stand-up circuit, especially with their satirical takes on Aussie cultures versus American cultures. And of course, I would be remiss if I didn't mention the great Hugh Jackman for his countless contributions to both sides of this debate. As Wolverine, he has carved out a niche for himself as a dark and brooding musclebound mutant superhero that men idolize and women ooh and aah over. And on the other side, as a Broadway star and on-stage singer, he has won over everyone from the theatre geeks to those who have never set foot on the Great White Way.

Frankly, I am happy for this recent subculture. Nerds have always existed in Australia; it's just that Americans were never introduced to them. It'd be easy to blame Hollywood for making the Land Down Under look like a place devoid of academics and packed with a glut of muscle and drunks. But as I have learned with my Rabbitohs friends and that one episode of The Simpsons that is set in Australia, Americans are still somewhat clueless about the land of koalas and kangaroos. And those well-dressed cosplayers on Glebe Island were there to show me that we're not so different after all.

In fact, my favorite moment came when I was checking out the artists' alley at all the self-published graphic novels. I still felt like a sore thumb since I wasn't dressed heavily in a homemade costume, but I still wore my Souths shirt with pride. One artist called me out for my Rabbitohs shirt and outed himself as a fan. When he heard my accent, he was stoked to learn I was an American. He was so impressed by my moxie as a Rabbitohs supporter, he nearly forgot about his stacks of books and line of people at the con. I jokingly told him that I had found out about this place at the last second and threw on the next best thing I had to a costume: my Souths shirt. I also told him that I had been planning on going as Reggie Rabbit, and he just laughed and laughed.

By the end of our conversation, he made me a deal on some animation cells I saw being sold near him; I bought three and he gave me a discount on the third one. Once again, my card-carrying Rabbitohs love saves the day! After a few hours of swimming in an ocean of nerds, I boarded the ferry from Glebe Island back to Darling Harbour with the knowledge that I'd be going home with both Rabbitohs merchandise and some rare animation cells. I was one happy Bunny.

CHAPTER 42
Bunny in Wondabyne

SEPTEMBER 17, 2014:

I have said before that the two things I always make time for in Australia are the Rabbitohs and the Hawkesbury River. Ever since I saw *Oyster Farmer* back in 2005, it opened up my eyes to just how surreal and beautiful Australia truly is, not to mention it introduced me to a part of the country I had never known about before. One of my favorite moments in the film came when Alex O'Loughlin's character, Jack Flange, disembarks the train at the Wondabyne station toward the end of the film. What made it such a cool scene was how small the station was. Actually, there was no road, ticket machine, or anything other than a platform and a tiny shelter. Since that scene, that tiny train station has been such a fascination, and not just because of my love for the movie, but because of how peculiar it looks.

Wondabyne station is the smallest and most inaccessible train station in all of Australia. It is the only train station that has no road access; the only means of accessing it are either by boat or via a hiking trail. Train passengers can only reach this station by making a personal request to the train guard and must then be located in the rear train carriage. The first two times I visited the Hawkesbury, I had gotten off at Hawkesbury River station in Brooklyn and not at the requested stop upriver. This time, I was determined to summon the courage to be dropped off in the middle of nowhere.

At Central Station, I loaded my backpack with bottled water, some energy bars, mints, crisps, and two bottles of

Powerade. It wasn't like I was preparing for a long hike on the Appalachians, but I never go anywhere unprepared, much less to a place I've never been. Frankly, I couldn't believe I was about to embark on this little journey. On board the train bound for Newcastle, I nervously sat back and waited for the train to pull into Wondabyne. After pulling out of Hawkesbury River station, I got up from my seat and walked toward the doors, awaiting my stop. Unfortunately, there was one little problem: the train didn't stop. Uh-oh! Just like that, I watched that tiny platform sail past me.

Not wanting to make a scene in a crowded train, I asked someone why the train didn't stop. They explained to me that Wondabyne is a "request stop," which meant that I had to alert the train guard of my stop and be seated in the rear carriage. And like an idiot, I smacked my forehead. I had boarded the train at Central without following proper procedure and blew it. But, that is the great thing about mistakes: you learn from them. The train arrived at Woy Woy station where I waited for the return train to Central. Well, this was an interesting way to begin a journey into the bush.

Take two. It turns out that my brief time in Woy Woy would yield an interesting surprise. On the return train, I found a seat next to tall bloke with a tattooed arm. He complimented me on my Souths jersey and was taken aback by the fact that I was an American and in this remote neck of the woods. Frank was his name and he was shocked to see a Yank in Australia sporting a Souths jersey, much less an American Rabbitohs fan in the Hawkesbury. In the brief time we became friends, he asked me what music bands I liked. Being in Australia, I excitedly told him that I was a massive fan of Midnight Oil. As if Frank wasn't already impressed by my Rabbitohs fandom, he was even more stunned by the fact that not only was I a fan of the eponymous group, but that I owned all their albums as well. He was positively awestruck. In spite of many Aussies feeling a bit jilted by the band's breakup and Peter Garrett's foray into politics, Midnight Oil still holds a special place in many Aussie music fans' hearts. Frank then showed me his tattoos and we talked about the Oils and AC/DC.

The train slowly approached the tiny platform at the edge of the Hawkesbury; I saw a tinny bobbing in the water and heard the electrified sound of a grade crossing as the train pulled into the station.

"Thanks, mate. If I wanna get another train back to Central, I just flag the train down, right?" I asked.

"Yeah, mate. You just stand behind the yellow line and the train will see you. The last car will stop. It'll make stops all day if they see someone," the train guard said to me.

"So just wave and do this, like I was hailing a taxi, right?" I asked as I waved my arms.

"Yeah, no worries" He said reassuringly. "First time here?" he asked.

"Yeah, first time here. I've always wanted to see this place. "They'll stop? Are you sure?" I asked again, just wanting to hear a bit of reassurance.

"Yeah, mate. Souths fan, are you?" he said, noticing my jumper and cap.

"Indeed I am!" I said, boastfully. "I'm from New York and I love the Bunnies!"

"Yeah, Souths are all right; I don't mind'em," he said nonchalantly. Well, at least he wasn't a Roosters fan. And just like that, the train disappeared around the bend, the electrical vibration in the rails slowly dissipated, and it was good and quiet. Well, all except for the sound of the river splashing up against the rocks.

I couldn't believe it. I made it. I finally made it! It was nearly ten years since I walked out of the Quad Cinema awe-struck by the surroundings of the Hawkesbury, especially the remote station of Wondabyne. What was once a fantasy was now a reality. This was no dream. This was real. I ran my fingers repeatedly across the platform and blue-painted bench just to feel that this place was tangible. I took a deep breath and for a few seconds, time seemed to stand still. The only thing that seemed a bit of out of place at this little station was the Opal Card ticket reader on the platform. Ever since this new piece of technology replaced the old paper tickets, getting on and off CityRail trains in Sydney was so easy. In fact, all I needed was to tap my card on the little screen atop the pole and I was good to go. It was pretty weird seeing something so high-tech in the middle of nowhere. It was like passing through a subway turnstile and ending up in an idyllic forest on the other side. At that moment, I held my head up and said, "I'm here. I'm finally here. I finally made it!"

I strolled alongside the pontoon and saw a tinny up close. It looked remarkably identical to the one I saw in *Oyster Farmer*. However, it was empty and void of any shellfish. The weather was so perfect, I took off my shoes and socks and dipped my feet into the river. I let out a big sigh and felt a tingle all over my body. The only sounds emitting from this picturesque tableau were the splashing of water and the warbling of birds in the air. I heard the laughing of kookaburras, the sounds of magpies, and the chortling of galahs.

After taking in the song of the river, I made my way across the Wondabyne platform and on to the surrounding Brisbane Water National Park for some hiking. The trail began on the opposite side of the river and went uphill. I turned around with my back to the trail and viewed the station from behind the trees. I was still in awe of how small and surreal Wondabyne looked. It felt, dare I say, magical to be wandering through the forest and wind up at a train station next to a riverbank. I mean, this felt like a scene from *The Lion, The Witch, and The Wardrobe* where Lucy steps into Narnia or *Spirited Away* where Chihiro gets off the enchanted train and journeys through Swamp Bottom. Forgive me if sound a bit corny, but this was kind of how I was feeling as I began my journey above the river. Along the trail, which was part of Brisbane Waters National Park, I found myself beneath what looked like pine trees; most unusual for a country like Australia, except these pine trees had skinny trunks and they didn't give off a strong pine smell that you get from Christmas trees.

Destinations along the trail included Pindar Cave, Kariong Brook, and Wondabyne. Walking trails also join the Great North Walk, which is a lengthy trail that stretches from Sydney to Newcastle for more extensive trips. The track that gives access to these areas leaves from near the station and is very steep. To say that it was steep would be a bit of an understatement. It wasn't like I was marching up a sixty-degree angle or climbing a mountain, but with each step, I began to feel a bit winded. I had to stretch my legs to get from rock to rock whenever there was a gap in the trail. The trail, however, was neatly marked by a flat, dirt path complete with steps carved out of rocks and some made from halved logs. The trail wasn't as long as the one I had done in Berowra, but that trail was a gentle, downward slope. This trail near Wondabyne was a straight up path that felt like it was carved out of the side of a small mountain so you were hiking sideways up it, rather than vertically up.

One nice thing about this hike was that I didn't feel like I was lost in the wilderness; since the hiking path went up, I could almost always see a clear view of the train station and the river. And since I wasn't venturing that deep into the bush, I could always hear the faint rumble of a train. And on occasion, I could hear the loud roar of a lengthy freight train pounding its way down the tracks.

About an hour after I began my hike, I took a break on top of a large rock in a small clearing near a larger dirt path. I recreated my brief respite at the pontoon on dry land with my back spread out over the rock with the verdant canopy overhead. This scene was too perfect. I was so far from home and all by myself in one of the prettiest places on Earth that almost no one knew about. It made me wonder why no one, let alone foreign tourists, have capitalized on this quaint region of Australia. I mean, a place this beautiful deserves recognition, at least among the tourist and backpacker set. It'd sure be nice if more people knew about the Hawkesbury and all its little hideaways. Then again, I think it'd be best if I kept this place to myself. Next to Redfern and Darling Harbour, this little slice of the bush is my own personal hideaway.

I spent more than an hour staring up at the sky through the trees. I had totally lost track of the time. Frankly, I wrestled with the idea of even moving from this spot. It was the same comforting feeling I had experienced back in Berowra. Alas, I had to force myself out of this comforting tableau of nature. I grabbed my backpack and headed back down the trail en route to Wondabyne. While the river was just in sight from high up on the trail, there was another site that was barely shrouded by the shrubbery. Just north of the railway station by the water is a tract of land that contains a sandstone quarry. I could clearly make out a crane and a few construction machines. It felt like a scene out of *Stand by Me*; I could even recreate the scene where the kids run away from the oncoming train, sans the bridge and dead body.

After what felt like a long and precarious march down through the bush, I made it back to the station. The challenge now wasn't just waiting for the train but figuring out how to flag it down. I only needed to remember what the guard on my train told me when I first got off that the oncoming train would stop as soon as it saw me. I did trust him, but I was taking no chances. I brought a little something to help me in case. It was a compass that had a built-in whistle with a compartment case. After waiting for about forty minutes, I blew an ear-splitting "*TWOOT*" as the train slowly came into focus from around the bend. Sure enough, the train came to a slow stop and I wouldn't have to worry about hitchhiking a boat from Wondabyne back to Brooklyn.

I felt a real sense of pride after my brief time in Wondabyne. I mean, I actually got off in the middle of nowhere and explored a remote corner of Australia all by myself, not to mention there wasn't another person around; I couldn't hear or see anyone at all. I only had the sound of Australia's avian wildlife and the wind to keep me company, and the occasional noisy rumble of a passing train in the distance. Still, it was something I would remember forever. While other camera-happy tourists were busy in the warm comfort of the Sydney Opera House or trying hard to blend in with the surfies at Manly and Bondi, I was miles away in a place where the tourist count was at zero. I was far from the all-too common tableau of refrigerator magnets and clichéd souvenirs that tend to rob people of an authentic experience.

Not to sound like I am poo-pooing Sydney's great tourist attractions that draw millions of people from around the world, but I am not like them. I had come here because I was inspired by an Australian rom-com, but I left feeling like I had discovered something so amazing that I am pretty sure I was not the first to discover. Still, I wouldn't be surprised if I was the only American who took time out from a busy footy schedule to escape to a quiet piece of the bush, even for a few hours. I encourage so many people who travel abroad to go out there and just explore. Go ahead, wander! Get lost and see what happens. I wandered into a movie theatre and fell in love with the Hawkesbury. I wandered into an apparel store in Alice Springs and fell in love with a footy team.

I couldn't leave without one little dip in the river. As the train pulled into Hawkesbury River station in Brooklyn, I got off and made a bee line for the river. I changed into my swim trunks and took in the coolness of the Hawkesbury as it caressed my body. It was another gentle reminder of why Australia is often referred to as the Lucky Country.

CHAPTER 43
Story on Page 1

SEPTEMBER 19, 2014:

My time in Australia was coming to an end. I should have been feeling sad, but that morning, I was anything but. I had received an email from the staff at Souths. I was not prepared for what I was about to read when I clicked on the link. It was my article that I written up for the Rabbitohs website. There it was. Or rather, there *I* was on their website. I wasn't dreaming; I was on a major sports website for a professional team. And not just that, alongside the article was the close-up photo of Reggie and I that was taken by my fellow Rabbitohs fan, Elizabeth Brown. As if meeting the entire team, the staff, Madge, and Reggie wasn't surreal enough, now this?!

I wasted no time sharing this article on social media every which way I could. I guess you could say that this was a proud moment for me. Incidentally, I had also received another email from the Rabbitohs Media Department saying that they wanted to see me before I left Australia. It wouldn't right for me to leave without bidding a proper goodbye to the gang at Redfern.

A few minutes later, I was walking from Redfern Station to Chalmers Street. On the fourth floor of the building, Tom and Jeremy from the Media Department were there with a little gift for me. No, it wasn't Grand Final tickets or that giant Souths motorcycle that they had front and center outside the elevators. They presented me with a Rabbitohs 2014 jumper and an autographed copy of "Glory Glory," an autobiography of former Rabbitohs captain and footy legend, John Sattler. Considered to be one of the greatest rugby league players of all time, Sattler won four Premierships with the Souths (1967, '68, '70, and '71), was captain of the team, and played with the Souths for nine seasons (1963–1972). On the field, however, was a man of great fortitude and toughness who had made some of the most memorable plays in footy history. Of all his moments, none is more iconic than the 1970 Grand Final between the Rabbitohs and the Manly Sea Eagles where Sattler attained legendary status in the game in which he played with a broken jaw to help the Souths to victory over Manly.

On September 19th, 1970, having lost the previous 1969 Grand Final to the Balmain Tigers, the Souths were desperate to win. Approximately ten minutes into the game, Sattler collapsed after being punched by Manly forward Zach Bucknall. He suffered a double fracture to his jaw but pleaded to teammate Mike Cleary, "Hold me up so they don't know I'm hurt." He was helped up and continued to play in the game. At halftime, the Souths were leading 12–6 when his teammates learned about his injury. Apparently, he refused treatment and insisted he continue playing. He told the side, "The next bloke who tries to cut me out of the play is in trouble," to prevent his teammates from trying to protect him from further injury. By the end of the game, South Sydney was victorious with a score of 23–12.

He later went to the hospital to receive treatment, but only after receiving the J.J. Giltinan Shield and making an acceptance speech on behalf of the team. It was all summed up with one memorable photo where Sattler was being heroically carried off the field looking like he had just gotten into ten hockey fights at once, or looking like he had just finished a bare-knuckle boxing match. For Rabbitohs fans, it was not just a memorable Grand Final moment but a symbol of just how tough and courageous footy players truly are. Sattler's injury and 1970 Grand Final win are now the stuff of legends. For me, I doubt I would have that kind of will to take a beating like that on the field, but his resilience is a real source of inspiration.

By the time I started watching the Rabbitohs, I had learned who Sattler was through social media thanks in part to other fellow Souths fans. When I first laid eyes on his broken jaw and bloodied mouth, I was, naturally, freaked out. I had seen terrible injuries in sports in America before. Most were mildly cringe-inducing, like Joe Theismann's crushed leg in 1985 or the time Mike Tyson bit into Evander Holyfield's ear in 1997. This injury, however, looked too brutal to be real. Even in a black-and-white photo, that image just sticks out in so many ways. Now I look at that photo and I am not only able to cringe anymore but I can feel a sense of pride from that Grand Final win. The next time someone in America mocks rugby for being too European or not brutal enough like football, or mocks the Rabbitohs for having such a cute-looking logo, I'll just show'em that image of Sattler's jaw and walk away.

As Tom and Jeremy handed me my gifts, I got up and looked them in the eyes and asked them, with all the sincerity in my heart, if there was room available at Redfern for an enthusiastic Yank who would want nothing more than a chance to work with the greatest team in Australia. I didn't have any skills as a sportscaster or sportswriter, and I was still working out the positions in rugby; to this day, I am still struggling to understand five-eighth and the duties of a utility. Nonetheless, I asked if there was anything I could do for the organization. I told them I'd be happy to man the gift shop or help out if Reggie could use a human sidekick.

Sadly, they said that there were no openings but they did promise me that if anything came up, I'd be the first to know. Whether they meant it or not, I still haven't forgotten them and neither did they. Just before leaving, I took one last look behind the doorway to the office pool and said to myself, *maybe there's a cubicle in there with my name on it. Someday.*

So I had another new Souths jumper and an autographed copy of a book signed by one of the Rabbitohs' best players in history. Considering that as payment for my article on being an American at a Souths game, I certainly couldn't complain. I had John Sattler's fractured jaw to keep me company on the long flight home.

CHAPTER 44
Parting Ways, Once Again

SEPTEMBER 20, 2014:

It was my last day in Australia. I woke up with a heavy feeling in my heart, not to mention a bad neck cramp. I barely ate anything at breakfast. I guess because I was feeling so blue over the prospect of leaving, yet again, that I had lost my appetite. It was such a beautiful day outside, but inside my heart, it was a dreary, overcast kind of day. I tried to squeeze in as much as I could in just a few hours; I had promised to have one last dinner with the Gotsis' later that night. I made a quick trip to Parramatta to make one last sweep at Peter Wynn's, just in case I had forgotten any extra Souths swag. Actually, I was hoping not, since I had so many red and green souvenirs. I had so many that I had to pack creatively so I could squeeze every last bunny into my bag. In fact, I was sitting on top of my suitcase the night before, desperately trying to seal it shut.

On the ride back, I watched the scenery of all the suburbs between Parramatta and Central. I was still an awe of how similar it looked to say, Queens or Nassau County when riding the Long Island Railroad on the way to Penn Station. I was really going to miss hearing the computerized voice on the train with an Aussie accent announcing stops. In fact, when the train pulled into Town Hall, I took a deep breath and sadly walked off the train as it left the platform. It always comes down to the little things that you tend to miss the most. In fact, as I reached the top of the escalator, I walked into BreadTop, this amazing Japanese bakery filled with all sorts of creative-looking carbohydrates. I bought about half a dozen pastries and saved them for the next morning while waiting for my flight. For the last few weeks, I had made regular visits to this Australian/Japanese boulangerie and had grown accustomed to its delectable goodies. I did, however, remain very wary of a pastry topped with tuna and egg. I wasn't going to miss that danger to olfactory senses but I did savor one of those pastries slowly and deliciously.

Instead of heading back to my hotel, I walked across Pyrmont Bridge toward the Australian Maritime Museum in Darling Harbour. I took one long, last look at the skyline of the CBD. I have to admit that I had grown fond of this skyline of steel and neon signs of Australian financial company logos. Nothing can compare to the skyline of Manhattan, and while I may be biased in saying that, the skyline of Sydney from Darling Harbour and Circular Quay is indeed quite close! Although there was a pastry in my stomach, I went for a scoop of gelato from a little stand by the Harbourside Mall. It was the one place in the city that served up a panna cotta-flavored gelato that always finished off a big meal. Why can't I get this in New York?!

At around 6:30 pm, the Gotsis family and I headed out for one last meal together. My choice for dinner was a tapas restaurant on Darling Harbour called Toros. If Sydney has taught me anything regarding the world of gastronomy, it's that you can find almost anything in this city. You would think that a city, even one as a big as Sydney, being so far away from every major western nation in Europe and the Americas would have limited access to a variety of dishes, save of course for some from the nearby Asian continent. Alas, many from the other side of the globe have made the long trek to this amazing city to lay their claim here and introduce the Aussies to cuisine that you'd otherwise have to fly twenty-four hours to experience. Surprisingly, the authenticity is quite extraordinary. I'm surprised that I am able to keep a tight figure and not come back looking like a bear with winter fat after months of hibernation. If I lived here, I'd turn into a foodie. A red and green foodie with a full tummy.

I introduced Isaac and Charlotte, Bill and Rachel's kids, to some of my favorite items from this place; I had dined here several times before. I spent dinner with my favorite family in Sydney. It felt just like I was back at Dolcissimo's or Millone's, only with Portuguese food instead of Italian. I was playfully shooing Isaac away from picking at my sofrito-smothered meatballs; they're just too good to share. I was, however, content to letting him sample my beef cheek and croquets. And just like that, it was like I was part of the family again. These outings with the Gotsis', I have to admit, are just one more reason I truly enjoy flying halfway around the world.

After finishing off nearly a dozen tapas and ice cream, I invited the family back to my hotel for one last goodbye. Inside my room, I had one last bit of business to take care off. I whipped out my poster which, after two weeks of transit through Sydney, was littered with autographs and signatures from fans and players alike. It was, however, missing the inking of the Gotsis family. I couldn't leave Sydney without having them give their contribution to my posters. Having the some of the Rabbitohs team members sign my poster was totally surreal. But Bill and Rachel's were probably the most heartfelt writings of anyone who inked my poster. I mean, yearbook quotes and sign-offs aren't this sincere and wonderful.

Down in the lobby, Rachel was getting ready to take the kids home. First off, she was changing them out of their clothes and into their pajamas. As I watched this adorable tableau unfold in front of everyone, Bill and I were talking to this nice family from India who were in Sydney on vacation. They said that they were from Goa in western India. I asked if they were from either Panaji or Vasco de Gama, the two largest cities in the tiny Indian state. Their eyebrows went up so high you'd think they were going to rise up to the ceiling like helium balloons. Bill wasted no time boasting about his American friend who had both a big brain and a proud love of Australian rugby league. I have to admit, I usually like to flaunt my geographical know-how to strangers whenever I go abroad. At least it shows to everyone outside America that we Yanks are knowledgeable about the world around us and that we take the time to learn. Also, I must admit, I get a real kick out of impressing people with how much I know about geography.

Once the kids were in their pajamas, Rachel and Bill slowly began their march to their car. We tearfully exchanged hugs; none more heartfelt than when Isaac hugged me and called me "Uncle Jah-wid." We bid farewell a second time and they promised me that they'd come to New York one day. I'm still saving a seat for Bill at the Meadowlands. Not to mention I would drive them across Long Island to my parents' summer home in the Hamptons.

SEPTEMBER 21. 2014:

The night my parents picked me up from JFK Airport was a night I shall never forget. I thought me leaving Sydney in the thrum of playoffs was sad enough. There was, however, one thing that topped my absence. My mom and dad dropped the bomb on me in the car: they told me that they had just sold our house in Rockville Centre. In just a few seconds, I saw my whole childhood flash before my eyes. It was as if time stood still. In just one fell swoop, my whole world came crashing down on me. I mean, I had just gotten back from an amazing odyssey in Australia and I was riding on an unbelievable high and it all came crashing down on me with one shocking piece of news.

For months leading up to my trip, there had been some rumors around my family that my parents were planning on selling their home in Long Island and moving into Manhattan. It was the only home I had ever known; I'm something of a sentimentalist. I had shrugged off these rumors and thought my sister, someone who is very savvy in real estate and interior design, had put this ridiculous idea into their heads. I wasn't even a quarter of a mile away from the Qantas terminal at JFK Airport when I found out what I had been dreading for a long time was actually happening: the Schnabl family was leaving Long Island for greyer pastures. I was so devastated that I totally lost my appetite. Even a full banquet at the diner couldn't alleviate my sadness. I had less than three months to get every last bit of my childhood packed up or thrown away.

Make fun of me if you dare, but this was a new surprise for me. I didn't know whether to cry or protest. I just felt that piece of heartache in my throat; I swallowed it hard, and I locked it up. The weird thing was that a few hours ago, I was really missing Sydney, especially since I spent some time fantasizing about me living along either the Hawkesbury or along the coast of Kiribilli. I mean, if I did live there, those would be my choices for where I would live. Well, that plus an apartment in Redfern for obvious reasons. But all that daydreaming disappeared once I learned I would have to say goodbye to the one home I had known for more than twenty-five years.

SEPTEMBER 26, 2014:

It was a quiet and warm morning, about a week after I had returned from my epic trip Down Under. The sky was slowly transitioning from darkness to dawn. I was waiting for the first train from Rockville Centre to Penn Station. This was the morning of the 2014 semi-final match. A chance for redemption after last year's loss to Manly after a blown lead by the Bunnies. This semi-final was no ordinary match. This was the Rabbitohs versus Roosters. Bunnies versus Chooks. Souths versus Easts. A classic rivalry tailor-made for the postseason. It wasn't the Grand Final, but it sure felt like it. The Australian that morning was, surprisingly, not as crowded as

I figured it would be; there were just under two dozen or so fans in attendance. Not the crowded subway car of fans that the Australian has during State of Origins, but at least I'd have plenty of room to jump up and down when the Bunnies won like I hoped they would.

Between how nervous I felt and the news of my family moving away from Long Island, I needed this win in the worst way possible. The Rabbitohs, however, needed this even more. They knew that if they couldn't win this crucial game, they would earn the terrible reputation for being perennial chokers; the only thing worse than losing a game would be losing to the Chooks.

The game began on an ominous note when fullback Mitchell Pearce would score the initial try in the first five minutes when he put the ball right in between the goal posts. One quick conversion by James Maloney and the score was 6–0 in favor of the Roosters. Not the start we were hoping for. Things only got worse when on the next play, Anthony Minichiello robbed Greg Inglis of the ball when he caught a punted kick from inside the 10-meter line and effortlessly scored the second consecutive try for the Roosters as well as a conversion by Maloney. Seven minutes into the game and it was 12–0 in favor of the Roosters. At that point, I was ready to go downstairs to the bathroom and explode in a fit of rage. Time was on our side, but our initial performance was embarrassing to say the least.

Madge must have flashed the team an angry glare from high atop the field because in just a few minutes, the team finally woke up and delivered their first try in the twentieth minute courtesy of Lote Tuquri; a narrow try that went up to the instant replay to decide the fate of Tuquri. Adam Reynolds would kick the conversion and we denied the Roosters a shutout with a new score of 12–6. With that try, I was able to relax for the moment. My eyes darted back and forth between the sides of the TV just waiting for us to charge up the field or hope one of the Roosters' players was sin-binned.

Ten minutes later, Alex Johnston gave us a huge sigh of relief when he and Adam Reynolds tied up the game at 12 all. Still, a tie game didn't do much to alleviate the pressure. One thing that certainly didn't calm me down was when it looked like Daniel Tupou dove in for a try just a minute before half-time. As the try went under review, I was praying that it would be denied. Under further review, a double knock-on happened when the ball bounced off of Lote Tuquri; the try was denied and everyone in the bar breathed a sigh of relief. The halftime siren blared and the score was deadlocked. I could only imagine that Madge was screaming at his boys in the sheds after allowing the Roosters to score on two back-to-back tries in the opening minutes. Well, whatever Madge did in the sheds must have worked because the second half was all about the Bunnies.

In the opening minutes of the second half, the Rabbitohs worked hard to not disappoint their fans for a third consecutive time. And so, at the forty-forth minute, Ben Te'o gave the Bunnies their third try and Reynolds brought us into the lead for the first time as the score read 18–12. Now we had our confidence back and I could breathe a sigh of relief. Perhaps another try or two would put us over the top. At the fifty-second minute, hesitant Bunnies were told to play on after a questionable "play the ball" call, which must have thrown the Roosters off. Greg Inglis easily stopped across the line and finally gave us his first try of the game which he followed up with his signature goanna lizard crawl. A kick from Reynolds put us two tries ahead with a score of 24–12.

The smile on my face began to grow, as did those of the other footy fans at the bar. But GI wasn't through yet, as he would give us his second consecutive try at the sixty-fifth minute when he caught a beautiful kick from Reynolds and put it down right behind the goal posts. Rabbitohs were leading

30–12. And at that moment, I was bouncing up and down. Two tries by GI? An eighteen-point lead? Pinch me, I must have been dreaming! But the ticking clock was a sobering reminder that there were fifteen minutes left. And as I learned bitterly last year, a lot can happen in a little amount of time as I was still reminded of that blown lead from the Manly game. I was hoping the Souths would continue to push ahead and play as if they were still behind or tied and not comfortably sit on a cushy lead. Reynolds gave us a penalty kick at the seventy-first minute and we had a 32–12 lead.

Any moment, I was about ready to get on top of the bar and start singing Botany Road. In fact, I could just hear it in the stands at ANZ Stadium as I saw Souths fans on the edge of their seat waiting so long throughout the game to start their traditional victory song. However, it was nothing compared to the wait endured by lifelong Souths fans that had been waiting forty-three years for a semi-final win. But, as quickly as we made those two tries by GI, the Roosters got two additional tries in the last three minutes; one by Aidan Guerra and the other by Minichiello. You might say we either got lazy or probably overconfident; a couple of consolation tries, perhaps? I knew that would make Madge mad. Did we learn nothing from Manly's four consecutive tries?

And lo, it came to pass as the final siren blared across Olympic Park that every red and green fan finally got to hear the most joyful phrase they had been waiting more than four decades to hear: "the Rabbitohs are going to the Grand Final!" Now, it was up to the Bunnies to see if they could upgrade that phrase to "The Rabbitohs have won the Grand Final!" While the red and green faithful in Sydney jumped up and down in the stands, I was screaming at the top of my lungs inside the bar. I was high-fiving every last Souths supporter inside and giving Matty a hug from across the bar. Just like that, that awful memory of Manly's victory from last year was expunged from my head. Redemption was sweet, indeed. We had to wait one more day to find out who our opponents would be. It turned out that we'd be facing the Canterbury-Bankstown Bulldogs after they were victorious over Penrith 18–12.

It was like a scene out of Watership Down: El-Hrairah against Rowsby Woof. Bunnies versus Doggies. The wily hare against the snarling mongrel. This was a sports story that was just made for the history books. And to think that fifteen years ago, thanks to a dirty deal by Rupert Murdoch, News Ltd., and the Australian Rugby League, the Rabbitohs were thrown into the dustbin of history as their beloved club was terminated. Thanks to the outpouring of support from fans, club legends, and the likes of Russell Crowe and Peter Holmes a Court, the Rabbitohs went from darkness, to spooners, to being on the verge of their first Premiership since 1971. I could not have been more proud of this team; their zero-to-hero story, in my opinion, would be the envy of American sports writers. I would not be surprised if ninety-nine out of one hundred Aussies would be wearing red and green out of solidarity for this club that had been waiting almost forever for a Premiership.

On my way out of the bar, I happily told Matty that I'd be back good and early for the Grand Final. There was no way I was missing this one. This was going to be the year of the Bunny. And after all the Rabbitohs magic that I had fallen in love with Down Under, a Grand Final win would cap off the perfect fairy-tale ending to an amazing season.

CHAPTER 45
21 at Dawn

OCTOBER 5, 2014:

The alarm rang inside my hotel room. It was 3:30 a.m. I threw myself out of my small bed on 37th Street where I was holed up all night long. I knew that riding the train in from Rockville Centre would be a ridiculous idea seeing how the game was on earlier than normal. In this case, I had booked myself a room for one night at the Holiday Inn just a block away from The Australian. Without missing a second, I threw on my jersey and hummed "Glory Glory to South Sydney" while I painted my face red and green. This would be a morning that I would either cherish for years to come, or one that would haunt me for years to come.

I have always been excited for champion matches in professional sports before. I was absolutely on pins and needles the night the New York Giants defeated the New England Patriots in Super Bowl XLII, thus ending the Pats' undefeated season. During the Rangers postseason, I typically pace back and forth so much, I break into a cold sweat. And when I was on my varsity basketball team in high school, I treated every game like it was a make-or-break one. This game, however, felt different.

I cannot remember the last time I put this much emotional investment into a team. I mean, here I was inside a Holiday Inn in Midtown, awake at 3:30 a.m., where I had booked a room just for the purpose of walking a block to a bar that in a few minutes would be stuffed to the gills with dozens of excited Aussies. When in professional sports have I ever dedicated this much to a particular team? I may have only been waiting a year for the Bunnies to make it this far, but I knew that thousands of miles away, I had scores of friends who had been waiting decades for this. They needed this way more than I did. I also knew that at this moment, Bill and Isaac were at that very game. I had seen a photo of them on Facebook where they had their faces painted in red and green, looking like a couple of rabid Rabbits. Now there's one cool dad! For a brief moment, I felt rather sad that I was not at ANZ Stadium. I had only left Australia two weeks prior, but in hindsight, had I known we'd go this far, I'd have booked an additional two weeks at the Four Points. Then again, I'm no soothsayer. Alas, I had no time for second thoughts or regrets. I had bigger things to worry about; for instance, getting to the Australian in time.

With my face painted and my nerves ready, I grabbed my Rabbitohs flag and camcorder. I stepped out the door and into the frigid air in the wee hours of the morning. It was pretty eerie seeing Midtown with hardly any cars on the road. I stopped to think what on Earth a cop on duty would say if he saw this red and green person strolling along through the streets looking like he was marching in a parade? Thankfully, my walk to the Australian was uneventful. With the hums of "Glory Glory" echoing in my head, I opened the door to the party.

I thought there'd be about a hundred or so fans there; roughly the same crowd that shows up for State of Origins every summer. I realized how wrong I was as I stepped into what felt like a Tokyo subway car at rush hour! It was packed with fans in a cacophonous orgy of cheers and swears. There weren't dozens or scores of fans, but rather hundreds! Balloons hung from the ceiling and from the bar; red and green for Souths fans and blue and white for Canterbury fans.

Thankfully, there were far more Rabbitohs fans than there were Doggies supporters. Then again, I wouldn't be surprised if some undecided fans were going with the Rabbitohs out of either solidarity or pity since we hadn't won a Premiership in forty-three years, while Canterbury's last appearance was in 2012 when they lost to Melbourne. I had read on Facebook and Twitter that most Australian newspapers and news sources were supporting the Souths for that very same reason; a red and green victory would be the emotional crescendo that would capture the hearts of almost every Aussie, whether a Souths supporter or not.

With that much support, we went from being the typical underdogs to the heavy favorites. I just hoped the pressure wasn't getting to the boys. I myself tried not to get too confident, but I just couldn't help but be so optimistic. There was some good news in our favor: Bulldogs captain Michael Ennis was absent from the lineup due to a broken foot he suffered during playoffs; the Doggies would be playing without a full deck. But it wasn't all in good news for us. Isaac Luke, Bully himself, was suspended from the match after he delivered a dangerous throw to Sonny Bill Williams in the preliminary-final against the Roosters. In his absence, Apisai Koroisau would be in as hooker; talk about big shoes to fill.

Just before the game, Russell Crowe stepped out onto the field. Former Rabbitohs captain and footy legend Bob McCarthy was presented a very special item. It was a big bell, resembling an old type of bell used by town criers in colonial days or by old-timey schoolmarms. Before the days of jumbotrons and loudspeakers, bells like this one were used to symbolically kick off a match. Instead of asking fans "Are You Ready for Some Footy?!" it was more like "Hear ye, Hear ye! Who doth ready to watch Souths and Easts tear each other a sunder?!" Hey, it does have a nice ring to it. Sorry, I couldn't help myself. Crowe had bought the bell for A$42,000 at a fundraising event back in 1999 and had given it back to the original owner, Albert Cliff, who later passed away in 2005 at the age of 101. Russell had promised Albert that the bell would not be rung again until the Souths were allowed back into the NRL after they were barred from the league following the controversial Super League decision with News Corp.

The Bunnies came back in 2002, only after endless lobbying, protests, and many bitter battles fought in and out of courtrooms. Crowe decided that the bell would not be rung again until the Souths made it into the Grand Final. For years, the bell sat silently with Crowe in Woolloomooloo until that glorious night. Bob McCarthy rang that beautiful bell in front of a sellout crowd of 83,833 fans inside ANZ Stadium. This was such a cool moment because it was yet another example of just how sentimental the Rabbitohs were and how much they take tradition seriously among their fans and elders. To those not in the know, it was an old, antique bell. To the red and green faithful, it was a priceless piece of history. It was almost as if Crowe and McCarthy had been waiting for years to break out that bell, but it still probably paled in comparison to waiting for a Rabbitohs Premiership.

I squeezed a spot at the end of the bar where I found Kate Rosalie Richardson and Shane with their Rabbitohs gear on. We all stood side by side in the small ocean of fans that filled the pub. We watched our beloved Bunnies take the field first; an odd choice, seeing how they finished above the Bulldogs on the ladder for the season but had elected to trot out first as a way to soak up the atmosphere of the stadium. I screamed my lungs out as I watched good ol' Reggie lead the boys into what would be their greatest battle yet. And right on cue, the Bulldogs marched out of the sheds and The Australian fell under an ear-splitting "Boo!" What followed was a loud rendition of "Advance Australia Fair," Australia's national anthem. It was an unusual moment since the national anthem isn't commonly played during NRL games, outside of certain events like the first game of the season or the ANZAC game, whereas it is practically ubiquitous here in America.

A special game like this one called for a special occasion

for the anthem to be played. The opening was big and brassy like an orchestra; everyone at ANZ Stadium and inside the Australian belted it out, including yours truly who had pretty much made himself into a bona fide Aussie. It would have been fun if they snuck in "Waltzing Matilda," just for good measure. Maybe next time. As lovely as that was, I was hoping that we'd be hearing "Botany Road" and "Glory Glory" by the match's end. I could hear my heart racing a mile a minute.

At precisely 4:35 a.m. local time in New York, the Bulldogs began the Grand Final with the opening kick. Less than ten seconds later, the first big moment of the Grand Final happened when Sam Burgess carried the ball for only a few meters before making facial contact with prop James Graham, who was acting as captain in Ennis' absence. Burgess' face, specifically his right eye socket and cheek, crashed into Graham's face, and suddenly, the whole bar gasped on cue and then went silent. Sam simply played the ball forward and slowly rose to his feet, gently touching the wounded area. A few seconds later, the camera immediately cut to a horrified Julie Burgess in the stands as she watched her muscular son nurse a potentially serious injury.

This couldn't be happening. The first tackle of the biggest game of the year and it looked like Slammin' Sam would be out early. Nothing comes easy when you're a Rabbitohs fan, much less someone on the team. But as I saw Sam slowly get back to work on the field while giving a heads up to the ref in regards his freshly bludgeoned face, one thing came to my mind: John Sattler. Yup, this looked eerily similar to what happened in 1970, only with less blood everywhere. Sattler played seventy-seven minutes with a serious jaw injury and it looked like Sam Burgess just might best that record. If there was a moment for history to repeat itself in our favor, then this was the night to do so. Well, at least I hoped it would be.

Or perhaps, Sam Burgess would pull off another improbable

sports injury moment from 1970: Willis Reed. Months before Sattler's jaw and the Bunnies Premiership win over Manly, the New York Knicks were playing the Los Angeles Lakers in the NBA Championship series. In game 5 in New York, Reed took a tough fall after attempting to make a basket. Reed managed to get up, but a leg injury forced him out of the game. New York managed to win that game, but game 6 was played without Reed, and the Lakers took that game and evened up the series. Game 7 in New York had Reed limping out onto the court just minutes before tipoff. He managed to score the first two baskets but didn't go on to score another point for the rest of the game; New York would go on to win and capture their first NBA championship. In the aftermath of it all, Reed was awarded the MVP of the series.

A few months later, Sattler muscled through an injury of his own and won the Clive Churchill Medal, the award given to the most valuable player of the NRL Premiership. Mind blown! All I had to do was keep saying to myself that this was the second coming of Sattler and I'd have nothing to worry about.

Around the sixth minute, Lote Tuquri looked like he would give the Bunnies their first try, which sent the bar into an uproar. Upon further review, however, his try was denied after it was revealed in the instant replay that Adam Reynolds committed an illegal high tackle on Bulldogs fullback Sam Perrett. The big, red "NO TRY" that flashed on the screen zapped all the jubilation out of us. The score remained zero all and it didn't do much to alleviate Sam's injury.

For the next few minutes, everyone in the bar looked like they were in the middle of the worst kind of stress of their lives. You know how when a woman is giving birth and the husband is pacing outside the delivery room? Or how about when someone is getting ready to skydive? Yeah, it was kind of like that. Everyone was waiting impatiently for something to happen. Well, at the nineteenth minute, it happened. The

Rabbitohs were awarded a penalty off an infringement from Bulldogs forward Josh Jackson, which brought the Bunnies thirty meters away from the try line. Luke Keary passed to Kirisome Auva'a, who threw an overhead pass to Alex Johnston, who delivered the first try of the Grand Final in the corner. The bar went nuts and the enthusiasm returned in a big way. Reynolds, unfortunately, missed the conversion, which didn't sit well with us; we needed every point possible. Still, it felt good to see us strike first and have a lead.

Around the twenty-fifth minute, Greg Inglis delivered one of the best runs all season; one that hadn't been seen since his juggernaut run against Brisbane in round 8 during the ANZAC game. He fielded the ball from a kick and began his charge upfield that went sixty meters untouched before he slipped out of bounds, ending what could have been an amazing Grand Final try. It did, however, put pressure on Canterbury. The Rabbitohs were awarded a penalty when Bulldogs forward Dale Finucane was penalized for hands in the play-the-ball area, and Adam Reynolds opted for a penalty goal. Reynolds made up for his early missed conversion and gave the Rabbitohs an additional two points; the Rabbitohs went up 6–0.

And just like that, the halftime siren blared and everyone inside the Australian breathed a collective sigh of relief. Granted, the score wasn't as high as we had hoped for, but the fact that we kept Canterbury scoreless this whole time was enough for me to applaud thunderously. I used the halftime to rush downstairs to hit the head and carouse with all the red and green fans inside the bar. I was showing off my Rabbitohs tattoos. Even though they were all rub-on, everyone thought I looked just awesome. In fact, it didn't surprise me how many mistook me for an Aussie with all the gear I was sporting.

By the time the second half came on, I was running scenarios in my head over how the Souths would come out victorious in this game. Best-case scenario, we'd keep Canterbury scoreless the whole game and make it a one-sided victory as we scored try after try. Or, to make things really nerve-wracking, I was worried the Bunnies would be playing defense for the duration of the game. It made me think of last year's debacle against Manly; defense seemed to be our Achilles Heel, but the first half of this game showed everyone how far we had come. Still, I was expecting Madge to encourage the boys to play every second as if they were trailing. There was never a good time in footy to run out the clock, no matter how ahead you were.

The Rabbitohs kicked off the second half with an amazing kick, which Canterbury's five-eighth Josh Reynolds caught, but he dropped the ball behind him; unfortunately, there was no knock-on. This did, however, put us within striking distance of a possible try from twenty meters away. At the forty-first minute, the Rabbitohs began an impressive drive which began with Adam Reynolds handing the ball off to George Burgess. After getting tackled just ten meters shy of the line, George Burgess handed it off to Adam Reynolds and the younger Burgess Brother, Thom. Unfortunately, he was tackled just five meters shy of the line. Next, John Sutton unloaded it to Kyle Turner, but went down just five meters away, again. The most exciting moment came when Luke Keary handed it off to John Sutton, who looked like he was going to score a big try after a brief charge up; he too was tackled just shy of the line. George and Thom, along with Jason Clark, tried to get it back with a few fancy passes but, alas, went down on fourth tackle. Lastly, on fifth tackle, Reynolds put a grubber kick on the ball as he tried to run for it in the end zone and put pressure on it. Unfortunately, he kicked it right into Bulldogs center, Josh Morris, but he was tackled in the end zone, which resulted in us getting a line dropout.

In spite of getting a second chance at another amazing drive, which including getting awarded six more tackles after the Bulldogs touched the ball while still in play, the Souths did something that I hated: they dropped the ball when Sam Burgess failed to catch a pass from Adam Reynolds on second tackle, which resulted in an ill-fated knock-on. Bad news for us Bunnies, but it gave Canterbury a scrum feed from their 10-meter line.

At the forty-seventh minute, South Sydney had the ball less than ten meters from inside their own line as they tried to move it as far up as they could. However, the worst error of our game came when Dylan Walker dropped it just five meters from the Souths line and it was picked up by Bulldogs interchange, Dale Finucane. Dropping the ball was bad enough, but dropping it so close to our try line was humiliating, if not infuriating, given the fact we gave Canterbury an easy chance at a go-ahead try.

At the forty-ninth minute, on fifth tackle, James Graham passed to Josh Reynolds, who kicked ahead toward Tony Williams at the right-hand side of the posts. He put the ball down on the line, which went up to the video refs for an instant replay. I was clenching my fists and praying that it would be a "NO TRY" in red letters on the screen. I held my breath and awaited the decision. The video refs put up the green light—TRY. Ugh. Sure enough, Trent Hodkinson made an easy conversion and the score was deadlocked at 6 All. That's when you could collectively hear everyone's knees knocking above the noise of the TVs. You could cut the tension with a knife. Except for a handful of fans in blue and white, I could see the look of pure anxiety on all the Souths fans' faces. Some looked like they were going to throw up, while others were struggling to just stand up on two feet.

With the game all tied up, it was only a matter of time before someone scored to unhinge everyone's nerves. Around the fifty-fifth minute, Apasai Koroisau, receiving a pass from Sam Burgess, made a brief surge up the field after finding an opening from dummy-half. He was brought down on third tackle just outside the 30-meter line. Luke Keary passed it to Chris McQueen, who then offloaded it to George Burgess, who was about twenty meters shy of the Canterbury line. That's when I saw George charging up toward the line like a stampeding elephant, or rather a gigantic Australian Bunny Rabbit; he delivered a beautiful try between the goal posts and the tie was broken. George's try could have been met with a standing ovation from the NFL crowd; he just knocked down several Canterbury players before slamming that ball down for the try like a gigantic running back or blocker. His fellow Bunnies met him in the end zone for a celebratory hug; the cameras cut to a bruised and puffy-looking Sam hugging George. Aw, cherished moments!

I quickly looked for someone to hug in the bar, so I hugged the closest person I could find. I didn't know who he was, but after the Bunnies took the lead with that monster of a try, I just needed to hold someone. Deep down, I like to think that George made that awesome try for his big brother as payback for what Canterbury did to Sam on the first tackle. Blood certainly does run thicker than water for both the Burgess Brothers and the Bunnies. A converted kick made the score 12–6 in favor of the mighty red and green and the entire bar erupted in a big cheer that was nearly orgasmic. Meanwhile, over at ANZ Stadium, an instant replay showed Madge in the coach's box jumping up and down in joy. It wasn't unusual to see Madge explode. This time, however, it was for all the right reasons.

At the sixty-first minute, we had a chance to up the score when Adam Reynolds was given a 41-meter penalty kick thanks to a penalty from James Graham after he shoulder-tackled Dave Tyrell. Unfortunately, he missed, and right on cue, the whole bar groaned. If I had to compare that awful sound to something, it was like when the audience on *The Price is Right* collectively groans when a contestant makes an awful bid on something, or when a stand-up comic bombs on stage and the audience is clearly annoyed. Now picture that sound and multiply the volume ten-fold. Thankfully, our groaning was short-lived when the Bunnies were awarded another penalty after Bulldogs prop Aiden Tolman committed a ruck infringement, where he had his hands on the ball of a tackled player, George Burgess. Reynolds redeemed himself with a two-point kick and the Bunnies took a 14–6 lead with seventeen minutes left. At that point, I was able to breathe a huge sigh of relief once I saw the new score. We had a modest eight-point lead over the Bulldogs and there was less than sixteen minutes to play. If we could just keep Canterbury away from the line long enough and perhaps notch one more try or penalty goal, we could close this forty-three-year book and write the happy ending we so have been wanting to pen. Still, this was no time to get cocky and play defense. The pressure was indeed mounting for both sides, however.

The Bulldogs looked ferocious in the sixty-eighth minute when James Graham tackled Souths prop Dave Tyrell (who had played in all twenty-seven games throughout the season) with a brutal head clash, which knocked poor Tyrell to the ground. The clock was stopped as the medics took the field and carried him off in a stretcher. As if Sam's facial tackle in the beginning wasn't enough, now this. In addition to his injury, the referee had ruled that Tyrell had lost possession of the ball and rewarded Canterbury with a scrum feed. Not once, but twice we gave Canterbury possession; first because of Tyrell and the second time because of a goal-line dropout thanks to a fumble on our behalf. If the Bulldogs were looking to enrage the Rabbitohs, well, I think that did it.

Just before the sixty-eighth minute, Thomas Burgess was put on report for an illegal shoulder tackle. I guess you could say that the redux of Sam's face via Tyrell's face clash with Graham really did fire us up. Still, an on-report tackle from one of the Burgess Brothers was not the kind of firing up we wanted, even with an eight-point lead and twelve minutes to go. One of the biggest scares of the game came when Canterbury was about twenty meters from the line and began an aggressive drive for the try with about eleven minutes to play. On fifth tackle, Josh Reynolds kicked it up and everyone held their breath. I think I saw everyone's pupils in the Australian dilate as they watched a possible game-changing try hang in the air. Thankfully, the ball landed in front of Lote Tuquri then bounced behind him into the hands of Sam Burgess, who unloaded it to Greg Inglis. However, when the referee blew the whistle, it was ruled a knock-on and Canterbury was awarded a restart. Sure enough, we would have a case of déjà vu when, just before the seventy-first minute, we stopped Canterbury from scoring, but in the process of our aggressive defense, we awarded them yet another goal-line dropout courtesy of Greg Inglis. Suffice it to say, I was ready to start chewing off my knuckles.

After what felt like an eternity of waiting to get possession again, Bulldogs second row Tony Williams attempted a flick pass in midair but Kirisome Auva'a got a hand on the ball, knocking it backwards. We all hoped that a player in red and green would get a hand on that. Thankfully, Apasai Koroisau was that player who robbed Josh Reynolds of a high shot in the process of grabbing the crucial ball from inside our 20-meter line. The Souths were on the attack once again. Not only that, but we were awarded a penalty after Josh Reynolds was put on report after it was revealed in the instant replay that he committed a high tackle on Auva'a's neck.

Ray Warren, one of the commentators for the broadcast said about the last eight minutes of play, "*Souths fans know they are only eight minutes from Glory Glory to South Sydney. I think they're rocking and rolling, but I've got a feeling that the finishing line might just be close enough for them.*" Some fans inside the Australian looked like they were in either a fetal position or were too nervous to rock and roll. At that point, I began nervously watching the clock tick downward, hoping it would speed up.

With seven minutes to go, Adam Reynolds, on fifth tackle, put up a high kick to the left and Chris McQueen leapt high to bat the ball back to Greg Inglis, who gently punted it. The ball bounced high over the head of Bulldogs winger, Corey Thompson, and Alex Johnston overran it as Thompson landed on top of him. From my perspective, the ball bounced in the upper-left-hand corner of the end zone and I couldn't see if it was still inbound; a referee was standing in front of the camera. That's when Auva'a was there and narrowly forced it down with a few inches to spare using both hands. I couldn't see him putting pressure on the ball and I was taken aback for just a second. When I saw several of his teammates hugging him in the end zone, I figured that it was good news and that we had scored. The try would be left up to the video refs but everyone seemed confident that we were about to take a big lead.

Once the instant replay came on, I got a much better look at Auva'a's try and it looked pretty legit, not to mention a real close call. He pounced on that like a cat on a mouse. He and the ball were practically a foot away from the upper-left-hand corner of the end zone. But would the video refs be swayed? Everyone waited nervously as the "Decision Pending" signal went up on the screen. We all held our collective breaths and the three magical capital letters came up...TRY! It was now 18–6 in favor of the Souths.

But it wasn't done yet. Adam Reynolds stepped forward for the conversion. He knew that the extra two points, at this stage in the game, would almost seal the deal for the Bunnies. After all, Reynolds hadn't been perfect in goals all night but he was making a big difference in clutch time. Announcer Peter Sterling summed up the collective feelings of concerned Souths fans by saying, "*It's only two converted tries, but if Reynolds converts this, they win.*" Reynolds wound up from outside the 20-meter line with Reggie Rabbit a few feet away watching him nervously; I saw the big bunny jogging in position, looking like the pressure was building up inside him. Well, he must have given Reynolds some good luck because Adam smashed that ball beautifully between the uprights and put the Bunnies up 20–6. That Provands-Summons trophy was starting to look more and more visible.

With only five minutes to play, one would think that the Bunnies would maybe try to put a one-point golden kick through the uprights to seal the deal. But in the last few minutes, that would not be the case. Nope, not by a longshot. After Canterbury momentarily regained possession, they were about ten to twenty meters away from a possible try, which we feared would give them a huge dose of confidence with only five minutes left. On second tackle, Josh Reynolds kicked it up, hoping they'd come away with a try. Instead, it was caught by none other than Alex Johnston, who ran with it up to the 20-meter line for the restart. Johnston, in classic fashion, sprinted with that ball up to the 40-meter line before being taken down. With six tackles to work with, our next assault on Canterbury began.

Up in the booth, the announcers were talking about how Souths fans had been waiting for this for forty-three years and were starting to get all gushy with praise for how long we have wanted this. Down on the field however, the Bunnies were playing as if it was the first five minutes of the match. John Sutton kicked ahead on third tackle and one of Canterbury's players ran right into the left uprights of the goal posts in comical fashion. The ball suddenly bounced to the right on-goal, where Adam Reynolds pounced on it and notched up another try. I was screaming "REYNOLDS! REYNOLDS!" channeling my inner Warren Smith from 2012. Sure enough, right after the score went up 24–6 on the screen, I shouted, "You can take me now, I have seen it all! I have seen everything!" I was jumping so high, you would think I could have launched myself onto the bar counter. And just like the game-winning moment from 2012, the entire team rushed to the sidelines to embrace the fans.

And speaking of embracing, after the cameras cut back from the instant replay of the try, we saw Greg Inglis putting his enormous arms over an emotional Sam Burgess as they walked back onto the field, looking like they were ready to cry. Madge was so psyched he blew out of the coaches' box to be with his team on the field as he hopped over seat railings and fans to be with his boys. The sheer magnitude of what was happening was finally sinking in: this team of red and green were about to put an end to forty-three years of heartbreak.

Greg Inglis put his fists up and threw his arms in the air, trying to get the already happy crowd even more excited while the announcers brought up the three year period when the Souths were barred from the NRL, which only added to the emotional magnitude of the moment.

Reynolds easily converted his own try and the Bunnies went up again 26–6. And right then and there, we were treated to what may be the most memorable and, dare I say, magical moment of the Grand Final. Sam Burgess, just bursting with emotion, got down on one knee and began weeping as he tried to hold his face up. For a second, he buried his face into his left hand, not wanting anyone to see him cry, especially with his face all battered and bruised from earlier. Still on one knee and with his eyes full of tears, Sam reminded me of a young boy whose team had just won the big game while his parents were watching him from the sidelines. I could only imagine the full range of joy and pride inside the massive British Bunny.

I like to think that his father, along with little Bailon, were looking down on him from heaven and watching his four sons and Julie and saying to God, "That's my boy down there!"

Frankly, I too was verklempt and felt a big lump in my throat from that one image. It reminded me of when Jim Craig, the goalie from the 1980 "Miracle on Ice" Olympic hockey team, won the gold medal and was skating around looking for his dad in the stands with the American flag draped across his back like a cape.

You would think that would be the perfect ending to a monumental game. Alas, there was still one minute left and the Bunnies decided to give their dedicated fans one last hurrah. Appropriately enough, Russell Crowe was in the stands, and the Bunnies looked to take a page out of *Gladiator* and ask the crowd, "*Are You Not Entertained?*" While Madge paced back and forth in front of Reggie, Luke Keary made a dash through the defense from thirty meters inside before passing the ball inside to Greg Inglis. And that's when Greg Inglis gave us one big finale in which he dove into the left corner of the end zone with a beautiful try accompanied by his signature goanna crawl in jubilant celebration. "And the goanna crawls!" I cried out. I watched happily as the team piled on top of one another even as Inglis' try went up to the video ref to see if Keary's pass wasn't a forward pass; it wasn't. The try counted though, and the Bunnies went up 30–6 as I watched Madge and Reggie happily hug each other. Reggie even pointed to Madge in front of the cameras like a hype man showing off his boss!

With only a few seconds left, the conversion attempt was given to Sam Burgess, who only narrowly missed it, just barely grazing the left upright with a good kick. Still, a touching way to go out on a high note, as it would be his last touch of the ball in rugby league before heading off to Bath in Union with the hope that he'd be back in the red and green very soon. And as the countdown to zero ticked away, right on cue, the Bunnies fans inside the bar broke into "Botany Road." It felt as if I was sitting side by side inside the stadium. Final score: South Sydney Rabbitohs, 30; Canterbury-Bankstown

Bulldogs, 6. The streak was over. The Rabbitohs had won their 21st Premiership.

In the medal presentation ceremony, the Clive Churchill Medal, named in honor of former South Sydney coach and captain, went to the most valuable player of the game. No surprise, Sam Burgess was the winner. He deserved it after playing on both adrenaline and sheer guts, not to mention enduring a broken cheekbone and drawing comparisons with John Sattler after he played through seventy-seven minutes of the 1970 Grand Final with a "gate-swinging" jaw.

The medal was presented to him from Joyce Churchill, wife of the late, great Rabbitohs captain and coach, all decked out with her late husband's red and green porkpie hat. When Sam got down and wept and showed the true love of both the game and his fellow Bunnies, I'd say that it couldn't have happened to a more deserving fellow. He was as real and genuine as when I introduced myself to him at the Oval less than a month before. If there was ever a model athlete to look up to and emulate, even if you weren't a rugby player, Sam Burgess was definitely the man, as were his brothers who tearfully joined him on the field with mum Julie. The win was not just a perfect fairytale ending for the magical season the Bunnies had, but it was a beautiful, if not bittersweet, swan song for Sam to go out on before his foray into rugby union on the other side of the globe. If Sam could notch up a premiership win with Bath and add to that a Rugby World Cup win with the English squad, he'd probably be for rugby what Pele was to soccer. But win or not, I'd always see him as the smiling, bruised Bunny from England whom I hoped would be back in the red and green jumper soon.

The pomp and circumstance of the award ceremony was filled with all sorts of memorable moments that could have given any Super Bowl moment a run for its money. You had Michael Maguire getting a Gatorade bath, and Russell Crowe trying hard to hold back the tears on the field. Can you imagine all the hardships and close calls he must have endured when he made his ownership stake in the team all those years ago? Well, it finally paid off for him in a big way. I couldn't help but wonder what he was relishing more: his Oscar win from *Gladiator* or celebrating a Premiership with the Souths?

By the end of the ceremony, John Sutton, the captain, hoisted the Provands-Summons trophy high in the air in what was easily the biggest show of pride that I have seen on an athlete in years. It was like the last scene in *Invictus* where Francois Pienaar lifted the Webb Ellis Cup in South Africa or when Mark Messier happily shook the Stanley Cup when the New York Rangers won in 1994. He was smiling so hard from lifting that thing that I followed suit; I smiled so much that my jaw was almost paralyzed with joy. The flames shot up from behind them and red and green confetti littered the green on ANZ Stadium. It wasn't a dream, it was real. Just before leaving the bar, I met up with Kate and Shane and we posed for a victory photo.

As I got ready to leave, time seemed to stand still. I began to take stock of everything from the moment I discovered the Bunnies in Alice Springs, to my winning the trip to Australia in 2013, to my meeting with the Souths organization, and all culminating with one of the greatest sporting matches that I have had the privilege of seeing. And I realized that later that day, I was going to a Giants game at the Meadowlands. How could I sit through an NFL game when I just watched a team break a forty-three year losing streak? I was at a loss for words. All I could muster as I headed back to the hotel was this: "Thank You, Reggie!"

CHAPTER 46
From South Sydney, With Love...

In the weeks following the Grand Final, I received a glorious bounty of red and green gifts from my adopted Australian family members. For starters, I got copy after copy of *Rugby League Weekly*, *Big League*, and various publications detailing the amazing saga of one of the greatest sports stories in Australia. Unsurprisingly, Sam Burgess and his battered face made most of those covers. In addition, many of those magazines all came with free posters of the entire squad celebrating their big win on the field; naturally, I had every one of them laminated and taped above my bed. It wasn't just the publications that I loved, but the fact that some of those packages came personalized with very heartfelt messages handwritten on a little note tucked away inside the parcel. Forget sealed with a kiss, this was sealed with a "G'day!"

A sweet couple from North Sydney named Bel and Sam McKean sent me a small care package that came complete with articles, stickers, facemasks, and a hand-knit scarf. Another one of my favorite gifts I received was a collection of handmade decals from an artist named Sam Aretem, a native of Bankstown. He was a Bulldogs fan by nature, but on social media he was responsible for all the colorful illustrations and caricatures depicting the results of all the weekly NRL matches. Sam Aretem, or *Aretem Art*, as he was known online, was someone I became a big fan of over the course of the season; whenever the Rabbitohs would win a match, I'd always look forward to his comical drawings depicting a gigantic rabbit devouring our freshly beaten opponents. In addition to art, he also customized his own decals and stickers. He was most kind enough to send me a collection of Rabbitohs premiership stickers that I wasted no time slapping on the rear of my car.

One night, when I was coming back from Manhattan, I found a folded piece of paper under the windshield wipers of my car in the station parking lot. Naturally, I assumed it was a parking ticket and I was thoroughly annoyed. That is, until I began to read what was inked on that piece of paper:

OCTOBER 19, 2014:

I met up with this Long Island Bunny named Tom Cawte just a few days later at a diner for some late-night coffee and chatting about the Rabbitohs and the Grand Final. He was a doctor working in Rockville Centre, of all places. What are the odds that I'd find a Rabbitohs fan—an Aussie transplant mind you—just a stone's throw from my backyard?

OCTOBER 10, 2014:

Not too long after the Grand Final win, I attended New York Comic-Con. Just like my recent nerd-a-palooza in Sydney on Glebe Island, I wore my Rabbitohs jersey and made damn sure every costumed character and fanboy/fangirl knew my red and green swagger. While combing the floor, the darndest thing happened when I ran into none other than the same Aussie bloke from Oz Comic-con. I knew it was him because I was scoping out the regulars when I overheard "Hey, Rabbitohs!" coming from behind a forest of heads. Sure enough, there he was. We Bunnies sure look out for one another.

I thought that was the freakiest thing that could have happened that day. Boy, was I in for a shocker. About two hours later, I ran into voice-acting legend and one of my childhood idols, Billy West, the man behind such cartoons like "Ren & Stimpy," "Futurama," "Doug," "Histeria!" and the "Red M&M." He was rather intrigued by my outfit, thinking I was some character he couldn't identify. I presented myself as an ambassador for the South Sydney Rabbitohs, the oldest and most winning rugby team in Australia. I added in the fact that they were the toughest, roughest guys to be called "The Bunnies" and he seemed to laugh at how that sounded. After gushing over how amazing he was, I had my picture taken with him. I like to think that I made a Rabbitohs fan out of one of the greatest voice-over actors in the world. Either way, it was a pretty surreal moment that I will never forget.

I thought it couldn't get any better than meeting a fellow friend from Australia and one of my childhood heroes in one day. It did get better. That evening, I went to a one-man show where this author named Matthew Clickstein had written a book about this history of Nickelodeon. Naturally, being such a nerd, I was in attendance and in my Souths gear as well. Hey, with a recent premiership win, I wanted to make sure everyone knew about this team's victory. During the show, I was introduced to yet another favorite celebrity of mine from my childhood—host of Nick Arcade, Phil Moore.

With my red and green on, he mistook my outfit for an early Christmas sweater. I told him that I just came back from Australia and that I was at a rugby match. He thought that I was from Australia and that I flew in just for this show, which warranted a surprising round of applause from the audience. So, I went with it. He too was laughing hard over the fact that a burly group of athletes were called the Bunnies, but he was incredibly kind and he too snapped a photo with me in my Souths shirt with him sporting my Souths cap. Meeting two of my childhood heroes in one day and turning them into potential Souths fans? Well, if South Sydney was looking for an American ambassador, I think I may have found my calling! A Rabbitohs Premiership win and meeting two legends of Nickelodeon in one month. Life was good, indeed.

EPILOGUE

One of my favorite words in the English language is serendipity. It is the act of finding the wonderful and unusual when you least expect it. And that is sort of what happened with me and the Rabbitohs. It wasn't supposed to happen. I never even planned on it. I didn't even know they existed. But it's funny how life works. My discovery of this amazing team and culture started something amazing. From the minute I laid eyes on that jersey in Alice Springs and when I walked into ANZ Stadium, I found myself transported to a world I wanted to be a part of. I had found not just a wily group of new friends, but a second family away from home. A pack of some of the wildest, funniest, kindest, and most dedicated people that I have had the privilege of befriending. They, along with the team, inspired me to write about Australia. They inspired me to get into rugby. They inspired me to start working out and getting buff like a Bunny. Hell, I was even inspired to get a pet rabbit. Truthfully, that has not yet happened, but I plan on it someday. I have made a whole horde of friends from different backgrounds and I can't imagine life without these fans.

With the Grand Final won and done and the next season months away, life resumed its usual banal existence. For me, however, it was anything but. I left my home in Long Island and moved on to greyer pastures in the concrete jungle on the Upper West Side of Manhattan. It was a time of much melancholy on my behalf, but I did my best to turn that apartment into a home. And by that, I mean I decorated the hell out of my room with as much Rabbitohs gear as I could, just short of painting the walls red and green. Having the mighty red and green all over my room combined with my boxing kangaroo flag really helped curb my homesickness and it made the move much easier. You might say that it became a full-blown Bunny Burrow with Australian flags, Premiership posters, and a full-on Rabbitohs doona (bedspread). I guess you might say that I was feeling homesick for Long Island but I was missing Sydney a little more. I had this really bizarre if not mischievous idea of slapping as many Rabbitohs stickers as I could all over the New York subway system as a way to promote the team.

As I prepared myself for the next season and as I looked through all my photos, something inside me clicked. Would I? Could I? Should I? Should I move to Sydney and become part of the Rabbitohs? Move 10,000 miles away from New York to other side of the globe? It sounded like a silly pipe dream, but it never left my head. It was the little things I missed the most. I missed walking down the street and going for a pub crawl with the fans. I missed hearing the voice on the train with an Aussie accent. It was official: I had left a piece of me in Sydney and it had somehow followed me back to New York. Yup, I was an Australian Bunny Rabbit, and damn proud of it. I wanted to make a Bunny out of as many Americans as I could. I wanted them to see just how amazing this team was. And even if I couldn't convince any New Yorker to swap their pinstripes for red and green stripes, at least I would show up to a stadium with my Bunnies cap on for everyone to see.

When I have kids, I will give them a choice of which baseball team to root for: Yankees or Mets. But one thing is for sure: they will sleep underneath a South Sydney doona, they will memorize "Glory Glory to South Sydney," and they will revere the rabbit as the toughest animal alive.

Thank you for sharing this journey with me. I hope you too have come away with some inspiration to follow one of the greatest sports teams around with arguably the greatest group of fans you will ever meet. It's good to be a Bunny, ain't it! *Glory Glory, my Bunny brethren!*

ABOUT THE AUTHOR

A South Sydney Rabbitohs fan since 2009, Jared Schnabl, a travel writer from New York, developed a love affair with the club after a visit to Australia in 2008.

After a second visit to Australia in 2013, he went to his first Rabbitohs game, not to mention his first footy match, ever. It was from this experience that he was inspired to write his first book—the one you are holding in your hands—to give an American perspective of a magnificent subculture that is rather exclusive to Australia, not to mention the many adventures he had Down Under, courtesy of the Rabbitohs and their fans.

Jared's passions and interests include pop-cultural history, rock music of the 1980s, world travel, rugby league, rabbits, and animated films.

ACKNOWLEDGMENTS

I'd like to thank...

- My family members, who I love very much and who always believed in me.
- Heather Grossman, who helped me overcome stuttering and helped me through every bit of academia all throughout my life.
- The cast of *Oyster Farmer*, whose movie introduced me to an amazing piece of Australia that made me want to visit and share it with the world.
- The South Sydney Rabbitohs, the fans, and the team; my book would not be what it is without their love, devotion, and athleticism.
- Brad Ryder, whose written works on the Rabbitohs made me feel like I could write like someone from Redfern.
- Charlie Gallico, whose devotion to the fans and rabbity antics on the field made for an unforgettable experience in Australia.
- The Gotsis Family for their kindness, hospitality, and love of the game.
- Tony de Quintal, the first friend I made in Australia, who showed me the way through the Lucky Country.
- The members of the Long Island Rabbit Breeders Association, for their love of rabbits and for being the first people in America I made into Souths fans.

- Jeff Weiss, my high school coach, for his toughness, his love of sports, and his discipline.
- The staff at Mascot Books, this long project would not have come to fruition without their help.
- The Australian NYC, for giving me a place to see my Rabbitohs matches from so far away.
- Jeremy Monahan, who introduced me to the inner workings of South Sydney's media department.
- Dr. Ben Accomando, who always pushed me harder to do better in life.